People,
Pooches
&
Problems

Our dogs can teach us invaluable lessons about facing reality, cherishing each day as it comes and loving all creation. Listen to your dog's message, and most of all, enjoy each other! *Dealing with Dogs/TV Ontario*

People, Pooches & Problems

Job Michael Evans

Photography by Kevin Smith

Additional Photography by
Levon Mark, Lionel Shenken/Visual Productions,
Dealing with Dogs/Campbellville, Ontario
and
Dealing with Dogs/TV Ontario

HOWELL
BOOK HOUSE
New York

MACMILLAN • USA

Macmillan General Reference
A Simon & Schuster Macmillan Company
1633 Broadway
New York, NY 10019

Macmillan Publishing Company is part of the Maxwell Communication Group of Companies.

Library of Congress Cataloging-in-Publication Data

Evans, Job Michael.
    People, pooches and problems/Job Michael Evans; photography by
  Kevin Smith; additional photography by Levon Mark . . . [et al.].
      p. cm.
    Includes bibliographical references and index.
    ISBN 0-87605-783-0
    1. Dogs—Training. 2. Dogs—Psychology. 3. Dogs—Behavior.
  4. Dog owners—Psychology. I. Title.
  SF431.E96   1991
  636.7'088'7—dc20   90-19966
                                                          CIP

Macmillan books are available at special discounts for bulk purchases for sales promotions, premiums, fund-raising, or educational use. For details, contact:

                    Special Sales
                    Macmillan General Reference
                    1633 Broadway
                    New York, NY 10019

10 9 8 7 6

Printed in the United States of America

To John Arcangeli

and in memory of
Charles Peter Hornek
and
Thomas Connor

Love lives on beyond "good-byes,"
The truth of us will never die,
Our spirits will shine long after we're gone,
And so the love lives on.
And so the love lives on.
—Barry Mann

Contents

Foreword

I FIRST BECAME ACQUAINTED with Job Michael Evans in 1985 when our local veterinary association invited him to Salem, Oregon, to share his expertise. Job presented a two-day seminar centered around canine behavior and training. The audience was an interesting mixture of veterinarians, Humane Society staff, dog trainers, animal control personnel and pet owners. The seminar was so popular that Job was asked to return with his program two years later.

I was pleased when Job asked me to write the Foreword to his new book, *People, Pooches & Problems,* but one of my first thoughts was, "Why me?" I had come to know Job and was enthusiastic about his approaches to training and understanding canine behavior problems. I enjoyed his books and readily recommended them to clients of my small animal veterinary practice. But it was not until I reflected on my personal experiences with dogs that I began to feel qualified to read Job's manuscript and write a comment for you.

I have practiced veterinary medicine for thirteen years and served six of them on the Board of Directors of our Humane Society of the Willamette Valley. My interests extended to attending canine training and behavior seminars and I found myself listening to behaviorists, veterinarians, competition obedience trainers, the pet-owning public and animal welfare people.

I have also trained. Our two dogs have AKC obedience titles, a Companion Dog on my Whippet, Tippet, and Utility and Tracking degrees on Banner, my Doberman adopted ten years ago as a puppy from our Humane Society. Through Tippet and Banner, I gained an appreciation for the potential and pure enjoyment that exists when dogs are loving and well behaved.

In 1987, I approached Job and asked if he would allow us permission to reprint, in our client newsletter, his excellent article on canine behavior problems, "RRRR: Radical Regimen for Recalcitrant Rovers." The article made good, clear sense and I thought it would help our clientele better understand their canine companions. We published the article and it generated a host of positive comments.

Job's article is the foundation for this book. True to form, Job not only describes what a healthy relationship between dog and owner can be, he is specific in suggesting how we can attain that goal.

With this book, Job Michael Evans has become a standout in a field of experts. What sets Job apart are his innovative training methods, his knowledge of the canine psyche, his ability to address canine behavior difficulties and his equally capable understanding of human nature. Job has trained both people and dogs, solved the most stubborn canine behavioral problems, authored a series of outstanding books and excelled as a public speaker.

I believe that good dogs and responsible pet owners are not born, they are educated. Most of the problems people and pets encounter are predictable and can be defined and corrected. *People, Pooches & Problems* opens a door to this kind of understanding and enjoyment of your dog, whether there are behavior difficulties or not. It will help you grasp the thought process of solving behavior problems and avoiding situations that create them.

At my veterinary practice we have a lending library. Prominent among the many titles are one or more copies of each of Job's books. *People, Pooches & Problems* will find a permanent home there as well. We look forward to continuing to share Job's wisdom and encouragement with thoughtful pet owners.

Stephanie Hazen, DVM
Salem, Oregon
October 1990

Note to Readers

Before embarking on any behavioral program for your dog, take it to your veterinarian for a complete medical evaluation. Since many medical and behavioral problems can overlap, it is important that you rule out any physical causes for problem behavior in advance of behavioral therapy.

Acknowledgments

I HAVE LONG WANTED to write a book on problem dogs and problem owners, and I originally thought the whole process would be a downbeat affair entailing endless days of composing critical prose. I soon found out that even problems could be joked about—perhaps problems *should* be joked about even as solutions are sought—and that very rarely is a dog problem the end of the world anyway. Everyone who has read my other books knows that I take the human/canine bond quite seriously, but I've always been able to see the funny side of the relationship. One reason for that is I have surrounded myself with smart, funny, sensitive people from the world of dogs who have greatly aided my dog work and especially the completion of this book. I'd like to thank them here.

My love and thanks to John Arcangeli, who typed and "computerized" the whole tract. I don't understand computers. He does. He even likes them. He has a Dalmatian, Sport (so named because "That way everyone in the Bronx will think his name is Spot"), so he must be sane. Sport is pictured throughout the book doing various naughty things—of course all the shots are fakes (and if you believe that, I have a bridge I'd like to sell you).

I'm grateful also to Carol Lea Benjamin, dog trainer and writer *extraordinaire,* for encouragement and endearing support, as well as to trainers Jack and Wendy Volhard, Marie Ehrenberg, Don Arner, Michele Siegal, Terese Van Buren and the members of the Society of North American Dog Trainers, a pioneering group of which I am a proud member.

Several members of the veterinary community refer clients with problem dogs my way, and I thank Dr. Lewis Berman, Dr. Sally Haddock, Dr. Jane Bicks, Dr. Peter Kross, Dr. Stephanie Hazen and my good friend Dr. Myrna Milani.

I am also grateful to the convention staffs at the Ohio State Veterinary Medical Conference, the Michigan Veterinary Conference, and the Illinois State Veterinary Medical Association Conference who enlisted me for seminars several years running—I've learned as well as taught at these excellent conventions.

My thanks to the staff at the American Kennel Club library, especially the head librarian Roberta Vesley, as well as to the members of the Dog Writers' Association of America. My research at the AKC library and my contacts in DWAA greatly aided writing this book. My thanks to my editors at Howell Book House, especially Seymour Weiss.

In Canada, special thanks goes to trainer Judy Emmert, head of Dealing with Dogs in Campbellville, Ontario, and her assistant trainer Joanne Nimigan. Ms. Emmert's popular TV Ontario series of the same name flooded her school's switchboard with training inquiries—and generated many photographs for this book! Most of all, I am grateful for the friendship and support my "Canadian connection" has given me on professional and personal levels.

Sincere thanks to my photographers the late Kevin Smith, Levon Mark, Lionel Shenken/Visual Productions, Dealing with Dogs/Campbellville, Ontario, and Dealing with Dogs/TV Ontario and especially to my canine models that withstood hours of photographic sessions and sometimes had to take a fake correction to illustrate a point for readers. You should know that some, but by no means all, of the shots of dogs doing dastardly deeds contained herein had to be set up. My canine models are certainly not up for canonization, but I wouldn't want anyone to think that Dalmatians, Dobermans, Collies or any other breed shown are inherently "problem dogs." Finally, my thanks to over 7,000 clients over twenty years who made me laugh, made me cry, but for the most part listened intently, were open to being educated, identified difficulties, changed some aspects of their own behavior and thus became people without problem pooches.

Job Michael Evans
New York City

Introduction

BY THE TIME this book sees publication I will be "celebrating" my twentieth year "in dogs." For that fact alone some people have remarked that I should have been committed. Perhaps they're right. But there's a difference between being committed and having a commitment. My commitment began in the early seventies at a monastery in upstate New York, and continued in Manhattan where I later opened my own dog training school.

During these two decades I calculate that I have individually interviewed over 7,000 clients with problem dogs. People, pooches and their problems have dominated my life. In the early years I interviewed my clients, took their dogs into the monastery kennels for boarding and training and then released the dogs to their owners with some "exit" lessons. I had no choice: I was cloistered and couldn't go to clients' homes. Later, in New York, I went directly into owners' homes to interview and train. I have carefully studied the methodology and psychology of how owners accept information and criticism about their dogs. This book is the culmination of too many years working with too many clients who own too many troubled canines. Yes, perhaps I *should* be committed.

The "flagship" chapter of this book is "A Radical Regimen for Recalcitrant Rovers," which I always abbreviate as the RRRR program. It's a twenty point "hit list" that is levied, or inflicted (the choice of verb is yours), on a problem dog and on a problem owner. The chapter is new to this book, but it did make the rounds in a very limited fashion in dog training clubs and within the veterinary community via my ubiquitous seminars. After hearing the RRRR in those seminars, many members of clubs or veterinary associations asked to reprint the RRRR for their clients. I agreed in a few cases because I wanted to "test market" the program nationwide. The response has been uniformly positive. The program works. It is a canine/human version of the tough love techniques recently popularized to correct failing teenage/parent relationships.

Seeing the results practical application of the RRRR garnered was a heartening experience. Earlier, when I would prescribe the program I always felt like the Big Meanie, called in to regiment the dog's life. But seeing others use it and have it work has taught me that what owners of problem dogs desperately need is succinct, concrete advice, dispensed in easy-to-remember steps. Trainers are sometimes oververbal. I try to make the complex simple.

The second core chapter is "Setting Up Set-ups." I don't mean to sound dictatorial, but I would recommend that you read it and *study* it. An understanding of these two chapters is absolutely essential if you are to grasp the theoretical underpinnings for *People, Pooches & Problems.* The concept really isn't that difficult. I'll be asking you to use your creativity and ingenuity to trick your dog into being naughty so that you can correct bad behavior. In so far as you are adept at trickery (let's face it, who isn't?) and at keeping the small details of the RRRR in mind, you should have success. Imagine that you've somehow copped the starring role of The Joker from Jack Nicholson in the latest *Batman* sequel. The Joker, of course, is also a trickster.

Fumbles and Foibles

The problem with owners of many problem dogs is that they either think too little or too much of themselves. Softhearted placating-type owners tend to think too little of themselves. Their lack of self-esteem makes it hard for them to grasp that they can stage a successful set-up. They are not used to being assertive or tricking anybody into anything. Instead they "enjoy" pleading and cajoling others, including their dogs, in order to get cooperation. Bombastic blamer-type owners, on the other hand, think way too much of themselves. They enjoy entrapment techniques because the execution makes them feel powerful. A middle course needs to be charted so that the dog is truly fooled by the set-up but not abused in the process.

I like to think that I can chart that middle course. I *have* enjoyed success in my dealings with my own dogs and the dogs owned by my clients. But this was not always the case. I once was a placating, cajoling, sniveling, shy dog handler. My family and academic background didn't exactly provide me with successful dog handling skills. A peek into my own early life with dogs—or more appropriately *without* dogs—might give you perverse encouragement if you think you are the world's worst dog trainer. You think you are? You're wrong. I once was.

Few good dog trainers are born. Most are made. Some of the greatest trainers in the dog fancy once disliked dogs or at least were supremely indifferent toward them. Nothing, and I repeat, absolutely *nothing* in my back-

"No dogs in this house," Dr. Evans had decreed, and indeed how could a dog find a place amidst this horde? No, this isn't a shot of the extras from *The Ten Commandments;* instead it's a photo of myself at far left with my siblings. *Author's photo*

ground slotted me for the career I now enjoy. Even as a child I was informed that dogs were out of the question. This was decreed early on. My heart-wrenching story might comfort you.

No Dogs in This House

"There will be no dogs in this house," Dr. Evans stated flatly, "It would not be psychologically good for the family—and besides, there are too many of you." We sat around the dinner table, my siblings and I, eleven of us, looking sadly at the floor, casting dejected gazes at each other. "Maybe one of us could leave," offered my brother John. "That will be enough," answered my father, "the subject is closed."

Well, we had tried again and failed. There would be no dog in the Evans household. And after Midnight and Lolita who could blame my father? Those two hadn't been shining examples of training.

We were allowed to procure two dogs during my years at home as "experiments"—and they were short-lived experiments. The first dog, Midnight, was a black Labrador from the pound who after being with us for three days ran out onto the highway and was squashed by the Good Humor truck. We were heartbroken—yet, we hadn't the slightest idea what we had done wrong. So much for Midnight.

Lolita the Loser

The next candidate, about three years later, was Lolita, also a pound mutt. She was some variety of exotic Afghan/Golden Retriever mix. The shelter personnel looked delighted and relieved when we picked her up and wasted no time attaching a leash to her and almost pushing us out the door into our car as soon as we had signed the necessary documents. My psychologist father had since proclaimed the family more "mature and stable" than at the time of the Midnight fiasco, and everyone expected Lolita to work out fine. On the way home, seven children cooed to Lolita, who licked back and looked demure.

When we arrived home, my father was in appointments. "In appointments" was a phrase that every Evans child understood as sacrosanct. Dr. Evans maintained his office in the home. We had to keep absolutely quiet when he was seeing clients. The office complex was in the lower level of the house, and we had to tiptoe above it. I spent my childhood in stockings.

Ever try to keep eleven children, a stressed mother, and a brand-new puppy quiet? Twice Dr. Evans stormed up from his office complaining about noise, at which point we would take Lolita outside to romp. Lolita would then run back inside the first available open door and invite us to catch her.

We remembered: The receptionist at the shelter had said something about Lolita being "hard to catch" because of her Afghan background. We began to discover what she meant. She had also warned us not to take the leash off the first day under *any* circumstances. Naturally, the first thing we did was take the leash off.

Lolita tore into the house with all eleven kids in hot pursuit. But she was long gone. She whipped through the entire house knocking over china, vases, precious heirlooms, and descended to the lower level of the house. She ran through the waiting room door of the office complex (which my dad had left open after one of his complaining trips), crashed into my father's office and flung herself onto the laps of the troubled couple he was counseling. My father, shocked, lunged for her. Lolita freaked out, dodged his grasp, ran into a corner and before the stunned couple and an even more surprised psychologist, defecated. Dr. Evans tried to make a lame joke about this being part of the therapy but the couple was too busy gagging to hear him.

Lolita was immediately returned to the shelter. She was greeted by the not-too-surprised receptionist, who, barely looking up from her *National Enquirer,* remarked to a coworker, "Well, Lolita's back." We made our apologies. I stayed after everyone had filed out the door to pet Lolita one last time.

Our next pets were two swans that had clipped wings and nested on the lake our house was located on. They hated children of any age with a passion, and would occupy our backyard, which sloped down to the lake. If we tried to go out to play, the swans would charge at us, hissing. We tried goldfish but we didn't take care of the tank properly. They all got a strange fungus and died. I grew up petless.

Unrequited Love = Frustration

Throughout high school and college I went without dogs. The tragic experiences with Midnight and Lolita plus a run-in with a heavily fanged German Shepherd Dog had converted me into a confirmed dog hater. If this was the way it was with dogs, what good were they? It was a defense reaction, I now realize, but my feelings were acute at the time. Dogs and I did not mix. I did not bother them and I hoped they would not bother me. If I saw a dog coming down the street I crossed to the other side. I closed my eyes during dog food commercials. I refused to buy anything in the supermarket stored in the same aisle as dog foods.

I detested the way dogs ran freely all over the quadrangle at the University of Michigan, totally out of control, breeding indiscriminately, while their student masters studied on the grass or did the same as the dogs. Before I made friends with people, I first attempted to find out if they owned a dog. Probably precisely because of my inner conflict, dogs never failed to come up to me, stick their faces in mine, snort at me, lick me, nudge me, paw me, grope me and do all the things that dogs do when they want to push someone over the brink. "Go say hello to Michael," my dog-lover acquaintances would enjoin the mutts. "Give him a *big kiss.*" The dogs always obliged.

During that time, I was juggling my interest in monastic life with anthropological studies. I loved the sections in archeology that dealt with canine fossils. I was chronic. The monasteries I visited raised animals or pursued other agrarian interests, and I could see myself in that kind of work easily enough. After all, the cheese-producing cows would sleep in the barn and I would sleep in my cell. *That* I could handle. But after visiting twenty-two contemplative monasteries, I managed to find something wrong with all of them.

Monastic life at that time was in a crisis of renewal, and the changes were being badly bungled in many houses. I was looking for a small, family-type community where brothers were a closely-knit group who had simplified work life and a rich liturgical life. Many of the monasteries I visited numbered over twenty monks, and I dismissed them out of hand. A group that size would be too large to sustain the deep relationships between the monks I was looking for, and I knew I had to have to live the life happily. Others had work occupations that were not inspiring—one house made cement blocks for a living, another baked bread. I wanted to be outdoors, close to nature. To me at that time, dogs were not a part of nature. They were a domestic frill inserted into otherwise peaceful and sane households. After two years of methodically searching for the right monastery, I had narrowed my choices down to two. One monastery was hidden seventeen miles off the main road in a canyon in New Mexico, far from family and friends and in a climate and terrain that were unfamiliar to me. That eliminated it from consideration. The other monastery was in upstate New York.

The monastery was New Skete, a collection of wood frame buildings which had been constructed by the monks themselves. In the center of the complex was a stunningly beautiful, eight gold-domed, Russian-style church. The place was surrounded by 500 acres of wilderness—silent, mountainous, serene. The brothers were loving and gracious. The liturgical services were touching. The monastery observed the Byzantine rite—and the beauty of the chant, the figures of the black-robed monks wreathed in incense, the intensity of the icons swept me away. This would be home. But there was a rude shock: The monks of New Skete supported themselves primarily by breeding, raising and training *dogs.* And they bred German Shepherd Dogs.

An Animal Laboratory

New Skete crawled with dogs. When I entered the community in 1972, about twelve dogs were in the breeding program, and there was room for four or five dogs of other breeds that came for training. Only four years after inaugurating the breeding program, the monks had already made a small name for themselves, and luminaries in the dog fancy were visiting the monastery frequently, trying to impart as much of their knowledge as they could to the monks. One woman, Marie Leary, a pillar of the German Shepherd Dog breed, remarked that the monastery was "an animal laboratory." She went on to add that she would rather work with the monks than many other novices in the dog fancy, "because I know they're serious, they will be working with dogs for a long time, they will probably be famous."

The brothers were originally farmers. The farm years spanned 1966 to 1969 and at one time or another the monks had goats, chickens, pigs, Holsteins, Herefords, sheep and even pheasants. Without realizing it at the time, the monks were receiving a grass-roots education in animal psychology and behavior. The monks had a mascot dog, Kyr, a German Shepherd Dog who had "flunked out" at Seeing Eye school because of a problem with his pedigree papers. He was a beloved pet, but he either ran away or got lost, and the monks never saw him again.

The house was empty without a dog, and other animals just did not fill the bill. Besides, the farm had to be phased out. It was not financially feasible and the monks were moving to a new location twelve miles away, high on Two Top Mountain. Brother Thomas Dobush, who died in a tragic automobile accident in 1973, had thought seriously about a breeding program, partly as an experiment (insofar as Brother Thomas "experimented" with anything) and partly as a means of livelihood—especially now that the farm was being phased out.

He contacted prominent breeders, procured some bitches and, on a very small scale, began breeding litters. More and more professional breeders and trainers recognized his sincere interest, which was spreading quickly to other monks, and visited. They imparted their knowledge graciously and openly, which is invaluable in a field that is self-learned. I was overwhelmed with the current that seemed to flow between Brother Thomas and the resident dogs.

Brother Thomas began to train the dogs to live in the monastery as a group and maintain quiet and order. "I don't want them in kennels," he said. "A Shepherd's mind will rot in a kennel." But there could be no fighting within the monastery pack. Each dog was assigned to a brother who was primarily responsible for its care. The dogs came to dinner, and as the monks said grace, they fell into down-stays and waited out the meal. During the meal, the dogs would remain anchored, and if one got up, it was immediately ordered to lie down. The dogs placed themselves behind the horseshoe-style refectory table, flung out along the dining room walls as if by centrifugal force. Feeding the dogs from the table was absolutely taboo. Even though I was afraid of the dogs, and held onto some lingering resentment, I wanted to feed them. I believed that if I fed them the dogs would "like" me, and it was very important to be liked by the dogs if you wanted to stay at New Skete. It never occurred to me that most of the dogs were simply not *interested* in me. I was just another guest, and a kind of regal aloofness is, in fact, written into the temperament section of the Standard of the German Shepherd Dog breed.

During my first meal with the monks, while I was still staying in the guesthouse and petitioning to be accepted into the community, the dogs eyed me with detached curiosity, calmly watching me as I took my place at the table, but they did not break their down-stays in order to greet me. One, Bekky, snoozed softly, and the others licked their paws, groomed themselves, looked at each other but did not get up. Not one gazed at my plate or drooled. "Good God," I thought, "this is incredible." I had never seen dogs behave that way, with such mastery, such self-control, such quiet dignity and poise. I realized that many of my negative feelings toward dogs stemmed from the obnoxiousness of *badly behaved* dogs who jumped up on me, or just didn't listen to anything I or their owners asked them to do. I began to think, for the first time, that maybe, just maybe, I could get to know and like dogs.

But as quickly as that thought entered my head, the old myths took over. Poised behind me were two large females, lying down a few short feet away, directly behind my chair. I couldn't turn around to see what they were doing without making a fool of myself in front of the other monks, but my nervousness mounted as I reflected on the myths and rules I had learned in childhood. These were German Shepherd Dogs. I half believed that before the meal was over, one of them would lunge at the table, steal a platter full of food and scamper away. But worse than this, German Shepherd Dogs *bite* people, sometimes even *eat* them. My mother had told me plainly: *Never* trespass on a German Shepherd Dog's territory. *Never* pet one. *Never* turn your back on one. Here I was, sitting, eating a meal, in a strange place, with strange people, with two German Shepherd Dogs lurking behind me. The end will be merciful and quick, I thought, I'll never know what hit me, and I forced another forkful of mashed potatoes down my dry throat.

Then the abbot checked to see if everyone was finished eating and rose to say the closing grace. The rest of the monks rose in unison, and we sang grace, but the dogs remained in position. When the last note was sung, the monks turned to their respective dogs and said, "OK!" and the dogs leapt up. Everyone was petting a dog, and a large self-assured bitch, Jesse, sauntered over and placed herself squarely in front of me. She did not jump, nudge or nuzzle, but she looked as if she definitely wanted something and wasn't going to move an inch until she got it. "Well, pet her," Brother Thomas said, "like this." And he took my hand and like a baby's moved my palm back and forth over the dog's forehead. We both laughed at my behavior and Jesse too seemed to be smiling. My defenses crumbled and I knelt down in front of her and ruffled the rich fur around her neck.

"You can't stay here unless you like dogs—or can get to like them," Brother Thomas commented. "Oh, that won't be any problem at all—no problem at all," I answered in the most blasé tone I could fake. "Good," he responded, "Maybe tomorrow you can help me with the training. We have two dogs brought in recently. One is a Labrador that soiled the house and the other is a Great Dane that bites."

My throat was dry again. A Great Dane that *bites.*

My Own Dog

I managed to stay out of the jaws of that Great Dane and began training other dogs. I was also given a personal dog to care for. She was a three-month-old German Shepherd puppy named Cita. She had been procured from a top breeder in Massachusetts and came from a long line of beautifully bred, even-tempered, exquisitely structured and genetically sound Shepherds. Even

The then Brother Isaac and the then Brother Job with puppies at New Skete Monastery. I finally had a "dog of my own" to spoil, and boy *did* I!   *Connie Vanacore*

Today, with my friend John Arcangeli and the spotted wonder, Sport.   *Eileen Evans*

now, after twenty years as a professional in the dog fancy—and remember, I *counsel* dog owners—I cannot tell you all of the stupid mistakes I made in attempting to raise my first dog. But, I will be publicly honest with you concerning my mistakes, if you will be privately honest with yourself concerning your relationship with your own dog. Is it a deal? I will tell you this: Within one month I had taken this otherwise sound, open, gracious puppy and turned her into a cringing mass of fetal jelly. Shy, unable to approach others, Cita was a wreck.

Brother Thomas came to me to have a serious discussion. He was a six-foot-two monk of Ukrainian background with a football player's build. He cut an imposing figure and was in charge of everything concerning the monastery dogs. He sat me down and told me in no uncertain terms that I was making a mess of my first dog. "Cita's littermate Cheer is doing fine," he said. Cheer lived five miles away at the convent of the Nuns of New Skete under the care of one of the sisters who had excellent handling skills. "The problem with Cita can't be genetic," Brother Thomas continued, "It must be environmental. There must be something in her environment that causes her to have these shy, spooky reactions. I think that something is *you.*"

He then went on to tell me that if Cita continued as she was she would never be able to be bred. She could never be shown to the public without embarrassment. The monastery prided itself on the temperamental excellence of its breeding stock. It was routine procedure to show prospective puppy owners the mother of the puppy proposed for them. Displaying Cita as she was would certainly not encourage adoption of her puppies. "I'll give you one month," Brother Thomas decreed. "During that time we'll watch and see how Cita does. If you make changes in the way you handle her, there is a chance that she can stay."

I sat silent and flabbergasted, filled with sadness. I had failed with my first dog. I asked Brother Thomas to please, please, please, tell me *everything* I wasn't doing to make Cita more sociable. "It's not so much the things that you *don't* do with Cita that make her respond so defectively," he replied. "It's specific things that you *do* that make her shy." Again I asked him to please, please, please, tell me all of the things that I was doing to cause the shyness.

Brother Thomas took a deep breath and looked at me wearily. "Well," he said, "I can tell some of the things that you do that have to stop if she's to improve, but frankly I can't tell you *all* of the things that you do that are detrimental."

"But why?" I asked. "Go ahead, tell me everything, I can take it."

"There are two reasons why I can't tell you everything. First of all I would have to follow you around the monastery day in and day out because there are so many little things that you do with Cita that are faulty and I would have to be by your side every minute to point them out. The second reason I can't tell you everything to do or not to do is that you are simply not emotionally prepared to understand or accept the information."

"Then tell me what you *can,* and I'll work on that," I said.

"OK, I'll tell you what I can," he replied. "But remember, one more month and then Cita goes to a new handler if her behavior doesn't change. . . ." Brother Thomas then launched in, "First of all, you have your hands on the dog all the time. You are constantly stroking and petting her. The two of you look like a couple going steady—and we're supposed to be celibates! My advice is to get your hands off Cita and pet her only when she deserves praise. Also, you have the dog on your bed all night. You know that is against monastery rules. We have small twin beds. We run a breeding program. The sheets get stained when the dogs are in heat. There's not enough room for both of you in the bed. Yet, you persist in this practice. How do I know? The brother who does the laundry has snitched on you. Get the dog off the bed."

Brother Thomas then cataloged over ten other specific "tips" that I had better follow if I didn't want Cita shipped off. I began to try to change my "love affair" with my puppy. I suppose I made some progress—but Brother Thomas was absolutely right: I was too emotionally bound up with the puppy to understand what I was doing. For instance, I'd be at community recreation talking over the day's activities with another one of the monks. All of the other brothers would have their dogs lying peacefully on down-stays some distance away from them. I, of course, would have Cita sitting right at my side, her adorable little head plopped in my lap, my hand fondling her forehead. I would hear footsteps from behind, and before I knew it the powerful arm of Brother Thomas would reach over my shoulder, grab my wrist and remove my hand from the dog.

Did Cita stay? Unfortunately, no. Unfortunately for *me* that is. Cita was sent to join Cheer at the convent. Brother Thomas wouldn't even let another one of the monks take charge of her. "We have to get this dog as far away from *you* as we can," he said bluntly. My first dog was sent to a nunnery. The shame! The humiliation! I was the only dogless monk in the monastery full of monks with dogs.

Within one month the sister in charge had changed Cita into a loving, outgoing adolescent who was shaping up to be a fine brood bitch. I had been a bad influence on my own dog. In this case, at least the dog could be rescued.

Most lay owners in the process of ruining a dog obviously do not live in monasteries under vows of obedience to superiors. There is no one to point out handling flaws or dictate changes. Even if a spouse were to point out handling foibles that would be the ruination of the dog, most probably the dog would still remain in the household. In a sense, Cita was very lucky to be able to get away from me. It's an old saying in the dog fancy—and a sad one—that very often one has to ruin a first dog before succeeding with others. I don't believe it *has* to be that way. If the neophyte owner is willing to get educated, it needn't be, unless the owner is psychologically or emotionally impaired. I was. I hope this book helps you not to be.

Public Confession: A Closer Look

Let's look at my situation a little closer—remember our "deal," I'll be publicly honest with you if you will be privately honest with yourself. What do you think was *really* going on between myself and Cita? What did Brother Thomas mean when he said that I was not "emotionally prepared" to accept the help that he would try to give me? Was the root of the Brother Job/Cita dilemma the various "things" I was doing or not doing with the puppy? Or was the true cause much deeper?

It has taken me years to figure this out, but I now believe that the real reason Cita got messed up and could not be rehabilitated—at least not by me—was that I was unintentionally *using* the dog to supply myself with a certain kind of support, love and affection one would normally expect only from a lover or spouse. In my case, I should have been looking for that kind of sustenance from the community and in my relationships with my brother-monks. I'll go even further. The truth of the matter is I should have been looking *inside myself* for affirmation and love. But the Job Michael Evans of 1972 was a very different person than he is today. He was, in fact, a shy, skinny, socially inept, twenty-one-year-old kid, with some serious communication problems. How many times have you heard the old saying: "Shy owner, shy dog"? I am living proof that this saying is often true.

The upshot? I think you can see the lesson clearly in my own story. Whenever you relate with a dog in a needy way, asking the dog to provide a kind of support that only another human can provide, or a kind of support that needs to be drawn from within, the dog inevitably breaks down behaviorally. The emotional and psychological stress is simply too great for an animal of another species. Faulty body language and insecure paralanguage miscue the dog and destroy the relationship. Dogs, naturally gracious, giving creatures that they are, attempt to accommodate us in our misguided needs, but inevitably they break under the strain. They cannot bridge the emotional gap between the species. We've put them in an emotional bind. They become shy, spooky, aggressive, destructive or simply frustrated.

A good experiment is to ask your closest friend to make mental notes for one week whenever you talk about your dog. If the name of a spouse or longed-for lover can be easily inserted whenever the dog's name is used, this might spell trouble. We must be extremely careful what we ask of our dogs. They are our charges and our responsibility. We are their stewards. They are also our friends, and we can be theirs. But they are not our mates or lovers. Believe me, I tried: It doesn't work. I hope that this "public confession" and this book helps you to examine and deepen your own friendship with your "best friend," and, if necessary, to balance that relationship.

A perfect balance once existed between the leader and the led—in fact, still exists, within the social structure of the domestic dog's nearest relative, the wolf. A look at wolf behavior is in order at this point. It will clear the air—and perhaps your head—for all that will follow.

1

Wolves and Dogs

PEOPLE WITH PROBLEM POOCHES should make an effort to get to know the dog's ancestor. It can be very helpful. There is an extraordinary amount of interest in wolves among dog owners these days. It's not that we're talking less about dogs and more about wolves—some observers say dog people talk too much, period—but that we're talking about *both* now. This is a heartening trend because the more we know about wolves, the more we can come to know about our canine pals.

This kind of thinking is now the dominant philosophical basis for most training texts. Most trainers now view the dog as a member of the pack, a social being, an animal that can be praised and disciplined using techniques modeled after those used in wolf packs. A number of dog trainers—but not all—persevere in their dogged insistence that a dog is a little machine-to-be-trained, and keep dishing out the usual folklorish, cookbook remedies for behavior problems. But the tide is turning against this kind of approach, and this is shown clearly by the popularity of training texts with a naturalistic approach. To learn more about your dog, learn more about wolves. And you can do this easily in many cities. If your city zoo keeps wolves, my advice is to put this book down *now* and hightail it to the zoo. Go ahead. If you really watch, you'll learn more about your dog there in one hour than I can teach you in ten.

My first experience with wolves happened when I was a member of that religious community and was sent, along with Brother Peter, on a fact-finding journey to St. Louis, Missouri, then the home of several canine endeavors of great interest. For one thing, Dr. Michael Fox lived there and was then teaching at Washington University. We went to meet him and his wolf, Tiny.

After a short talk with Dr. Fox, he told us we would soon be meeting Tiny, a large grey Timber wolf, and we piled into the backseat of his Datsun, presumably on our way to meet the wolf. We had driven about one mile when I noticed a long tongue out of the corner of my eye. The tongue was licking my ear. Thinking it was a dog, I instinctively reached around and put my arm around the animal without fully turning around. But it quickly became apparent that if this was a dog, it was a breed that I was wholly unfamiliar with, and a very large breed at that. I turned around and my eyes met a pair of wolf eyes. We were about five inches apart. The wily Dr. Fox had forgotten to tell us that Tiny was already present—and when he noticed what was happening, he commented, "We're on our way to a large park to take Tiny for a walk," and added, "You should feel complimented. She doesn't usually relate well to men right away—men have too much ego." I did feel complimented, but I also felt like someone who had been set up for a blind date—in this case it was a success. The illustrative point is that ego, indeed, does frighten animals, and especially wolves, and it was truly better to let Tiny introduce herself, rather than attempt a frontal approach. This is something to remember with some dogs, too, especially aggressive ones. Sometimes when I am training I try to set up a situation so that the aggressive dog can choose to come or not to come to me. If you show absolutely no reaction, and especially no eye contact, toward the aggression, and yet are positioned so that you can save yourself from an attack, many times the aggressive dog will come over to you. This can be the basis for a training relationship that will later include elements of control and discipline for aggression, which can be increased incrementally during the training process.

Wolves can show us the way in many training procedures and problems, but their input must be evaluated on the basis that they *are* in fact different from domestic dogs in many of their behavioral manifestations. A good illustration of this is the walk we took in the park with Tiny. Dr. Fox had her on a rope attached to a regular dog collar of the wide, flat variety. At one point Tiny spotted a Beagle romping around on a small knoll and expressed great interest in approaching the dog. We had tried to stay in areas of the park where people would not see us and be freaked out by the wolf, and where we would not disturb dog walkers, but here was this Beagle, totally unattended and totally enjoying itself by rolling around on something that looked exceptionally dead and probably exceptionally smelly. This was just too much for Tiny to resist and she made a beeline for the Beagle. She had Dr. Fox literally in tow, and I wondered inwardly why he didn't use a training collar on the wolf and simply give a leash correction to stop the lunging—a true trainer's thought. But instead, Fox controlled the situation by letting the wolf zip toward the dog, but slowing the wolf down by exerting steady but gentle pressure, and finally turning the wolf away by making a large arc. I later realized that it is simply futile to stop the prey reaction in an adult wolf—it can only be controlled by prevention or diversion, not by the kind of force we use as trainers of domestic dogs. The concept of "timing"—so extolled among trainers and so important to the training process—just doesn't have the same significance to a wolf. This ability to take tactile correction, to adapt to and understand carefully timed corrections, is one area where the domestic dog has branched off, behaviorally, from the wolf.

Nor can wolf pups be leash-trained in the same way as domestic dogs. This was explained verbally and graphically to me on a visit to Wolf Park, a nineteen-wolf research facility outside the little village of Battle Ground, Indiana. Pat Goodman, second in command to Erich Klinghammer, who heads the park, was working with six wolf pups, trying to accustom them to the leash without at the same time convincing them to hate it. "They need *some* kind of leash work," she said, "because they will at some point be in contact with the public because of the educational programs we have here. But most training texts are not helpful—you cannot use a choke chain and you cannot dictate a heeling pattern." We worked with some of the pups, Pat instinctively giving directional tugs on the leash, giving the wolf pups freedom, within limits. It was a joy to watch her, and to see the pups respond to direction. In some ways they reacted as many young pups react at the first experience with a leash. They stalled, they squawked, and then they came along. But the impetus provided by the trainer was totally different from the greater amount of pressure that could be exerted, and more quickly, by a trainer of a domestic dog. And wolf pups didn't really care if they "got it"—there was not the desire of the domestic dog in their eyes or in their reactions. I mentioned this to Pat Goodman and she replied, "Well, why should they care? They're wolves, not dogs." Her simple answer again batted the point home to me, and made me appreciate both the amazingly cooperative spirit of the domestic dog and the integrity of its progenitor.

During my visit to Wolf Park, I did see one area of wolf interaction that validated what I had previously written concerning discipline for dogs. Techniques like the Shakedown and the Alpha-Wolf Roll Over came to life for me in a new way when I saw the wolves demonstrate them on each other. These discipline techniques are detailed in *How to Be Your Dog's Best Friend* (Monks of New Skete, Little, Brown, 1978), but it was one thing to write about them and another thing to see them. Mostly, the wolves did variations on these techniques. For instance, a dominant wolf will not always throw a rival or pushy subordinate to the ground and pin it in a full rolled-over position. Most disagreements don't come to that, but the dominant wolf might use eye contact to "cast a wolf down" or simply approach and put its head over the withers of the wolf it intends to discipline. The message, however, is clear: If you don't stop your behavior, I will execute the full discipline technique.

There is a point here for dog owners who misunderstand the use of discipline. Once you have your dog in line, which may include having a few episodes with him over the behavioral transgression, the dog should know clearly that you will go through the whole process if necessary. Trouble is, many dog owners *do* go through heavy discipline when they could have gotten away with vocal control, eye contact and partial discipline and stopped any bad behavior neatly with just those. Because training texts must teach corrections in a rather literal way, due to the limitations of the medium, there is often no way to show dog owners how to modify, subdue and adapt discipline so that the dog and dog owner are not in a constant state of war. Again, the wolves can show us the way. Spend an afternoon at Wolf Park or at a zoo that houses wolves and watch for nothing except how social order is maintained. You'll be fascinated—and you'll have to watch closely, for it is happening. But rarely is discipline a big event, a prolonged encounter or an ongoing trauma. It is swift and sure—and when you discipline your dog it should be swift and sure. The dog should get the point, and the discipline should have a beginning, a middle and an end, and not last more than a few seconds. I recently got a call from someone who had read an article on discipline and proudly announced, "Well, I used all the techniques on Rascal. I took him into the den and we had it out for an hour." The owner may have felt he had accomplished something, but I'm sure the dog just felt it was a game—the equivalent of big-time wrestling, and great fun.

The study of wolves can help dog owners in many other more subtle ways. You can gain a deeper appreciation of canine anatomy by studying wolves. Look at their structure, the way they move, the gait, the stops, the drive behind even the slowest trot. Look at their heads, and especially at the eyes. It's not a good idea to stare at a wolf for a long time, but if the wolf isn't looking at you, try to take in the eyes. They are iridescent, luminous eyes, full of teaching ability and knowledge that can be tapped into only by intuition and patience. Look at the way the wolves hold themselves, also—quite different from domestic dogs, and not all are equally self-assured and composed. The main exercise should be just looking and watching, seeing, and even as the poet Rilke says, "inseeing."

Before you go, bone up—read Barry Holstun Lopez's *Of Wolves and Men,* David Mech's *The Wolf: The Ecology and Behavior of an Endangered Species,* Dr. Fox's *The Soul of the Wolf* and anything else on wolves you can get your hands on, especially if it is illustrated. And then go, watch, insee.

If you ever have the opportunity to visit with wolves directly, à la my encounter with Tiny, do accept the invitation. I had a recent encounter with four wolves at Wolf Park, where I was allowed to enter the wolf enclosure after being briefed in proper behavior and asked to sign a paper saying I would not sue the park for any damages sustained while with the wolves. It is a necessary precaution because wolves are wild animals and stupid humans can easily mislead them by faulty body signals and other quirks. I was asked not to wear any earrings (no problem). My beard was, however, a potential problem, but Dr. Klinghammer thought it was short enough to pass. Wolves like to grab on to anything that hangs out, and when they grab it, they might want it, and there will be little convincing them at that point, that they can't have it. The thing they want could be your beard, and by extension, your face. There were other precautions, and when I was fully prepared, Dr. Klinghammer, Pat Goodman and I entered the wolf enclosure. Dr. Klinghammer continued to lecture to fifteen visitors who sat on bleachers and who had come to participate in the raucous Wolf Howl nights held every Tuesday and Thursday.

As soon as we entered, the four wolves flung themselves at us in greeting, jumping up immediately to nibble my beard. The jump was a driving, hard-hitting landing, somewhat like being thrown a cement block—again, so different from the jump of the domestic dog. Even chronic jumpers tend to inhibit their jump a little when they meet a person of authority (most trainers can attest to this) but not these wolves. Once they jumped up, they stayed and they started to lick and nibble. It was wonderful, uninhibited, sustained licking—a full face bath. I wondered how to turn it off, and Pat Goodman indicated that I should place my hand over my cheek, rather than try to push the wolf away as one would a dog. We stayed for about twenty minutes, while Dr. Klingham-mer continued to talk to the crowd, explaining the dual myths currently plaguing wolves. On the one hand, there is the "Little Red Riding Hood" syndrome in which wolves are seen as evil and treacherous, and on the other hand the more recent, developing myth (shared by some dog people) that wolves are really just Boy Scouts in fur coats, "just like dogs" and incapable of harm. Neither is true, as I so clearly knew from my own experience.

We exited, carefully slipping out of the pen, and the wolves returned to the center of the enclosure. I felt absolutely honored to have been with them, and as I glanced back with an affectionate look, I caught the eye of one of the aged wolves, who had been especially welcoming and warm in her wolf way while I was in the pen. Our eyes locked for a few moments and through her I thanked all wolves for the gift of the dog, and most of all for being themselves.

Every wolf was born of a bitch. So too with every domestic dog. Most wolf and domestic canine youngsters are also raised by a bitch. She is the first leader figure: the Alpha. Even orphan wolf and dog youngsters carry in their genes an ardent desire to lead or be led. But, usually, the bitch in either species imparts the basics they need to know.

2

Bitch Basics

EXPERTS aren't absolutely sure about the lineage of the domestic dog, but we are next to certain that dogs descend from wolves, *Canis lupus.* Maybe there's *some* other blood mixed in, but as you read in the last chapter, if we take our behavioral cues from the wolf, it's hard to go wrong in making some comparisons between wolf and dog behavior. Wolves live in packs. In every wolf pack there is an *Alpha* or leader wolf. This wolf is the head honcho. However, I hasten to add that sometimes the Alpha wolf is a female. The Alpha keeps order in the pack and keeps members of the pack on friendly terms. Just because we've domesticated dogs does not mean that we have changed their desire to lead or be led. If you can't function as your dog's leader, you probably should reconsider dog ownership. If you can't handle the job because of a lack of leadership skills, your dog will try to assume the role. The result is trouble.

This isn't a moral choice on the part of the dog, it is a genetically dictated response. The dog is looking for leadership, but if it is absent, the dog will attempt to lead the pack itself. Even if you live alone with your dog, it will consider you "the pack." Of course, you want to be your dog's friend, but your friendship must always include elements of leadership and ongoing demands for obedience and cooperation.

A bitch controls her litter of puppies in somewhat the same way an Alpha wolf packs a wallop with its pack—usually through low growls, various kinds of eye contact and occasionally physical punishment. Recently there has been some criticism of dog writers like myself who watch wolves closely and adapt wolf maneuvers to domestic dog dealings. We've been called, and not always in a complimentary way, "wolf watchers," and the criticism is trotted out particularly when we pander punishment Alpha-wolf style. It's said that very little physical punishment actually goes on in wolf packs, so the comparison is unwarranted. But that's exactly the point: I'm not advocating punishment as a *way of life* with your dog, but rather as a valid occasional ploy you must pull to get rid of problem behavior—which is exactly the way punishment is used among the dog's wolf ancestors.

Eye-Eye Sir (or Ma'am)

A leader wolf stares down a packmate or a naughty puppy with a hard cold look that practically freezes the offender in its tracks. This stare is often teamed with a low growl. *Grrrrrrrrr.* The leader never barks, yodels, screeches or screams at this critical juncture, but instead will lock eyes with the culprit and emit a low serious tone. The eye contact will be sustained for just a few seconds, and then the leader will look away maintaining an aloof expression. It's a transparent minidrama from the point of wolf watchers, or those experienced in watching brood bitches, but most subordinate wolves and puppies learn to respect "the look."

I've emphasized eye contact in all my other books, and now I'd like to go into how to obtain it in some detail. Don't skip over this section if you have a problem dog. You may think that your dog already looks at you enough. Trust me—it probably looks at you only when it wants something, or thinks it will get it. Often, when I bring up the subject of eye contact to owners of problem dogs, they will immediately state, "Oh he looks at me all the time." Closer examination shows that the problem dog does, indeed, look at the owner "all the time," but that this same dog usually wants something all the time, and knows how to get it—by looking forlornly or demandingly at the owner. This is not the type of eye contact we want. Because eye contact between problem dog and problem owner is often used by the dog in a *manipulative* way, a new kind of eye contact must be practiced in a formal way using the following steps:

- Take the dog *alone* in a room. There should be no other person, no other dog around. Remember, I said *alone* with you, no matter how artificial that may seem. If there is another person or another dog in the room, the dog may use that person or pet as an excuse not to look at you. Suddenly, your spouse will become the most interesting person on the face of this earth or your dog will become suddenly entranced with your kitty cat—*anything* to avoid making eye contact with you.
- Put your dog on a leash and sit the dog in front of you. If your dog doesn't know the sit command, a little upward tension on the leash will tend to hold the dog in the sit position. You want your dog on leash, because if it isn't on leash, it is free to walk away. You'll be demanding eye contact and the dog will simply saunter off. The leash prevents this.

The first step in getting eye contact with your dog is to make sure all excess hair is trimmed back or held back in some fashion—otherwise you can't read your dog—and I wouldn't be so sure this dog could read you through that veil of hair! *Kevin Smith*

Hold your dog in the sit position by keeping some upward tension on the lead. Touch the dog's muzzle and immediately bring your finger up to your eyes—this rivets the dog's attention on you as Alpha.

Judy Emmert / Dealing with Dogs/TV Ontario

Having your dog in the sit position is also important because when a dog is sitting it will tend to look up into your eyes. If the dog is standing it will tend to make eye contact (depending on its size) with your kneecaps or ankles, which don't have eyes.

- Now, holding your dog in the sit position with some upward tension on the leash if necessary, bend down and touch your index finger to the side of the dog's muzzle. Immediately bring that same finger up to your temple. The purpose is to help the dog orient on your eyes by following your finger up from its eyes to yours. Sometimes it helps to "quarter-frame" your eyes with your thumb and index finger, clearly indicating the portion of your face you want to highlight.

- Simultaneously with the muzzle touch, emit an animated sound (similar to the type one would use with a horse) and then add a sentence that includes the dog's name and a request for eye contact, such as "*Psst,* Tippy, look up here at me right now." The animated sound gets the dog's immediate attention, the dog's name makes the pet know that this means *it,* and the sentence helps the dog to "lock in" with your eyes even more solidly. Choose a *sentence* though, because just the phrase "Tippy, watch me," might not give some dogs enough time to make full eye contact. It is very important that after bending over to touch the dog's muzzle, you straighten up your body completely to a fully erect position. Get those shoulders back, to force the dog to make the effort to look up at you. You should not be bending over the dog at this point, pleading with the dog for eye contact, but rather have a fully entranced animal sitting at your feet literally craning its neck up toward you.

- Once you have three to four seconds of "sealed" eye contact, end the exercise with some light verbal, not physical, praise. A simple "good dog" will do. Don't go overboard with praise just because the dog locked in with your eyes. The message to your dog is "When I say look at me, you *look.* This is to be an accepted part of our relationship from now on, just as it was between you and your mother." And, I might add, just as it was, and still is, between the leader wolf and pack members.

- You should be in and out of the "eye contact room" within one or two *minutes.* The point is to trot the dog into the room, get eye contact and get out. *Dazzle* the dog. The speed with which you demand, and get, eye contact from the dog makes a deep impression on the dog and prepares it to give you eye contact quickly during the course of a set-up. Some dogs might seem a little shocked and even perturbed about being dragged into a room and made to lock eyes with their owners. But, believe me, a certain dramatic swiftness when practicing eye contact is very important. There is a scene in *To Sir with Love* in which Sidney Poitier propels a recalcitrant student out of the classroom and into the hall, makes eye contact with him, issues a growling

By practicing eye contact you'll get an "overflow" of it in your general relationship with your dog. Day by day you'll notice your dog looking up at you, as if he wants to be told what to do—or simply out of love for you. *Kevin Smith*

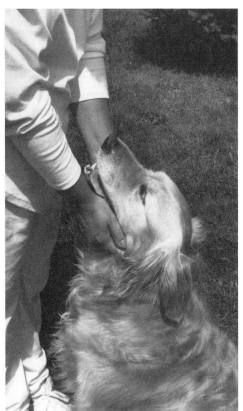

Occasionally there is a dog that simply refuses to make eye contact. Check all your techniques and if all else fails simply force the issue by cocking the dog's head up toward your eyes. Remember, hold the eye contact for only three to four seconds. *Dealing with Dogs/TV Ontario*

warning and then trots the student back to his seat. That student never misbehaves again in the film.

- By practicing eye contact, you'll start to get an overflow of it in your general relationship with your dog. Day by day, you will notice your dog looking up at you more responsibly, as if it wants to be told what to do. You'll find a corresponding *decrease* in manipulative eye contact designed to get you to give a treat, pet, walk or just drop whatever else you might have been doing and pay attention to Sweet Sam. Responsibility will replace manipulation, and one is just as satisfying to the dog as the other. In fact, many dogs become bored using manipulative eye contact because their owners respond *so* predictably. They welcome the challenge of responsible eye contact as taught herein, and their stress level is actually lowered because they no longer have to eye their owners into submission.

- Occasionally, there is a dog who won't make eye contact, even if the above structure is carefully adhered to. "He just won't give me eye contact" is a statement I sometimes hear from clients or at seminars. The usual complaint is that the dog simply looks away, looks at the ground or even at the sky, but avoids the owner's eyes. If this is happening double-check your timing and structure. Are you alone in a room with no distractions? Do you have a leash on your dog and are you holding the dog in the sit position? Are you nagging the dog in a whining tone of voice? You might try simply tilting the dog's head up toward your eyes by scooping one hand under its chin and using the other on its forehead for leverage. You might have to settle for a one or two second "lock" and call it a day. Whatever eye contact the dog grants you, don't engage in prolonged entreaties, begging the dog to look longer. This will only cheapen you in the dog's eyes and ruin the effect of swiftly granted eye contact. Ideally *you* look away first, breaking the "spell."

- Remember, the whole point is to leave the dog dazzled, thinking "What was *that* all about?" Don't worry if the dog appears bewildered—that is exactly the response you want, besides, of course, its undivided attention. The dog will find out later what "that" was all about when you use eye contact in steps one and four of set-ups. If you need to fine-tune set-up steps one or four, make sure you return to this section on eye contact.

No Collar, No Correction

You might think it is the height of stupidity for an owner to complain about a problem dog but have the dog walking around the house, constantly doing naughty things, without a collar on the dog. But it happens all the time. I've walked into literally hundreds of households where I am immediately jumped on, pummeled, goosed and occasionally bitten, but when I reach for the dog's collar I find I am dealing with a nude dog. Of course, I can't give any kind of correction and the dog knows it. Owners of such collarless culprits have a bizarre array of excuses for why their dogs don't wear collars:

- *"It wrecks his fur."* It's interesting that clients with this excuse often possess beautifully groomed but badly behaved dogs. The interiors of their houses are often first-class in decor and style. The dog is seen as an ornament whose esthetic beauty must not be tampered with. This line of reasoning is simply ridiculous. Exquisitely groomed and coiffed canines at shows like New York's prestigious Westminster still wear collars. Go to a first-class pet store or get a top-notch dog supply catalog that describes which collar is best for which dog. But *do* get a collar on your dog, because you will never be able to stop bad behavior if your dog constantly runs away, dive-bombs under furniture and cheapens you with chases.
- *"He knows when it's on and only misbehaves when it's off."* The solution is simple. Leave the collar on whenever the dog is in your presence. The dog might not misbehave for a while because he "knows it's on," but, trust me, he will. Besides, you might have gained yourself a few days of peace simply because wearing the collar put the dog on good behavior.
- *"I'm afraid it will get caught on something."* OK, this *is* a possibility, but it's still not a valid excuse for having a collarless dog. Simply take the collar off when you leave the dog alone or unsupervised and put it on at other times.
- *"I like my dog to feel free."* How very sixties! I know this excuse sounds strange to some readers, but I hear it all the time; often from unreformed hippies or other antiestablishment types. Owners of such dogs often send their children to Montessori school, stock their kitchens with tofu and, yes, love their dogs deeply. Something about leather or metal irritates these owners. The thought of placing a collar on the dog is revolting. But all the love in the world won't help you to catch your dog, not to mention correct it, if it is smarting off. So take that red bandana off and put a real collar on.

Correct Collars

The type of collar is important. Assuming you've gotten over any fur or freedom hang-ups you might have had, choose a leather buckle collar for very young puppies or toy dogs and a training collar (sometimes commonly, but incorrectly, referred to as a "choke chain") for older or larger pets. Be sure that the collar is not too long. This is the most common mistake lay owners make in outfitting their dogs. Almost always the collar is too large or too long. I've seen training collars on Cocker Spaniels that belonged on Great Danes, and I've seen collars on Great Danes that belonged on Shetland ponies. Every

This collar is too long. It might do for a Great Dane, but not this Dalmatian. Make sure the training collar is no more than two to three inches oversize when pulled tight. *Kevin Smith*

inch of "slack" on a collar delays a corrective jerk on it by one or two seconds!

I prefer a metal collar with pounded flat links. If the links are pounded flat and not rounded the collar will have smooth clean action that tightens and telegraphs a correction swiftly. Nylon training collars are OK, too, especially if coat damage is a major concern. Whichever type you choose, make sure that the collar is no more than two or three inches oversize when it is pulled tight on the dog's neck. Since most dogs have foreheads that are wider than their snouts it's likely that the collar will be very snug passing over the dog's head. It also means that the collar might be hard to remove unless you bring the collar up to the dog's ears. Gently fold each ear under the collar, working it over the dog's forehead. By the way, using the scruff of your dog's neck as a "collar" is not acceptable, especially when correcting a dog, even though the bitch used the scruff this way. The bitch used her mouth, grasping the scruff of the pup's neck with an inhibited bite, but in a way that tightened the neck skin similar to the way a training collar does. You cannot possibly duplicate this bitch technique effectively because you cannot use your mouth to grab your dog. Well, I suppose you could try—and you're going to get a lot of laughs. So use your collar or the shake technique (of which more later) instead. Mastering bitch basics doesn't mean that we have to duplicate everything that mom did exactly. We can use our human ingenuity, plus properly fitted equipment, to train and discipline effectively.

The *width* of the collar is also important and also often ignored. A thin jewelry-type training collar—even one with pounded flat links and good, clean action—will be useless in correcting a large dog. Conversely, a collar that is too wide will "clunk up" on a small dog and deliver a correction that is too harsh. Again, visit a quality pet store or peruse a good supply catalog.

Putting the collar on correctly is essential, otherwise the collar can't "telegraph and teach." Stand with your dog at your left side and with both hands dangle the collar in front of its muzzle. When you hang the collar in front of the dog's face it will look like the letter P turned sideways. The rounded part of the P will be facing the floor. Take a careful look at the photograph in this chapter. Of course, if you are using a simple buckle collar you don't have to worry about this aspect, but you do have to be sure that the collar is snug. When the collar is pulled sharply, be sure it absolutely cannot pass over the dog's head. There's nothing worse than a failed set-up that went awry because of a malfunctioning collar—except of course a dog who is injured because an owner used a collar that was too large and tragically slips off.

The Terrific Tab

Just as some parents fail to keep tabs on their children, some dog owners fail to keep tabs on their dogs. Now that you have a collar on your dog (you do, I hope, have a collar on your dog after the lecture I've given you), I want to go one step further and suggest that you put a "tab" leash on your dog. The concept is very simple: Take a leash and snap it on your dog's collar. Now take a pair of scissors and cut the leash off so that it droops down to touch the floor when your dog is standing. That's your "tab." Don't make the tab too long, otherwise the dog might get tangled up in it. Although this might mean you have to cut up a good leash, it is well worth the sacrifice. Now you will have a way to get your dog if it starts to act up or act out. It doesn't matter if the dog looks like a fool walking around with the tab on—get one on, pronto.

If your dog decides to chew the tab, you might have to get a metal chain leash, have a locksmith cut it off and attach that to your dog's collar. It's amazing, but my clients often find myriad reasons for not attaching a tab to their dogs. That's why I mention attaching a metal tab if necessary. Whatever tab you choose, get one on your problem dog immediately and leave it on for the next two weeks.

That's right, for the next *two weeks*. Take the tab off when the dog is alone, but whenever someone is in the household the tab should be immediately attached. No ifs, ands or buts. You never know when the dog might act up. Just instruct everybody in the family that Tippy has to be tabbed to ticket taboo behavior.

That's the purpose of the tab: It helps you to get a "grip" on your dog when it's naughty. For instance, if Chuckles steals a Frito and dives under a table, you can more easily retrieve the dog and discipline it if you have a tab to grab. If Tippy is enamored of charging at the sliding glass door that faces out onto the street and barking at anyone who passes by with another dog, the tab will enable you to come from behind and haul the dog off its assault. If Conrad is in the habit of sending you around and around through the kitchen, dining room and living room (all of which form a circular route), the tab will help to short-circuit Conrad's circuit because you can grab the dog more easily if the tab is flailing behind it. You couldn't if you had nothing but a collar to grasp.

Cheap Chases

By the way, problem dogs love to cheapen their owners by sending them on circular chases. They seem to get a kick out of it. Because many homes and apartments are set up with a free-flowing layout, the "route" is easy for the dog to memorize (any idiot could do it) and the dog delights in having the owner chase it around and around. Many owners actually think this type of track meet is funny, but I can assure you every lap you and your dog run cheapens you in the eyes of the dog—especially if the dog is clenching something that it's stolen from you. I must stress that if you think the chase is funny, and you prefer not to believe that you are being cheapened, you will probably not have the necessary motivation to correct problem behaviors that stem from these very chases. Remember, *chases cheapen owners*. So, if you laugh during a chase the dog will sense your weakness and perceive your inability at leadership. You might very well have the dog that you want. In this case see the chapter "Do You Have the Dog You Want?"

But, if you've truly had it with chase scenes, you will readily see the value of the tab leash. It makes corrections so much swifter and efficient. After a while the dog begins to realize that you have a way to retrieve it even when it runs for its traditional hiding places, ones that were previously inaccessible to you. Owners of extremely crafty dogs might need to put a very long tab on the dog, and might need the services of a private trainer. Oh, by the way, tie a *knot* two or three inches from the end of the tab so that if you grab it midchase the tab doesn't slip *pfffft* through your grasp. The knot also helps if you need to plant your foot on the tab.

The Shake

I hope all you ever need to correct your dog will be eye contact, a low tone of voice and perhaps a tab leash. But, if you're reading this book, chances are those ploys haven't worked. You might have to employ some physical bitch basics. A mother dog would grab her puppies by the scruff of the neck and give a very sharp shake. The shake wouldn't last more than two or three seconds, tops, and the bitch would use an inhibited bite so as not to puncture the skin of the scruff. I believe you should simply *invert* the procedure. Grab from underneath the dog's neck, then elevate the dog and shake firmly. I don't want you to mimic the bitch exactly in her scruff shake because I do not want your puppy or dog to become hand shy. Approaching with your hands underneath the dog's neck is less threatening.

The way the shake is executed is extremely important. Interloop your fingers underneath your dog's collar and at the same time gather up some of the skin underneath your dog's neck. Now, suddenly lift your dog's front paws up off the ground while at the same time shoving your dog's backbone into the ground like a stake. This sudden, swift, upward thrust and downward stab startles many dogs into submission. It also makes certain that the dog's center of gravity is in the lower third of its body, which will enable you to dangle the front paws in the air as you shake. The front paws don't have to be more than one or two inches off the ground. The point is to simply disorient the dog in the front while at the same time pinning the dog firmly to the ground in the rear.

The shake should be "Al Capone" style, in and out toward your body, not side to side, and should not be exaggerated or flamboyant. Remember, just because you are getting physical doesn't mean you are allowed to get loud or violent. No screaming or shrieking! Keep your voice low and growllike as you shake and don't go over three or four *seconds* of shaking. I repeat: No screaming. In our culture most of us are trained that when we get physical, we can get loud. This applies more to the Western male of the human species than to many females, and probably comes from cultural indoctrination pertaining to sports that involve physical contact. But among dogs the opposite is true. When a bitch gets physical with her puppies she uses a very low growl, if she uses any growl at all, and the growl is very quiet, almost spookingly quiet, yet

An effective shake: Interloop your fingers under the dog's collar, "plant" the dog into a sit, lift the front feet slightly off the ground and give an "Al Capone"-type shake. Remember, keep the correction short and humane—no screaming and no hysterics!
Charles Hornek

An ineffective shake: The dog is not being grasped firmly and it is climbing up on its owner—and probably thinks the whole ritual is funny. Compare this dog's eye expression with the Yorkie's above. You'll see submission and respect. Here you see play and even dominance.
Kevin Smith

The swat is more drastic than the shake and is reserved for big canine crimes: aggression, constant destructive chewing, housetraining infractions in older dogs and other "mortal sins." Remember, always go for the softest correction possible, but don't cheat your dog if you know you need to get tougher. *Charles Hornek*

firm. It's often difficult for humans—especially some macho males—to comprehend that loudness and extreme physicality doesn't mean that their authority will be respected. Welcome to a new species, mister macho, you've met your match, and you'll have to quiet down and calm down or resign yourself to an ongoing battle with your dog. The shake is never successful when overdone: Drama, surprise and timing are the keys.

The Swat

A more serious way of disciplining your dog is a swat under the chin. It's often easiest to stand with the dog on your left side so that your right hand can deliver the swat and your left hand can grasp the dog's collar. This correction stems from a basic correction by the bitch in which she swatted the puppy on the head or shoulders, usually with her paw (although I have seen bitches discipline large litters of puppies with their *tails* as well as their paws and mouth). We are again simply *inverting* the bitch's swat so as not to produce hand shyness in the disciplined dog.

How hard is the swat? Well, since the correction is more drastic than the shake, usually if you don't get a response like closed eyes or a yelp from your dog, the correction just wasn't hard enough. The swat is more immediate and startling than the shake. There are some dogs who will accept the swat but not the shake and vice versa. Many owners opt for the shake instead of the swat because they do not like the idea of striking their dogs. I sympathize with you, but must stress that sometimes the time it takes to put the dog into position to give the shake enables the dog to squirm away and the correction loses impact. The swat is much more immediate and forceful. Yet, it is fully valid because it is bitchlike. You do your dog a disservice if you use the more delayed shake when a firm, quick, startling swat is what the situation really calls for. This is especially true in the case of disciplining aggressive dogs. The problem, of course, is that often only an experienced trainer can effectively swat such a dog under the chin without getting bitten. If this is the case with your dog, you need to employ a trainer, or simply use collar and leash corrections. In other cases, especially with young puppies, the shake or only the slightest swat will effectively deliver your message. In general, it's best to always go for the *softest correction possible.* But you'll cheat your dog if you refrain from getting tougher when soft corrections are not working.

The Centering Spot

There is a special spot on your dog's head. Tapping it may help you warn your dog out of bad behavior *before* you have to deliver a physical correction. Massaging it will help calm your dog. I call it the "centering spot." It is located on your dog's forehead just above his two eyes. Perhaps your own mother tapped this spot on your forehead before you entered a store or another area where she thought you might act up. Mine did! I find tapping the spot to be quite powerful in warning dogs out of problem behavior. Several firm taps on the centering spot seem to focus many dogs and make them more appreciative of warnings and directions. In staging set-ups for bad behavior you'll notice that I stress the concept of emphasizing *phonics*—key syllables that need to be accentuated when giving the dog a warning or a reprimand. This is precisely when the centering spot should be tapped with your joined thumb and index finger, as in "Don't even *think* (tap) about it, *Spot* (tap), and I *mean* (tap) it!" Tapping the centering spot helps you to literally tap the warning or reprimand into your dog's brain.

It's interesting that this spot is called a Chakra point in Far Eastern religions. For instance, a Hindu woman will draw a spot on her forehead in this precise location to show that she is "centered"—meaning that, in that culture and religion, she has a husband and family. Jews at the Western Wall in Jerusalem routinely press their foreheads to the wall in prayer, melding the centering spot and the stones of the wall together. Christians, while in deep prayer, often bow their heads and press their enclosed fingers to this same spot. Look at a cross section of a dog's brain and the human brain—in other words, if you cut open the two brains like melons and lie them side by side—and a trained observer can see that there really is very little difference. The center, toward the front, is where both species feel emotions like love, hate, guilt or shame. Could it be that our dogs share with us a common centering spot? I certainly believe so, and have found that tapping this spot as a warning or a reprimand certainly seems to center many dogs. Of course, there is no way to scientifically prove such a theory. But, you didn't buy this book to read scientific theory—you bought it to tap into the lived experience of a longtime trainer. I can only tell you that the centering spot is the niftiest spot I've found on a dog's body—and not just for disciplinary purposes. It's amazing how many dogs go into practically a trancelike state, similar to hypnosis, when this spot is *massaged* as a form of praise, rather than tapped. Try this spot out for discipline *or* praise and you'll see what I mean. By the way, this is a spot I've seen many bitches "kiss" on their puppies. That's another bitch basic.

Some Final Cautions about Folklore Remedies

Responding like a bitch does not mean getting overly harsh with your dog! Practices such as hanging dogs by the leash, kicking them, throttling them and otherwise abusing them are inhumane, ill-advised and simply deprive the dog from learning anything. Usually, these "corrections" are manifestations of human anger, period! Anytime a dog is fighting for its life, for the basic right to *breathe,* that dog cannot possibly *think out* what it's done to deserve such a correction. It's a correction without any connection—quite apart from the deplorable "quality" of the correction itself.

Dogs are also often repositioned or restrained instead of corrected, and this can send mixed messages to the offender. Typical examples: the aggressive dog who is simply restrained lest it attack another dog or a human, or the obedience dog who breaks a sit-stay or down-stay and is simply repositioned in the correct space without any scolding.

The use of food in training is, of course, a controversial topic. In my opinion, you will not convince your dog to regard you as pack leader by the use of food. Verbal and physical praise are quite sufficient as rewards, and no bitch ever corrected a puppy by promising or withdrawing food. Funny—a full review of the existing literature shows food training to be a relatively recent phenomenon. It was rare twenty years ago. Your dog should work for you because it loves you, is bonded with you and wants to please. Let me tell you a super secret: Dogs are the greatest opportunists on the face of God's earth, and they are *thrilled* to get food for doing simple things they know they could do easily without food incentives. But please remember that dogs are also the most benign, forgiving, gracious creatures on the face of God's earth, and they will forgive you and perform, even if they don't get that cheese ball.

In short, if a correction is so harsh that you yourself can't imagine learning anything from it, the correction is probably incorrect folklore. If the advice has an air of finality behind it and doesn't allow for the fact that the dog and owner can revamp behavior, it's probably incorrect folklore. And, if you are advised to simply *reposition, restrain* or *feed* your dog rather than correct it, you might just have won the folklore lottery.

Finally, with the exception of overly harsh corrections, there seems to be a reaction from certain quarters against physical punishment in training—in some instances, a deep prejudice. But physical punishment *is* an acceptable way of dealing with unacceptable behavior in dogs and any good brood bitch can attest to it by her actions. Bitches physically punish their pups when they need to, and have no moral qualms about doing so.

If we are to master bitch basics, we might have to examine our attitudes toward physical punishment. While physical punishment is rarely needed, it is occasionally called for, and while "becoming a bitch" might not be acceptable in dealing with fellow humans, it is appreciated by your dog—after all, they do it among themselves, and have for almost 15,000 years. Don't worry that your dog will "hate you" if you get physical. Remember, its mother already got physical, and the problem might be that no one else has, at least not in a way that allows the dog to connect a correction with a connection. Remember, hands down, prevention beats correction. Read on.

3

Prevention or Correction?

YOU'VE ALL HEARD the saying "An ounce of prevention is worth a pound of cure," and only a fool would disagree. Books on problem behavior in dogs abound with preventative tips that can be used to circumvent dog difficulties such as not coming when called, pulling on leash, destructive chewing and a host of other maladies. I'll give you a hit list at the end of this chapter of preliminary maneuvers that you can employ to circumvent such problems. But first things first. Chances are that if you are reading this book you might be past the point of prevention and feel "condemned" to correcting your dog. Well, don't. Correction can be more difficult, to be sure, but there's nothing immoral about it! Besides, if I *only* preached prevention you'd join the ranks of frustrated dog owners who buy books in hopes of finding out how to stop bad behavior in its tracks, only to be told what you *should have* done, not what you need to *do now*.

You'll find that the emphasis in this book is on correction and not prevention. This certainly doesn't mean that I don't care about prevention. Along with the tips I'll give you for preventing problems, you'll find instructions galore in my other books, especially in *The Evans Guide for Housetraining Your Dog* and *The Evans Guide for Civilized City Canines*. But for some readers of this book, it might be too late for prevention. Again, it's not exactly a kindness for an author to list preventative measures that *should* have been taken months or even years ago. The owner of a problem dog who has moved past prevention and needs immediate correction is then left in the lurch. As distraught owners read over everything that *should* have been done, they sink deeper and deeper into despair. They accuse themselves of having blown it and can decide that it's too late to do *anything* now. They start up an internal mantra that goes something like "I *should* have done X when Rascal was Y years old, but I didn't, so now Rascal does Z. . . . I *should* have . . . I *should* have . . . I *should* have."

Psychological Put-downs

In fact, some problem owners love to look back at what they should have done or what could have been. Placating owners, especially, enjoy this type of self-castigation. It's a way of blaming themselves for the dog's problems. It adds a seemingly wonderful sense of hopelessness about the overall situation and justifies inactivity and even despair. Many owners of problem dogs have a love affair with despair. It's at least predictable.

The psychological roots of "should have" mind games reach down too deeply for me to analyze, but I can assure you the paralysis that results will do absolutely nothing to correct your dog. In my opinion, unless a dog is genetically defective, seriously ill or pathologically violent, it is *never* too late to attempt correcting problem behavior. First step: Give up all "should haves." Owners who enjoy reciting the "should have" litany need to find another form of prayer. They should instead meditate on staging sterling set-ups that will help eliminate undesirable behavior. I'll help you with factual information and with a theoretical framework that defeats most dog problems. I can offer you encouragement, sympathy and support. But if your personal psychological problems entrap you in the past, or if you actually enjoy beating yourself up because of what you should have done and didn't, you might be unable to appreciate the information or inspiration presented here. If you are caught in this game of psychologically putting yourself down, please realize that I mention it not to make you feel even worse, but so that you can realize that there are limits to what can be accomplished in a book on people, pooches and problems. While some reviewers have noted an emphasis on human psychology in my writings, I prefer to leave therapy to therapists. If you need one, get one.

Don't torture yourself as you read over the following preventative tips. Chances are, you didn't do a lot of the things listed, but there is still plenty that you can do now. Read over the list, which is presented in shorthand style, and as you bump into techniques that *should have* been employed, simply note them and use a given tip if possible. But if you can't use a tip because of a dog's age or the severity of its behavior, don't blame yourself, just resolve to do better next time. You can read the list to help you with your next puppy. If you are a far-sighted owner of a new puppy or a young "secondhand" dog, you're in for a real treat because most of the following tips are best begun during puppyhood.

Make sure your puppy thinks the world of *you*— so it'll want to come to *you*. Begin indoors using a hallway that will "funnel" the pup toward you. Remember: positive body language, positive tone of voice and positive eye contact!

Judy Emmert/
Dealing with Dogs/
TV Ontario

The best preventative measure to guard against your dog jumping is to never let the puppy begin to jump up. No matter how "cute" you think the behavior is, you can't have it both ways.

Judy Emmert/
Dealing with Dogs/
TV Ontario

35

PERFECT PROBLEM PREVENTION

Coming When Called

I believe that obedience to the word "come" is not completely a purely mechanistic response on the part of the dog but rather a manifestation of what the dog thinks of its *owner.* Your dog's opinion of you begins to be formed in puppyhood. In short, if the dog thinks you are somebody *worth* coming to, it'll come when called. If it thinks you are a littermate, or a complete bimbo, it won't. The preventative trick, then, is to teach your dog from the beginning that you are the star of the universe—its at least. Beginning as early as nine or ten weeks of age (when most puppies start to gain full depth perception) have a short five-minute "following" session with your pup. Your pup has a natural inclination to follow you, so maximize on this. Trace a simple figure eight, being careful to shuffle instead of walk, especially if your pup really hangs in close. You don't want to trample it! Pat your leg and move sideways suddenly, saying "come" as you do. Stoop and turn toward the pup after you say the command so that the pup winds up sitting in front of you. Praise heartily, but not for a lengthy period of time. Repeat another figure eight. Move sideways again, stoop and call.

Walk a straight line with your pup, but suddenly put yourself into reverse and walk four giant steps backward. The pup will probably forge ahead and it will take a few seconds until it notices you aren't by its side. As the pup turns to locate you, stoop and simultaneously say the dog's name and the word "come." Repeat three times.

When your pup is playing in an open field or wherever its play area may be, do not call and then immediately confine it. This will only teach the pup that when called it is always confined: end of play period. "Shucks," the pup will think, "I just won't come the next time." Instead, call the pup and then release it to play again. Every play session should be a little different—sometimes the pup gets leashed and/or confined on the first recall, sometimes on the fifth, sometimes on the third. Variety is the spice of successful recall training.

Another good tip: Have the puppy sleep in the bedroom. This increases bonding, which is the basis for steady recalls. When I cowrote *How to Be Your Dog's Best Friend* with the monks of New Skete, this was the first chapter I penned. In fact, "Where Is Your Dog This Evening?" was my first effort at any dog writing. Having the dog sleep in the bedroom might seem unconnected with success in the recall, but since your dog is coming to *somebody,* and granting the dog access to your personal "den" really makes you look like somebody super, it makes sense that recall rewards would be reaped from this simple practice.

Remember, if your pooch is past the puppy stage and is having a recall problem, begin immediately to retrain using the methods in chapter 18, "To Come or Not to Come." The follow-me preventative method won't be of much value, but use the in-bedroom sleep and the don't-call-and-always-confine methods.

Jumping Up

The best preventative measure to guard against your dog jumping up on you or others is to never let the puppy jump up on you or anyone else to begin with. This applies no matter how cute you or others think the behavior is. Teach the pup early on that you will only praise it if it presents itself in front of you for affection—never if it mauls you. See chapter 14, "Praise Problems"—the corrective measures can be used on pups as well. If you simply never encourage the behavior, you'll have very little reason to haul out heavy corrections for jumping up. Remember, no one else thinks the jumping is cute—even if they say they do. Trust me, they're lying.

Avoiding Aggression

Few dogs just wake up one morning and decide to turn on their owners. Unless the dog is genetically defective, the build-up to aggression is much slower, and thus more difficult for the indulgent or uneducated owner to detect. But there are things you can avoid. Don't play tug-of-war games with your puppy with *any* object. There is a new strain of thought in some training circles that says that such games are OK, and that dogs are *naturally* somewhat aggressive. I don't buy the argument. Dogs live in a specific culture—ours. They must not use their mouths on anything except their food and their toys. Making exceptions only results in double messages and a lack of boundaries, which the dog senses are changeable. Do not encourage any growling, overbarking, tug-of-war games or violent roughhousing no matter how much the pup seems to enjoy it, no matter how much the breeder may tell you that such activities are "normal" to that given breed. You are simply increasing the chances that you will wind up with a biter.

Socialize the *hell* out of your puppy or secondhand dog. Excuse the "French," but I repeat, socialize the hell out of your dog. The statement isn't really that far off or that risqué—for living with an aggressive dog *is* hell, and early socialization and exposure are the keys to avoiding such a state. Get your pup out to shopping malls, plazas, train or bus stops and other people-congested places early on. Park the dog in a sit. Keep some upward tension on the leash to hold the dog in the sit position, and when greeters approach (as they will, if you park yourselves long enough) *loosen up* on the leash and allow interaction between parties. Don't keep the leash tight—this telegraphs anxiety right down the leash into the insecure dog's cranium. If the dog jumps on the person, correct it. If the dog retreats, scoot it around from behind you and issue the sit-stay command with a strong flash of your hand in front of the dog's face. Allowing early retreats can produce a "fear biter" later on. And, if the young pup should growl or exhibit any aggression, *send the dog to the stars* with a firm swat under the chin. Blunt? Not at all. This is where it all starts, this is where canine aggression is born—and all too often the owner is the midwife. This is where it needs to be aborted. Your pup must know from the beginning that growling at, lunging at, snarling at or barking at *anyone* or *anything* without your express permission is *unacceptable* behavior.

Resolve from puppyhood on that whatever (short of physical abuse) someone else might do to your pooch does not justify any aggression on its part. If you make this a house rule, and an absolute dictum, you will not be psychologically swayed when a weird guest or set of circumstances seem to trigger Alfred to be aggressive. Instead, without even trying to figure out what is "bothering" poor Alfred, you will go into immediate corrective action. Alfred will learn to keep his aggression to himself, where it belongs. Most of all, examine your own motivations in getting a dog. If the dog was procured simply to provide a "service" for you such as protection, you might unintentionally have created an atmosphere that encourages overprotection. This is an old, well-known scenario among professionals in dogs. Usually the script features a placater-type "soft" owner who is scared of crime, a given neighborhood or life itself, and procures a large dog of a protection-oriented breed. However, if the original motivation was a desire for companionship rather than protection, the relationship would be off to a better start. In no other behavior problem do the psychological undercurrents in the owner's mind turn the tide of events as they do in problems of canine aggression. Your motivations, needs, desires and expectations as an owner plus your determination or lack of determination to seek out early training are pivotal here. If you don't want a grouch, train early and train hard.

Circumventing Chewing

If you want a puppy who will go through only a natural chewing and teething stage and then keep its mouth to itself, find a reputable breeder who puts his money where his mouth is. In other words, if you buy a quality puppy from a quality breeder, it's my firm belief that the temperamentally sound pup can easily assimilate corrections for chewing—even corrections after the fact. Brain power comes out of good breeding. The smarter puppy can more easily be humanely corrected early on.

Avoid the temptation to provide the newcomer with zillions of chew toys. You will unintentionally teach the pup that *everything* is a potentially chewable item. Obviously, do not let the pup chew on *you* at all. It's a small step for the pup to deduce that if it's OK to chew on you, it's OK to chew on your belongings.

A smart owner will also avoid the temptation to make a production number out of saying hello or good-bye to the pup. If you make these really commonplace daily events into high-powered or heart-wrenching scenes you'll simply set the dog up to become frustrated. Of course, the classic release valve for frustration in puppies is to chew—often a scent-soaked item—in order to get "closer" to the owner and relieve anxiety. When you leave, give the pup a brief pat, and when you return, no matter how excited the dog is, simply say a sweet, sincere hello and go about your day. No, the puppy will not hate you for playing it cool—and you'll be doing yourself and the pup a favor.

If the pup is chewing on something unacceptable, reprimand it in a growllike tone, but don't feel you have to immediately run and shove an acceptable item in its mouth—and do *not* praise it simply because it stops chewing on the illegal item. If you want to offer an alternative after reprimanding your dog for inappropriate chewing, offer the acceptable item only 50 percent of the time. The rest of the time let the pup learn to inhibit its own chewing compulsions. Remember, you won't be home to pop an "OK" item into its mouth all the time. At those times, the pup will have to seek one out itself or simply wait and chew nothing.

Be careful about toys. Don't buy or offer any that have a squeaker that can come dislodged. Certain breeds, especially some of the terriers, love to "kill" such toys; there are squeak toys available that have inverted noise makers that cannot be swallowed. Also, please, no foam or supersoft toys, and obviously, no old shoes or items of clothing from your wardrobe. The puppy can't tell the difference between old, beaten-up tennies and Guccis, B.V.D. underwear or Calvin Kleins.

Shunning Shyness

If you have a brand-new puppy that is acting extremely shy, my advice to you is to immediately, as in *now,* call the breeder and discuss the situation. Instead of calling with vague complaints of shyness, make a list prior to the call as to the *specific* instances of shyness. This will give the breeder something to go on, and will enable him or her to distinguish between what is a matter of the pup simply adjusting to life in a new environment and without its littermates and true genetic shyness. I stress immediate action because genetic shyness is the hardest to "train out" or modify, and even with training, such a dog may always be a management problem. It would be better to return the pup and start anew. There's also a chance that a mismatch has occurred and a shy person has wound up with a shy puppy—which is always a prescription for disaster. While you should know when to return the pup, it is also imperative that the breeder learn proper placement procedure.

Problems of shyness call for remedies similar to those used for discouraging aggression. Socialize your puppy or secondhand dog early on. Again, get out to shopping malls, train or bus stops—wherever people congregate or pass by—and just park yourselves. Keep some upward tension on the lead and sit the dog on your left—the tension will hold the dog in the sit. However, do *not* choke the dog with tension on the lead, and if someone approaches, *loosen* the lead, but do not allow the shy dog to retreat behind you. Often, your leash manipulation will be a combination of tightening and loosening the lead in order to keep the shy dog who wants to retreat in place, yet not telegraphing anxiety down the lead by having it too tight. Obviously, owners of shy dogs need to enroll in obedience class as soon as possible. The trick—and the hardest part—of getting your dog to shun shyness is to be tough and not to coddle the shy dog at all. If shyness has already set in, set-ups are in order, and you will need obedience training in order to execute them. So, off to class with the two of you!

Lying Down

In *The Evans Guide for Housetraining Your Dog* I detailed a method for getting your potentially messy canine resting comfortably by your side—before the dog has learned the words "down" or "stay." Besides the housetraining benefits, the technique has many other dividends. Be sure your pup is at least four months old before trying this technique. Attach a six-foot-lead to your pup, and bring the dog around to the side of a chair. It's best to start with a dining room chair rather than a low-slung couch, as the height of the chair will discourage the dog from bothering you. Take the other end of the lead and place it underneath your buttocks. Push your pup down to the ground. Measure out just as much lead as the dog needs in order to hit the dust—that's your goal. Correct the dog for any naughtiness. If the pup jumps up on you, whip the leash down hard and say, "No!" If the pup pulls on the leash, your dead weight will stop the dog from pulling any further. If the dog bites on the leash, whip the leash diagonally up and toward your body and say, "No!" No nonsense during this quiet time. Sooner or later, the dog will start to figure out that it might as well lie down—as you allow no other alternatives. I suggest having a young puppy hold such a thirty-minute down (yes, that's *thirty minutes*), beginning at age four months, forever. Yes, I repeat, *forever.* That's right, one thirty-minute down a day for *life* beginning at age four months. This must be an owner-enforced down—not just a time when the pup or older dog is snoozing and lying down anyway. Naturally, as you train commands, you will not have to sit on a leash anymore. But, for now, anchor your dog with the dead weight of your body. Trust me, you'll be investing in a solid future of steady, unwavering "free-lance"—that is, off leash—long downs, because your dog will already be comfortable holding the position for a lengthy period of time. Later you'll be able to use this expertise on your dog's part to take it to many, many places you would otherwise not even *think* of taking it— because you will be confident that you can "park" your dog. In short, park early and save later!

Walking Nicely on a Lead

Early leash training is the key. Your initial method can be quite simple. Attach a six-foot leash to your puppy's collar. Be sure the pup is at least four months old and wearing a buckle collar, not a choke collar. Drop the lead. Let your pup walk around like this for ten minutes each day. At some point, the pup will step on the lead and "correct" itself. The pup will look startled. Do not praise or coddle the pup at this point even if it screams when it steps on its own lead. Since you are not holding the lead, you will not look like the bad guy who choked the pup. It's amazing how quickly many pups learn on their own to somehow (there are a variety of methods) keep that lead over to the left or right side of their bodies—rather than get zapped by stepping on it yet again. Of course, this is exactly what we want: to have a pup that respects the lead. Go one week using this method. In week two, come from behind and gently pick up the lead and walk a few steps with the pup. You might also simply stop, without correcting the pup with a huge tug. As early as the fifth month, teaching a more formal "heel" can and should be started. Do it in class or from a book, but do it.

"Preaching to the Damned"

I recently told a fellow trainer that I was going to include a section on prevention in this book because I didn't want to simply offer corrective tactics. "Besides," I added, fantasizing, "perhaps, just perhaps, there will be new owners of puppies far-sighted enough to invest in a book on problem behavior just *in case* they ever have problems." "Magical thinking," my trainer friend replied. "Owners don't turn to problem books until they have one. Every puppy owner thinks—at least for the first two months—that everything their puppy does is saintly or just a *little bit* naughty. A section stressing prevention will be preaching to the converted, and the rest of the book will be preaching to the damned." I disagree. I do not consider naive puppy owners "converted" to anything except infatuation and romance. Nor do I consider an owner of a problem dog "damned." If this chapter caught you at the right time, great. Use the material presented here and you might not need the rest of the text, but you can never be sure. Remember, most dogs, no matter how preventatively trained, socialized, schooled, disciplined and educated, will *try everything at least once.* At least you'll be ready to administer corrections armed with the rest of this manual.

For those of you with older, terribly naughty or even criminal canines, you have a choice: You can read over this chapter and use the fact that you might not have done (or had the *chance* to do) this, that or another technique, and collapse into despair and inertia or catatonia, or you can say to yourself, "So what about the past and what I or somebody else did or didn't do? I have the dog I have the way it is today—and if I want a better dog I can build one. I can train, or I can complain.

4

A Worthy Cause

EVERY PROBLEM POOCH has a *reason* for misbehaving. Dogs do not sit around deliberately trying to think of how they can thwart their owners. There usually is a *cause* for bad behavior. Experienced trainers learn not only to evaluate actual bad behavior but to ask, "What is *driving* or *motivating* this problem dog?" Inexperienced owners, however, concentrate only on the *symptoms* or *results* of the unpleasant behavior. They just want to get rid of the unpleasant aspects of the behavior as soon as possible: If the dog continues to have a *cause* that it thinks is a worthy one for doing something obnoxious, that's the *dog's* business, and not something many owners want to be bothered about.

In fact, this book itself concentrates on alleviating the symptoms and the results of bad behavior by staging set-ups to weed them out. But, we must never forget the fact that the dog has reasons for the way it acts. Unless the underlying causes of bad behavior are addressed, set-ups can be staged until the cows come home, but the dog may still misbehave. So before designing a set-up, ask yourself: "*Why* is my dog misbehaving?" Let's look at some examples.

- Let's say your dog barks when you leave your apartment. In fact, it does more than bark. The dog yodels, screams, shrieks and screeches so dramatically that your neighbors are ready to lynch you both. A set-up to alleviate these intense vocalizations is easy enough to concoct. You would issue a warning to the dog as you leave, exit, explode back into the apartment at the first whimper, humanely discipline the dog verbally and/or physically, repeat your warning and leave again. Set-up steps 1, 2, 3, 4, 5. Simple, eh?

Let's look into this situation a little more deeply. If you are in the habit of trying to soothe your dog out of barking when you leave the house, coddling it, cooing to it gently and pleading with it not to bark, you might be in fact setting up a situation that will *encourage* the dog to bark. You will be intensifying the natural anxiety the dog feels when you, its pack leader, abandons it. This "separation anxiety" is the cause of the barking. The resulting operatic performance is just the result or a *symptom* of the real problem. Since you can't avoid leaving home (after all, someone's got to buy the dog food), thus alleviating separation anxiety completely, you can at least alleviate the dog's stress by avoiding overly dramatic hellos or good-byes. For more on overbarking, see the sections that deal with separation anxiety elsewhere in the book. For the purposes of this chapter, I think you can readily see how very important it is to look for the underlying cause of the barking rather than just correcting the dog for it. If you continue to emotionally overload the dog when leaving, and only stage a set-up to correct the barking, chances are the set-up will fail—or the dog will express anxiety in a different way. For instance, it might start to engage in destructive chewing, bed wetting, or even self-mutilation. You will have corrected a symptom but not the cause.

- Or let's say your dog has gotten into the habit of leg-lifting on everything when you are away from the house. A set-up to correct the symptoms of this problem is also easily devised. You would issue a warning upon leaving, return later, discipline if there is evidence of leg-lifting, reissue the warning and leave again. As simple as set-up steps 1, 2, 3, 4? Not necessarily. But again, let's look a little more deeply into the matter. There might be several causes—worthy ones in the dog's eyes—for the leg-lifting. For instance, let's say you simply haven't walked the dog enough, or on schedule, and its bladder is bursting. That seems to me to be a worthy cause for letting loose! Or let's say you leave a large amount of water for your dog when you leave home. Out of anxiety, some dogs drink a lot of water immediately after their owners leave, not realizing that they will have to "hold it" for several more hours. Or, let's say that your relationship with your dog is so corroded that the dog has you permanently slotted as submissive, and leg-lifts to establish territory and maintain its dominance over you.

Unless you identify and address underlying causes your set-ups will probably foul-up. You could get the dog emptied out and walked on schedule. You could leave less water, or leave a bowl of ice-cubes that will melt down slowly, preventing your dog from tanking up out of anxiety. If you sense that your whole relationship with your dog is marked by such a lack of leadership that this is the cause of the leg-lifting, you could place the dog on the Radical Regimen for Recalcitrant Rovers (RRRR). The point is, unless you identify the cause or causes for the objectionable behavior, simply staging set-ups probably won't stop it. Remember that sometimes there are several causes for a given canine behavior and all of them have to be identified and, if possible, alleviated.

All for the Cause

I mention the concept of cause and effect at an early point in this book for a good reason: Domineering "blamer" owners with problem dogs are often thrilled to learn how to stage set-ups to correct the *results* of bad behavior but don't want to take the time to look into what *causes* it. The relationship with the dog then becomes a battle in which the dog has to submit to set-up after set-up and is sometimes literally beaten into submission. Symptoms and results of bad behavior are corrected, but the dog continues to live on a level of supreme frustration.

That said, and those owners warned, I will also say that sometimes it's just not possible to fully address the cause of bad behavior. For instance, most owners have to leave their dogs alone, at least temporarily, so the basic cause for some overbarking and destructive chewing *can't* be changed. The problem behavior must still be corrected. Or consider, for instance, a genetically defective dog. The genes cannot be manipulated. If genetic defects are the root cause of shyness or aggression, set-ups might help only to a degree. The root cause of the difficulties can't be considered or corrected because it is untouchable. But it's still almost always worth trying to correct the bad behavior itself. But not knowing the cause, or not being able to allay it, can prevent full rehabilitation.

Trainer Tips

Often, a professional trainer will know very well what the cause of undesirable behavior might be but will mention it only in passing and immediately concoct remedies to stop whatever it is the dog does that is annoying. This is OK as far as it goes. After all, you *are* paying the trainer or specialist for some relief. However, a good trainer will not only provide you with specific techniques and tips for specific problems, but will help you to understand what is driving the dog—in short, the cause of the problem. You will then have a much deeper understanding of your dog's dilemma.

Remember, though, not to get obsessed with the cause of the bad behavior. Sometimes you will just not be able to change it. Very often a good trainer will, while mentioning the underlying cause of the bad behavior, appear to downplay it, and will want to get right to work on the symptoms and results of the behavior. This is not necessarily an oversight or an evasion. The trainer is, after all, employed by you to eliminate problem behavior—with your cooperation, of course. Give it.

On the other hand, beware of trainers or behaviorists who discuss *only* the causes of behavior, but never help with remedies for the problems themselves. It is of no use for a professional to come into your home and reveal to you that your dog overbarks when you leave because of separation anxiety, collect a fee and leave. You will be a poorer person who still has a barking dog. This syndrome is especially common among professionals who have received only academic training and have little or no direct training experience with real, live problem dogs. A diagnosis will be dished out, but little else. Diagnosis without direction spells disaster.

A Human Analogy

Just as domineering blamer-type owners could care less about the cause of a problem, placater-type owners will use the cause as an excuse not to correct the problem behavior itself. I've had some clients who actually seem to *enjoy* the frustration of not being able to alleviate an underlying cause of a bad behavior and feel it is "unfair" to the dog to correct the manifestations of bad behavior when nothing can be done about the cause for it. While I sympathize to a degree, once a sincere effort has been made to research the cause of the dog's behavior, I feel it is a disservice to simply give up on the dog or give the dog tacit permission to continue irksome behavior.

Let me paint my philosophy concerning cause and effect in canines by giving you a *human* example of how a leader figure might confront the phenomenon. Let's say you are a parole officer. You have a sixteen-year-old client: a criminal who steals, specifically, items from stores. This client was assigned to you after being caught and sentenced to community service and to counseling sessions with you. You delve into your client's background in order to understand and help this young person more completely. You ask many, many questions trying to find out the *cause* for the shoplifting. You learn that your client comes from an impoverished background, is a member of a disadvantaged minority group, grew up in a ghetto and hung around with friends who are also fond of filching. You begin to understand that peer pressure, racism and classism are all possible causes for the stealing. Some of these causes can be changed and some cannot—at least not by you alone. What should you do? Sympathize and tell the person it's OK to steal because of everything he's endured? Tell the youngster to try to "cut down" on shoplifting "just a little"? Of course not! Instead, you are going to tell your client that if there is any more stealing, you will, in your capacity as parole officer and leader figure, correct the behavior with punishment and incarceration. You might appear to be unsympathetic to the underlying causes for the behavior, but you know you are doing the right thing.

The above situation mirrors the attitude I have toward problem dogs. If a dog is displaying unacceptable behavior I am sensitive to possible causes for the behavior, but I will not allow the dog to continue with it. In my early days of dog training I made excuses for problem dogs because they had solid reasons for doing what they did. Now I walk a middle course. I try to examine the cause, without *over*examining it, and go directly to work on the problem itself.

I suppose one could say that the original, root cause for all of the problems that we experience with our dogs is that we ourselves domesticated them. Perhaps we should have left them to their own devices in the wild. But we *did* domesticate them, didn't we? So, it is our responsibility, as their stewards and leaders, to make them as comfortable as possible in human society, in return for the great deal they give us. It's also our responsibility to correct them humanely if they abuse the covenant we made with them thousands of years ago. For better or worse, we are together, we two species. We might not always understand the other's causes and reasons, but we are honor-bound to compromise, and, if necessary, correct.

5

Do You Have the Dog You Want?

O FTEN terribly troublesome dog behavior problems result from an owner allowing eighty zillion little problems to go unchecked. Well, at least the *owner* perceives the little problems as insignificant. Little incidents of bad behavior are excused because the infractions really aren't that bothersome. Worse yet, an owner might think that some of the small-time naughtiness is comical and cute. These are the same owners who go into catatonic shock when they read over the twenty points of my Radical Regimen for Recalcitrant Rovers. About ten of the twenty points in the RRRR program mention various forms of obnoxiousness that dogs engage in that many owners think are cute. Some owners read the RRRR and think that I am telling them not to allow their dog to be cute anymore. This disappoints them deeply. In short, there are owners who really don't want to change bad behavior. They think the project is too overwhelming and will squash the personality of the dog. Essentially, these owners have the dog they want. Here are some examples.

- Munchkin loved stealing Fritos from the coffee table. He had done it for years. He does it in front of his owners. He does it in front of guests. And of course he does it when he's left alone in a Frito-filled room. It took some sleuthing to have the owners even reveal this instance of major bad behavior. I asked, *"Does your dog do anything you know in*

Do you have the dog you want? Are you "unintentionally" training in bad behavior? This owner enjoys feeding her "favorite" crackers and cheese.

Judy Emmert/
Dealing with Dogs/
TV Ontario

It's party time! Now the "favorite" is joined by dog number two. On with the festivities.

Judy Emmert/
Dealing with Dogs/
TV Ontario

Suddenly the phone rings in another room and our owner is called away. . . . Do you have the dog you want?

Judy Emmert/
Dealing with Dogs/
TV Ontario

your heart is naughty but you still find funny?" Both husband and wife looked down toward the floor with embarrassed grins on their faces, hesitating to answer. Finally the husband raised his eyes sheepishly toward me and said, "Well, there's this Frito thing . . ." And both the husband and wife burst out laughing. They thought the behavior was cute. But there's only one problem. The reason I was sitting across from them, employed as their trainer, was that Munchkin recently lunged at the husband when he tried to retrieve a piece of steak that had fallen from his plate onto the dining room floor. Munchkin, who naturally resided during meals under the table (instead of off to the side on a down-stay where he belonged), felt that the piece of steak had been delivered from heaven expressly for him. "Will he turn on us?" the wife asked. "No," I answered, "but you'll have to stop laughing at his Frito stealing or he'll be filching much more than pieces of steak." The wife couldn't see the connection between Frito filching and the mounting aggression of the dog. She had the dog she wanted.

- Chuckles was a "humper." He belonged to a twenty-six-year-old single man. And of course wasn't neutered. All this owner had to do was cross his legs and angle his kneecap in a certain provocative way and Cocker Spaniel Chuckles promptly mounted it. The owner would then swing his crossed leg as Chuckles grasped his calf in his entwined paws and enjoyed the "ride." Chuckle's sexual mounting became a kind of party tradition. The gentleman was even asked by his friends to bring Chuckles along for various "shows" around the city. When the owner called me to explain the problem, at first I thought it was a prank call or a joke, especially when he became rather graphic in his description of Chuckle's escapades. "What do you think this is, a porn line?" I asked. The owner then explained that it was indeed a serious problem. He revealed that recently, when he tried to scrape Chuckles off his leg in order to get up and answer the phone, Chuckles had growled at him. I explained that the first step in eliminating this problem would be a change in attitude. The owner could no longer laugh at, enjoy or condone *any* sexual mounting. Later I found out that the owner had stopped the mounting for a while. He was afraid the dog would turn on him. But Chuckles had resumed his "appearances" around town and the client had not followed my instructions to neuter him. After Chuckles growled at him a second time the owner called me to complain. After double-checking to see whether my previous advice had been followed, I said simply, "I don't think there's much more I can do for you. I think you have the dog you want."

- Muffin was a "nudge." She liked to gently push her mistress on the leg, on the arm, even on her rear end. Muffin's favorite nudge maneuver was to wait until her owner was holding the morning paper with one hand and a cup of coffee with the other. Muffin would circle behind and stick her head underneath her owner's armpit, nudging the owner's arm upward. The owner had learned, after being scalded a few times, to fill her coffee cup up only halfway. She thought Muffin's behavior was cute. Of course I didn't even find out about the morning scenario until I carefully interviewed the owner and asked my famous question: "Does your dog do anything you know in your heart is naughty but you still find funny?" Why was I called in for a consultation? Three times in the last week Muffin had destroyed the morning paper. Ripped it up into a million tiny pieces. Nothing else, just the morning paper. On those same mornings, it turned out, the owner had not had coffee and had read the paper with *both* hands, depriving Muffin of her morning nudge. Muffin was jealous of the attention paid to the paper. The nudgery had to stop or the destruction would continue and probably expand in scope. This owner immediately saw the connection between the small instance of bad behavior that she thought was cute (nudgery) and the larger problem that was potentially developing. She did a set-up to trick Muffin into nudging (it wasn't hard to do). The owner ceased to think that the behavior was cute, and on a deeper level, she decided that she really didn't have the dog she wanted.

- Conrad constantly hurried his owners. When it was time to go out for a walk he would start dancing around a full half hour before the owner even picked up the leash. Something as simple as the owner getting up and turning off the TV would set off Conrad's whirling dervish act. Conrad was a 120-pound Saint Bernard. The more Conrad whirled, barked and crashed around the apartment the faster the owner hurried to get him out for a walk. Conrad would then drag his owner to the park where he was immediately unleashed and allowed to tear about like a madman. The neighbors had even gotten into the habit of watching these Ben Hur chariot race walks for sheer enjoyment. The owner, and indeed the whole neighborhood, thought the behavior was cute. Only by asking my famous question did I find out about the dog's "hurry up" routine—the owner had simply asked me to teach his dog to heel, but obviously much more behavior modification was needed. You see, Conrad had finally floored his owner on the way to the park and the owner had a broken nose to prove it.

All of the above forms of cuteness are actually forms of *dominance*. When Munchkin steals, Chuckles humps, Muffin nudges or Conrad dances, they are *leading* their owners. These dogs immediately understood their owner's laughter as *submission,* because of the way dogs interpret light, lilting, whiney sounds. These seemingly insignificant actions fed directly into the development of more serious behavior problems. From the point of view of a trained trainer, "terminal cuteness" in a dog, especially if it is encouraged and condoned by the owner, quite predictably backfires. But many owners can't see the connection. And some of these owners already have the dog they want.

It really goes quite deep: Small infractions allowed to slip by lead to bigger problems. But the bigger problems can't be solved until the small infractions are identified and stopped. But that can't happen if the owner insists on seeing the small infractions as cute. It all comes back to the fact that the owner has to have a change of heart and a new view of the dog's behavior. This psychological mind shift can only occur when owners really decide, once and for all, that they don't have the dog they want, and they are going to do something about it. Sadly, it sometimes takes a bite, a growl, some thievery or one nudge too many before some owners reach that point. Then they hire me, and I tell them that the big problem they *think* is the problem isn't the only problem, just the tip of the iceberg of little "cute" problems they will have to correct.

Well, Do You . . . ?

If you are reading this book there's a big chance that you have a problem dog or know one. Ask yourself, "Do I have the dog I want?" Then reflect on everything, and I mean *everything,* the dog does during the day, especially those actions that you think are cute. Could they really be forms of dominance? And do you really want to eliminate them? This is the first, essential step in stopping a big behavior problem: revamping the way you view the little things your dog does.

Do you have the dog you want? If you've decided after reading this chapter that you don't, and you really want to create a dog you *would* want, get busy training and stop complaining. Get busy educating and stop bellyaching. Go into action setting up set-ups to cancel out behaviors that you once thought, but no longer think, are comical.

Remember, you can't have it both ways. You can't let slip by zillions of incidents of dominant behavior and justify them as funny when nobody else thinks so. The first step in getting rid of problem behavior in a dog is not working on the dog, but working on yourself.

On the other hand, if you *do* have the dog you want, I suppose that's OK, too. Live with it that way. Just don't endanger me or others. And don't invite me to visit your Frito-less house where all that will happen to me is that my knee will be raped, my coffee spilled and my feet trampled by your thieving, oversexed, pushy or hyperactive canine controller. So live like a hermit with your problem pooch, since no one will want to visit. You'll be lonely, frustrated and controlled by a dog that you will probably grow to dislike. But you *will* have one consolation: You'll have the dog you want.

6

Do Dogs Feel Guilt or Shame?

WHEN I TEACH SEMINARS in the United States and Canada I often conduct an informal poll of the audience. Without necessarily telling them in advance my own feelings, I ask them if they feel dogs can understand being disciplined after the fact for wrongdoing. I ask them to raise their hands if they've ever disciplined their dogs after "criminal" canine activity. I don't want my opinion to prejudice their vote, and I don't want the feelings of others around them to sway their vote, so I ask the seminar participants to close their eyes before the poll.

Then I ask them: "How many of you have ever disciplined your dog after the fact—you came home and found defecation, urination or something chewed or stolen, and disciplined your dog?" Regardless of what they have read in dog training books 90 percent of the audience always raise their hands. To verify what I am seeing I usually ask one or two participants to open their eyes and look around the room.

Then I ask, "Of those who raised your hands, how many of you feel that disciplining your dog after the fact had the desired effect. In other words, the dog didn't do the same naughty thing again, or at least not so quickly?" Of the 90 percent who had their hands up for the first question about 80 percent keep their hands in the air. In short, dog owners routinely discipline their dogs after the fact and claim success, but most dog training books instruct against this. Why this discrepancy?

Time Games

When I was researching my housetraining tract, *The Evans Guide for Housetraining Your Dog,* I spent hours at the American Kennel Club library poring over everything that had ever been written on the topic. Different prescriptions were dispensed pertaining to the amount of time that can pass between a canine offense and a human correction. Many authors simply said disciplining a dog after the fact is totally taboo and should *never* be done. The theory, of course, is that dogs live in the here and now and can't remember the wrong they have done.

That was one extreme. Then the "time games" began. Various authors stated that a dog *can* be disciplined after the fact but only if not more than two or three or four or ten or even 15 minutes had passed between crime and correction. Interesting, isn't it? Who interviewed the dogs to find out exactly what time span they can comprehend? And if the dogs *were* interviewed, who got interviewed? Dalmatians? Chow Chows? Pekingese? Basenjis? (I hasten to add that Basenjis can't bark, so they could hardly talk, let alone confess.)

The time games became so bizarre that in one book an author suggested that you could still discipline your dog for defecation if you discovered it later on—but only if it was still *warm.* Now, how can you tell if the mess is still warm? Should you *touch* it? Should you put a meat thermometer in it? And if you do, what is the correct temperature reading? Medium? Medium rare? Well done? It all gets a little ridiculous and tedious, doesn't it? Ridiculous *and* tedious. Tedious researching it, tedious writing about it here, perhaps tedious reading it and certainly tedious and frustrating for anyone who has to live with a dog who supposedly "can't be disciplined after the fact."

I'm spending time going over what's in the existing literature because disciplining dogs after the fact is one of the most controversial areas in dog behavior and training. During my research I found only three major authors who condoned it. Everyone else said no to the idea or started playing those silly time games. But 90 percent of the reading audience disagrees with them according to my informal polls. Noted author Carol Benjamin *(Mother Knows Best, Dog Problems)* talks about the concept of "evidence." If you have evidence you can convict your dog of a crime. I like to use the word "proof." The concept is similar. In fact, I've discovered that many guide dog trainers routinely advise their blind clients to discipline their dogs for infractions discovered after the fact. Guide dogs might appear to be saints, but they are still dogs and occasionally forget themselves. But the blind master might not discover a chewed pillow until a sighted person brings it to his or her attention. The guide dog who has "sinned" is reprimanded humanely even after the fact. Are "regular" dogs incapable of comprehending what a guide dog can comprehend? Is it possible that we have sold our dogs short in terms of their capacity for understanding discipline after the fact?

Why It Works: Some Background

Before I tell you how, when, where and why to discipline after the fact, bear with me while I give you a little more background on why it so often works. I decided to do some private research, and asked my psychologist father to educate me on the etiology of "guilt" and "shame." What he said, and what I do with the information when it comes to disciplining dogs, might help you to correct your problem pooch.

First, understand that we are going to be talking about guilt and shame in their purer, more primitive forms. Wise parents bring guilt and shame out of the closet. We should do as much for our dogs. Here we go.

Guilt, as experienced in humans, can begin around age five to seven (rarely before) and operates as a kind of undercurrent. *Guilt* doesn't exactly wash over a person every minute of the day, but nevertheless keeps the person in a state of sadness and confusion. *Shame,* on the other hand, is a much more immediate phenomenon, and shame is always felt, and felt deeply. Think about how often you've heard people say, "I was so embarrassed I could have crawled under a table" or "I felt so ashamed I could have died!" Interesting how we humans feel so ashamed about being shamed that we often invoke life or death comparisons—"I could have *died!*" You might be guilty all your life, but you are *shamed* for a moment—even if the moment seems like an eternity. Got the difference?

Now, given what we know about dogs and how they like to live life in the here and now—being much smarter than we stupid humans—I would venture to say that dogs cannot experience ongoing guilt, but they can be made to feel shame, or to feel ashamed. That's why I believe in carefully structured discipline after the fact—because the dog *can* be shamed. In fact, there is one breed—the Pharoah Hound—that *blushes* when excited or reprimanded.

The difference between guilt and shame hinges on *discovery.* You can be guilty all day or all year, but you are shamed when you are discovered. Someone could be having, for instance, and extramarital affair, and feel very guilty about it, but the guilt doesn't exactly stop the affair from continuing. But if your mate *discovers* you in bed with your lover, you are bound to feel more ashamed than guilty, for the moment at least. That's why it's so important to keep your cool and not scream when you discover evidence of wrongdoing on the part of your dog. More on that soon.

The distinction between guilt and shame is important. If you understand it you will be able to give corrections with connections. Don't kid yourself for one minute that your dog feels an ongoing sense of guilt over what it did or even plans to do. Your dog can be made to feel shame but it's unacquainted with guilt. Guilt is a human invention stemming from human culture—dogs couldn't care less about it. Just think in terms of simple shame, the kind of shame you felt when you were less than five. Little children are incapable of feeling guilty, but they *can* be shamed. Dogs are like little kids in this respect. They too can be shamed, but they do not feel guilt.

People who want their dogs to feel ongoing guilt—and there are many—like to say, "He does it all for spite," and then they will usually add, "He knows when he's done wrong" or "He knows he's guilty" when all the dog is doing is looking ashamed. Watch what you think about your dog and certainly what you say about it, because if you really believe your dog is "guilty" and "does it all for spite" rather than simply showing shame and frustration, you will tend to deal with your pet on a moral plane. You'll then get very angry and abusive rather than dealing out fair, calm corrections that clarify issues for the dog rather than confuse them.

Follow these steps:

1. If you come home and you find evidence of defecation, urination or something chewed or stolen, you can try disciplining after the fact if you have "proof"—but you must not react to the proof until you get the dog *to* the proof. In other words, don't explode into the house and scream or whine at your dog. The dog will simply run away and you will *think* you have corrected it. I assure you, you have not. Instead, say nothing. Go get the dog. The dog may still flinch when you approach. That's because your body language is hard to disguise, and perhaps you have a past history of screaming at the proof before getting the dog to the proof. Just approach the dog calmly even if it flinches.

2. Without saying anything yet, bring the dog by the collar over to the proof. If the proof is a chewed or stolen item, pick it up and brandish it in front of the dog's face, softly but firmly scolding the dog. Remember you want to mimic the growl of the bitch in your tonality. *Grrrrrrrrrrrrr.* For really recalcitrant thieves use the swat-under-the-chin correction.

3. If the proof is defecation or urination the method is slightly different. Of course you can't pick it up, so simply tilt the dog's head down toward the mistake *without* shoving the dog's nose in it. With your other hand point to the mistake and give your growl reprimand. Again, for older dogs who consistently fall off the housetraining wagon, the swat correction may be in order at this juncture.

4. Now, trot your dog to the desired area for defecation or urination, unless this is impossible. If the proof was a chewed item, or if the dog eliminated, but it is simply not possible to march the dog to the desired area for elimination, simply isolate the dog. Return and clean up the mess, using vinegar and water (50/50) for housetraining accidents (*never* ammonia). Don't let the dog see you cleaning up. Your body language looks submissive as you kneel, grovel, scrape and scrub, and that won't win you any Brownie points in the dog's eyes.

5. Leave the dog in isolation for thirty minutes. If it barks, yodels or screams when isolated you will have to correct it for that also. Isolation after serious canine crimes such as destructive chewing or inap-

propriate elimination is necessary. These infractions are almost always attempts on the part of the dog to claim territory within the household. By isolating the dog you are telling it, "This small room or crate is all you get, and if you chew my things or soil my house, you'll be confined. The rest of the territory is *mine* and I, as the Alpha figure, simply grant you access to it. You make a mistake on *my* territory—Boom!—you get disciplined and demoted in territory." Don't worry that isolating the dog will make it "hate its crate" or a particular room. As Carol Benjamin says, "when your mother sent you to your room after you caused trouble, it didn't make you hate your room." I'd only add that perhaps it made you "hate" your mother—for a while—but maybe you didn't misbehave so soon afterward!

Some Qualifications

If your dog continues to commit crimes while you are away, and certainly if it does the same naughty things right in front of you, and you've tried disciplining the dog after the fact and/or during the act, your dog is probably telling you that for some reason it simply cannot understand the corrections. Double-check your corrective style by rereading chapter 11, "Why Set-ups Sometimes Foul Up," and simply arrange the dog's life so that it does not have access to your personal belongings. Also see chapter 12, "Creative Avoidance," and practice it for two to three weeks. This will probably mean more confinement or the use of a crate. There are some dogs who simply cannot be shamed—during or after an act of mischief—but this is rare.

Finally, remember to keep your cool when disciplining during the fact or after the fact. No screaming! No hysterics! This is correction time, not Oscar time. No Academy Awards are being presented for Most Dramatic Canine Correction. Your on-site growling sentence should never be longer than three to four *seconds*. Remember, dignity is never despised by dogs, it is always respected. Yelling at your dog is a good way to cheapen yourself. The dog can tell that you've lost your cool. Your lack of control doesn't elevate your Alpha status, and may make the dog escalate into violence. On the other hand, if your correction is too soft, or if you break down laughing because you think what the dog did was cute, the dog will understand the signals you send as submissive. Wimpy owners often have to act angry even if they aren't.

Many dog writers have not and will not take the risk of going out on a limb and discussing discipline after the fact, even if they themselves do it at home with their own dogs and have raised their hands during my poll (and some have). But I am not ashamed to bring up shame in dogs. I'd be ashamed if I didn't. I suppose there is always a chance that some domineering owners will unfairly and overharshly discipline their dogs. They will reap what they sow. The dog will continue to defecate or destroy, and these owners will continue to believe that the dog is guilty. My responsibility as a dog trainer and writer is to bring to you my *lived* experience with dogs and share with you what has worked for me and many others, not just deal in theory and abstraction. If dogs cannot be shamed, and truly cannot understand discipline after the fact, why does it so often work so well for so many owners and so many dogs?

If you've got a problem pooch that acts up only when you are gone, and you've been wondering if and when you can correct such a dog—take heart, you often can. But hold the thought—and the discipline—let's take a look at *you* first.

We may never know for certain whether dogs feel guilt or shame. My personal observation is that the cannot feel guilt but can be shamed. *Kevin Smith*

7

Your Owner Personality or How to Drive Your Dog Nuts in Five Days or Less

---

DID YOU KNOW you can drive your dog bonkers simply by being who you are? If that sounds like an insult, please don't take it that way. As you now know, I drove my first dog stark, raving crazy simply by being the shy, nervous personality I used to be. She was an open, friendly, outgoing three-month-old German Shepherd puppy when she was placed in my care at the beginning of 1972. By mid-1972 she had picked up on my insecurities and resembled fetal jelly more than the happy puppy she started as. I was a first-class placater with my new charge and projected my personality onto her.

I've since owned many more dogs. While I still have my handling foibles, I have been able to learn enough about them to avoid frying more canine brains. Ironically, a system I developed to help other trainers and dog-owner counselors classify owner personalities has helped me to stare down my own faults. I first introduced this classification system in *The Evans Guide for Counseling Dog Owners*. That book is geared to the professional, who, in any capacity, has to talk with dog owners. In this book, I'll talk more informally about owner personalities. They are the placater, the blamer, the computer, the distractor and the leveler.

These classifications are the terms of the late Virginia Satir, a pioneer in the field of family therapy. I first met Dr. Satir when I was about ten years old and she did a series of seminars with my father, who was also doing family therapy. Satir says that placating, computing, distracting or leveling are near-universal patterns of communication people use with each other in order to avoid the threat of rejection or elicit obedience and cooperation—in other words, to get what they want. I theorize that people also employ these ploys to get what they want from their dogs.

- You can *placate,* so the dog doesn't get mad at you, so the dog will perceive you as being "fair," with the hope of getting obedience and cooperation.
- You can *blame* the dog, so that it will regard you as strong, in control and not to be trifled with.
- You can *compute,* be very logical, orderly, concise and unfeeling, and hope that the dog will see the eminent "sanity" of your approach.
- You can *distract* yourself and others from the dog and its problems and just ignore bad behavior as if it were not there.
- You can *level* with your dog, acting as leader, steward and Alpha, while at the same time deepening your friendship with your dog.

It's important that you diagnose your owner personality because it often influences your "paralanguage": the emotional overtones your dog ascribes to the way that you sound. And the way you sound, the tonalities that you use in your speech, are often directly influenced by your owner personality. If you placate, you will tend to whine at your dog, and the dog will regard you as a littermate, an equal, a peer. Your set-ups for bad behavior will lack authority because your underlying owner personality is not taken seriously by the dog. If you blame, your voice will tend to be either too loud, with accompanying oververbalization, or hard, tight, succinct but tense, and the dog will fight this misuse of leadership. Your set-ups will be overproduced, possibly hysterical and bombastic, and will only frighten, not teach. If you compute, your voice will probably be dry, flat, unanimated and clinically cold. Your set-ups will be technically accurate but their staging will lack the drama and surprise that are essential. If you distract, you will be in an ongoing state of ambivalence about the dog, and your voice will be lilting, sing-songish and lacking in authority. Your set-ups will be flops. If your paralanguage is off, the dog will tend to regard you as a littermate instead of a leader, as a bimbo rather than the boss and, in extreme cases, as an ass rather than an Alpha.

It sounds complex but it really isn't. How you think of yourself inevitably influences how you sound to others—and to your dog. Sound like a wimp and you'll probably get taken advantage of. Boss others around and you'll get into fights. Try to be superlogical and Murphy's Law—If anything can go wrong, it will—will get you every time. And simply ignoring life or distracting yourself from it will lead nowhere.

The Placater

A large percentage of problem dog owners are placaters. They are over-verbal with their dogs and talk in long, whiney sentences. They plead with the dog to "be good" and their whining tonalities are usually decoded by dogs as the sound of a littermate. Whines, wimpers and yelps are infantile sounds that littermates make among themselves when they are cold, hungry, lonely or stressed in some way. Most placaters don't even realize that they are whining at their dogs.

If you are a placater you are probably enamored of the word "but" and the phrase "if only," as in

- "But he won't *listen.*"
- "But I *tried* that."
- "If only I had gotten a Maltese instead of a Rotteweiler."
- "If only I had gone to that third obedience class, maybe he wouldn't still pull me down the street."
- "If only I had *tried* harder, I could have changed the rainwater into wine, but I didn't *try* hard enough."

When I train trainers in seminars I play recordings of placaters taped during counseling sessions. The words "but" and "if only" can be heard frequently on the tapes. Placaters are basically passive and these terms give them excuses for not going into action. In extreme cases placaters reduce themselves to food ploys in order to gain even a shred of obedience from their dogs. The dog will only come, lie down, sit or simply leave the owner alone when a food reward is offered.

Placaters have low self-esteem and do not see themselves in a leadership role with the dog. The placater wants to be friends with everyone. But dogs want more than friendship: They want leadership.

How to Help Yourself

If you are a placater your first task is to educate yourself concerning the concept of paralanguage. Just reading this book is a good start, but because books don't talk it might also be therapeutic to simply listen to yourself as you deal with your dog. Studies show that a full 35 percent of dog owners talk to their dogs *all day* as if they were fellow human beings. I'm willing to bet that at least 90 percent of that 35 percent are placaters. Because some of the problem behavior your dog exhibits might stem from its hearing faulty paralanguage too often during the regular course of a day, my suggestion is to simply not talk to the dog without reason for one month. Save speaking to your dog for commands or for giving praise when it is truly warranted. If you are a placater, simply drop point number twenty in chapter 9's RRRR program—no jingle for your dog. Your placating has probably already jangled its nerves. When the dog experiences long stretches of silence interspersed only with occasional command words and praise phrases, its attitude toward you will change. At first the dog might be bewildered, but it will soon learn to listen more intently. After all, something you have to say might actually be important! The benefit for you is that, even unbeknownst to yourself, you will find yourself placating and pleading less, and will inevitably move more toward the owner personality of the leveler.

You have a great advantage if you are a placater. It is very likely that you have a self-deprecating sense of humor. You're capable of laughing at yourself and you should choose educational tools that are funny, sympathetic to your stance but offer no-nonsense advice. Placaters like to laugh, especially at themselves and this is OK as long as there is also some education going on. While I hope that this book is funny enough and sympathetic enough for a placater to learn new ways of handling the dog, and at the same time have a good hoot, I realize that other books might be welcomed also.

Finally, in order to help yourself pull out of placating, remember not to be too rough on yourself. Besides choosing funny yet helpful training books, choose a trainer who does not criticize you directly or harshly. Know why? As a placater, you will tend to simply agree with the criticism, but simple agreement, simple acquiescence, will not necessarily mean that you have learned anything, only that you have acquiesced to the criticism in an attempt to placate the trainer! Placating can become a vicious cycle that carries over from how you relate with your dog into how you relate with those trying to help you with the dog. The untrained trainer doesn't realize that the key to effective criticism, especially with a placater, lies in humor and technique. Luckily, it is usually easy to find a funny dog trainer who will help you without clobbering you with direct criticisms. The reason for this (and this is a closet secret in the dog fancy) is that many trainers are former placaters!

The Blamer

The blamer is a faultfinder, a boss and a dictator—but the sad thing is that the blamer doesn't know it. Blamers feel that they are superior and like to use all-encompassing terms like "always," "never" and "all" when describing their dogs.

- "Tippy *always* disobeys."
- "He *never* comes when he is called."
- "He does it *all* for spite."

As a blamer you will probably catch yourself using such drastic terminology. Be honest with yourself and you will probably admit that you often begin sentences with the dog's name or the personal pronoun that pertains to the dog. By putting the dog's name first in a sentence, or at least somewhere in the sentence, it enables you to blame the dog more effectively. You probably aren't even aware that you do this. It might just be part of your overall personality. As the character Ouiser Boudreaux says in *Steel Magnolias,* "I'm not crazy. I've just been in a bad mood for forty years." However, you should realize that such an overall stance in life is bound to have ramifications for your dog. Dog problems are very rarely the fault of the dog alone. They are almost always the result of human/dog interaction.

If you are a blamer you might have trouble in obedience classes or with a trainer because you will tend to criticize everything being taught. You will come into class or engage a private trainer with a know-it-all attitude that will, in fact, thwart the very help you are seeking. Because you will question every technique and move the trainer makes, you will probably not do your homework in between classes and will fall behind the rest of the group. Then you will blame the trainer or the other members of the class. What blamers have to realize about themselves is that they almost always blame everyone else for their dogs' bad behavior rather than themselves. Blamers always assume they are never the one causing any of the problems.

How to Help Yourself

If you recognize yourself as a blamer you should probably realize that you might have a set of problems more complex than can be handled in this book. That's for you, or your therapist, to diagnose. I hasten to add that in some cases of extreme blaming the result is a battered dog. There is a grim ecology present in the households of some blamers. It tallies like this: Husband beats wife; wife beats children; oldest child beats youngest child; youngest child beats dog. In this case, professional help is needed.

Usually, however, things have not gotten that bad. For a blamer, sometimes a simple examination of conscience and a commitment to training will do. You might take ten to twenty minutes before each training session with your dog to meditate or at least sit quietly. Read over your training lesson and rehearse in your mind what you plan to do with your dog that session. Resolve in advance that you will not become testy or agitated if the dog doesn't respond just as you would like. Blamers often have short fuses and bring incredible tension and nervous energy into training sessions. Of course the dog picks this up. The session turns into a shambles. Blamers often laugh at the idea of meditating, but they are exactly the persons who could profit from it. Blamers are often really very insecure and unhappy persons underneath the difficult exterior that is presented to the public. But the dog, even a dog the blamer deems "stupid," often sees through this mask and sees a person who needs to be secure and safe and needs a friend. Unfortunately, many blamers get into such dominance fights with their canine charges that they never decipher the truce messages that the dog telegraphs.

Blamers should be especially sensitive toward trainers. If you've decoded yourself as a blamer, even if you have to bite your tongue, give the trainer a chance to explain fully any technique that will help you. You don't have to like or love your trainer, or for that matter a training book you might read, just try to be civil and empathetic with the trainer's or book's goals. One more closet secret: Some dog trainers are former blamers!

The Computer

This personality is very reasonable, very correct, calm, cool and collected. This owner could be compared to an actual computer. The vocal tonality is dry, flat, a monotone. If you've ever heard a voice-activated computer "talk" you have an idea of the vocal quality. Dogs, however, adore vocal modulations, especially a higher pitched voice for praise and a lowered voice for reprimands. The computer offers none of this. Computers very carefully choose their words and actions. Giving praise is a supreme difficulty because the computer is rigid physically and mentally.

Computers love to read and memorize training books. They expect everything that is said in the book to be the gospel truth and allow the author little or no leeway. They often view dogs as little robots who can be ordered about if only all the right words are said at just the right time. Sometimes professionals in the hard sciences exhibit computer traits. Lawyers, especially, often take a linear, computerish view of life. The syndrome also occurs among some physicians and even veterinarians. I am not announcing anything new— medical schools now have to teach physicians bedside manners while lawyers flood seminars that promise to teach them kinder negotiating skills and simple human warmth.

However, computers have several good points going for them. When they seek out training they usually listen very carefully to everything the trainer has to say. They do the prescribed homework with their dog between private sessions or classes. If they are not sure about something, they ask. Correct information is extremely important to the computer. Just as proper data must be fed into a mechanical computer in order for a project to be successful, the human computer doesn't feel he can train his dog successfully unless he has proper data. In the computer's world life goes like this: First there is A and after A is, of course, B. Then we proceed naturally to C, followed by, of course, D. Order. Logic. Correct sequence.

The problem with this world view is that dogs don't necessarily operate this way. The dog might say instead, "No, no, no—we're *starting* at B. Then we're going back to A. But, I'm not sure—we might go on to C." This of course throws the computer for a loop. The computer becomes especially frustrated if a training book states an A-B-C-D scenario, and then the dog performs otherwise. That's why my philosophy of dog writing is never to say, "Do *this*, and your dog will never do *that* again." Instead, I allow for more leeway in dog/human interactions and will suggest, "Try this, try this and try this. If that doesn't work, then try this, this and this." I don't kid myself that training texts can be absolutely accurate or exact, no matter how badly computers desire them to be.

You might wonder why a computer gets a dog at all. I think I've finally figured it out. Computers want to recapture a side of themselves that they sense they have sacrificed. One accusation hurled at dog people to "explain" why we keep dogs is the old chestnut that says the dogs are simply our substitute kids. This criticism is often levied by non–dog owners. But there might be some truth to it. A look at the dog fancy *will* reveal a large number of single persons and childless couples. But a second look quickly reveals the presence of many families with children who also choose to keep one or more dogs. Perhaps the real reason that people keep a dog is not so much as a substitute kid, but instead as a way to get back to the kid in themselves—the free, open, honest person who gave spontaneous unconditional love to all, who loved to play (in fact, *lived* to play) and who led a carefree life. The dog is both an actual manifestation and a cultural icon of these traits. This was, in fact, Freud's reasoning behind why people get dogs and I think it is accurate. The personality type that has most sacrificed the kid in itself is the computer. And computers know it. They sense that the kid inside is "on vacation" or might even be dead— that's why they get a dog. So you see, the motivation behind the computer's acquiring a dog is really quite healthy. While the behavior toward the dog might *seem* cold and distant, computers are really quite taken with their dogs and love their pets.

How to Help Yourself

If you've diagnosed yourself as a computer, you need to get into a training class and watch good dog handlers in action. Watch the instructor and the better handlers in the class. Listen to the amount of praise they give and instead of judging them as gushy Pollyannas, watch how the faces of the dogs light up and how obedience to commands picks up. You might ask the instructor to work with your dog, which might be somewhat surprised at being handled in a vivacious way. Even if you feel uncomfortable about praising your dog, give it a sincere try. Remember the inner reason you got your dog to begin with was to free yourself to enjoy life more fully through and with your friend. You owe your dog not only training, but sincere praise, tons of warmth and gratitude for all it has given you.

The Distractor

We've all met off-the-wall dog owners—people who seem unaware that they have a badly behaved dog. We see such owners being dragged down the street, or we see them driving along with a horde of unruly ruffians boomeranging around the back of the car, sometimes occupying the passenger side of the front seat—or even the driver's seat—barking wildly, totally out of control. Meanwhile the owners will be listening to the radio, talking to friends or simply humming to themselves—anything to distract themselves from the shenanigans of the dogs.

Obedience class instructors know distractors well. They are the members of the class who, even after several sessions, still do not have their dogs under even minimal control. While all the placaters, blamers and computers in the class will have begun correcting their personality foibles and paralanguage problems, and have their dogs sitting calmly, the distractor has a rotating pooch and a dislocated arm.

Distractors love to give double or even triple commands that confuse the dog. Double commands are phrases like "sit down" or "c'mon heel." Since "sit" and "down" are two distinct body positions, there is no way a dog can adopt both at the same time. "C'mon" might be used as a term of encouragement, but it is also a word that sounds suspiciously like "come"—which means that the dog should present itself directly in front of your body. It's awfully hard for the dog to do that if it's trying to stay by your side to heel. Watch out for double commands, especially if you are a distractor.

I once had a distractor as a client who, even after repeated admonitions, persisted in giving double and even triple commands. During our last lesson together I asked her to do some off-leash work with the dog, a Cocker Spaniel, who was standing about ten feet in front of her. "Tell the dog to sit," I said. My client said "sit" in a wimpy voice that the dog totally ignored. The client looked to me and I told her to give the command again. Using the same ineffective tonality she whined at the dog, "Sit downnnnn." Again the dog stood staring at her with a blank expression on its face. My client stamped her foot in exasperation and again looked to me for advice. I told her to give the command once again. This time she got angry and bellowed at the Cocker, *"C'mon, sit down!"* At this point the dog went into a full crouch. The front portion of his body was slightly more elevated than the rear, which he dragged on the ground as he began to crawl subserviently toward his mistress. He looked like a guerrilla snaking along the jungle floor. The frustrated distractor threw up her hands, stamped her feet again, turned to me and said, "See, he's stupid. He doesn't know his words!" "Excuse me," I replied, "He knows his words very well. He's coming, sitting and lying down. You *did* give three commands. That's his version of it." The distractor now looked totally baffled, and I thought to myself, "This is a damn smart dog. He's found a way to obey all three commands. He probably figures, 'I don't know what she wants—I'll give her a little of everything and see if she'll leave me alone.' "

How to Help Yourself

First, try not to do more than one thing at a time when you are working with your dog. Distractors need to meditate a bit before starting a training session and clear their minds of all distractions. Take the phone off the hook, drive to a quiet area, do whatever you have to do to concentrate on the training session alone and not be drawn away from it. While in general I do not like the idea of sending the dog away to a training camp to be educated, distractors sometimes need a break from their dogs. Just be sure if you do this that the same trainer who takes your dog in releases the dog to you. Consistency is very important in your training efforts because, let's face it, you're distracted and have a lot on your mind. Finally, if you have diagnosed yourself as a distractor and do not currently own a dog but are simply thinking of getting one, *don't*. Wait until the elements of your scattered life fall together more cohesively so that you can offer a dog the consistency and leadership it deserves. Try goldfish, but don't forget to feed them.

The Leveler

A leveler offers to the dog friendship *and* leadership. The voice is controlled and reasonable. The relationship between the dog and the leveler is honest. The dog clearly sees the leveler as the Alpha figure in its life and responds happily. Some owners are natural-born levelers and others are reformed placaters, blamers, computers or distractors who assimilated correct handling from a book or picked up paralanguage skills by listening to and observing levelers interacting with their dogs. There are three hallmarks of the leveling response:

1. When giving an active command or praising the dog, the leveler's voice will tend to rise higher in tonality—without whining or yelling. For instance, a praise phrase like "good boy" will be delivered in an animated tonality more like "Goooooood boy!" A command word that needs an active response such as "Come!" will be delivered in a slightly elevated tone. Dog's like voice modulation and respond well to it. The opposite is also true.
2. When giving a static command or reprimanding the dog, the leveler's voice will tend to sink lower in tonality—without yelling. For example, a command word such as "stay" will be delivered in a deep or "husky" tone of voice rather than a light one. The darkened tonality will definitely suggest to the dog that no movement is desired. A discipline phrase or a reprimand will also be delivered in a lower tone. Again, some levelers adopt these tonalities quite naturally and others learn from experience. Don't worry if you have a naturally high voice. It's the *difference* between the way you normally sound and the higher or lower voice modulations that will impress the dog. Just remember: active command or praise go higher, static command or reprimand go lower.
3. When reprimanding the dog, levelers do not yell. Instead, the leveler will change tonality but not increase volume. If you yell, the dog will literally start to structure reality around your yelling. The dog will reason that you don't really mean it unless you yell. Since dogs do know the difference between the two species, it becomes noticeable after a while that the two-legged members are addressed in normal conversational tones, while members of the four-legged species are yelled at. In short, if you yell enough, you will simply produce a dog

that will literally learn to *wait* for you to yell. Levelers don't yell. They level with their dogs using paralanguage that the dog understands.

So, that's it, our rundown of owner personalities. In my experience, 50 percent of owners placate their dogs, 30 percent blame their dogs, 15 percent compute with their dogs and just .5 percent distract themselves from their dogs. That leaves only 4.5 percent of owners who, without any work, reading or education will naturally level with their dogs. It should be quite clear that for most of us, dog training skills are *learned* skills. And we should be thankful they *can* be learned, otherwise our dogs would be doomed to living in a bizarre world where they are constantly placated into obedience, blamed for everything, overreasoned with, forced to decipher distractions they cannot understand or simply ignored. Once again, remember, your owner personality influences your paralanguage, and your use of paralanguage will give you problems or peace.

8

Look, See, Observe, Memorize, Insee

I T'S A BIG STEP for owners to admit that they are a placater, blamer, computer or distractor. It's an even bigger admission to allow that because of these personality problems one's perceptive abilities might be limited. But inability to see clearly and fully lies at the root of many pooch/people problems.

It's amazing the number of clients I've had over the years who claim that erratic behavior on the part of their dog is totally unpredictable, unexplainable and spontaneous. I'll hear, "She just explodes over nothing and tries to bite people," or "He steals my things so quickly there is just nothing I can do about it." Owners of problem dogs often have a vested interest in believing, and getting other people to believe, that their dogs misbehave so quickly, so suddenly that nothing can be done to even anticipate the bad behavior. After all, if this is the case, then the owner is excused from doing anything about the misbehavior. An owner can justifiably claim difficulty in arranging a set-up if the dog truly engages in completely unprovoked, unexplainable behavior. Then it's back to complaining or off to the pound with the dog. But, as trainers have said for years, "Train, don't complain." I'd only add, "Set up. Don't screw up."

Part of training your dog is to open your eyes and go beyond simply looking at your dog to *seeing* its behavior. The fact is, many owners of problem dogs can't even see what's right in front of them. Their dogs will already be lunging, growling or snapping at somebody before they even consider verbally, not to mention physically, reprimanding the dog. These owners can't see the dog escalating into aggression or some other form of bad behavior because they literally don't know what to look for. Once educated as to the signs of upcoming aggression you might think that these owners would be faster on the draw and able to discipline their dogs more speedily. But the problem goes even deeper than lack of education as to trouble signals. Trouble signs can be memorized—but if your vision is impaired, we're in trouble.

The sad fact is, not only do many owners of problem dogs not know what danger signs to look for, they don't know how to look, period. The situation becomes quite serious because the owner is blind to seeing the true nature of the problem dog's behavior. Some trainers simply drill these owners and their dogs in obedience commands, forgetting that the owner's basic ability to perceive visual reality may be retarded.

If that sounds like a severe judgment, it's meant to be. In an era of endless remote-control options for practically every aspect of life—including selecting a TV channel or activating the coffee maker from bed—our ability to sit still and look, see and observe has been extremely compromised. This lack presents serious difficulties for our dogs because the core of all animal study is the ability to *truly observe* the animal's behavior. Owners of problem dogs are not exempt; in fact, they need such skills even more than other owners.

The eminent naturalist Konrad Lorenz once noted, "You must love the animal you are studying, and in order to love it, you must go beyond just looking at it." This seemingly innocent and obvious statement caused an uproar among academic naturalists, who were used to quantifying animals and delivering the behaviorist's party line—that animals are just little machines and it is a waste of time to speculate about things we can't catalog, and far better to limit our study to what we *can* see: the input, the stimulus, the response. Konrad Lorenz, talking about "loving the animals you are studying," blew some academics away. The man must be a romantic, a hedonist, a communist or something worse.

But decades after Lorenz made his statement about loving animals we are really not much better off in our ways of dealing with animals—including dogs, although we will protest to high heaven that we do love them. We stammer and stutter and stamp our feet and say again and again, "We *do* love them. We do, we do, we do!" The problem, however, is an inverse one for dog people. I accept all that stuttering and stammering and stamping of feet. I know that most dog owners and professionals *do* love dogs—but I am far from convinced that the majority of lay persons or even professionals know how to *study* a dog.

The Steps to Inseeing

Most of us never get much past the point of *looking* at something or somebody. But if you do, you are on your way to a visual adventure that will enrich your life and enable you to stop problem behavior by recognizing it promptly. You will, for the first time, be able to see your dog!

Here's an example of what I mean: Let's say you're driving home from work one day. It's a regular, old, run-of-the-mill day. Nothing special about it. You come to an intersection and stop at the red light. You stop at this same red light 365 days a year, sometimes twice in one day. But today, perhaps because the sun is exceptionally bright, you turn toward a building on your left and notice some ornamentation on the roof of the building. It suddenly strikes you that you've never quite noticed that ornamentation before. Congratulations! You've just graduated one step from looking to *seeing* what has been right in front of you for days and even years.

Most people would simply drive on at this point, perhaps vaguely noting that they should take more time to stop and look at the world around them. But because you want to embark on a visual adventure, *you* won't simply drive on. Instead, you pull over to the side of the road, get out of your car, cross the street and look even more carefully at the ornamentation. You notice that it is baroque in style and you recall your college art history courses. You notice the interplay between the sunlight and the ornamentation. You see the shadows the ornamentation casts on the rest of the roof. You note some pigeons strutting near the ornamentation. Congratulations! You've just gone one step further from looking to seeing to *observing*. Observation takes more time, you note, but you're grateful you've taken the time because the image of the ornamentation stays clearly in your mind even as you walk back to your car.

Now, if you were to pursue this visual adventure even further, you would, when you came to the next stoplight, be able to close your eyes and still see the ornamentation just as it was a moment ago. Your mind's eye has *memorized* it. If you were determined to take this exercise even further, perhaps you would go home, sit down and write something about the ornamentation. Everyone comes to this last step of *inseeing* in their own personal way. Perhaps you would write a poem about the building or its ornamentation. Maybe you would make a journal entry about the ornamentation, discussing its meaning to you—if only that noticing the ornamentation clearly indicates that you have to take more time to stop and truly look, see, observe, memorize what you've observed and try to insee.

Try this exercise at the next intersection you commonly cross. Better yet, try it with your dog. Try it first when the dog is just hanging around doing nothing. Then you can graduate to the more complex activity of observing your dog in action. Remember, if you do not know what you are looking at, you will never be able to anticipate bad behavior and issue an advance warning as step one of a set-up. Sometimes issuing an advance warning is impossible anyway, no matter how acute your observation skills are, but many times it is the owner's inability to see danger signals and signs that makes a set-up foul up. This is where a professional trainer with a trained eye can be of great help.

The Payoff

There is another payoff in perfecting your visual skills. You will fall more deeply in love with your dog insofar as you go beyond simply looking at him or her. With a little discipline you will be able to reach new levels of observation that will culminate in beautiful moments of inseeing. Inseeing is a term originated by the poet Rilke. I chose to reproduce his definition at the beginning of *How to Be Your Dog's Best Friend* (Little, Brown, 1978), which I coauthored while with the Monks of New Skete. Brother Nil, then a monk at New Skete monastery and a German classics scholar, conducted a series of talks on Rilke for the monks and alerted me to this quote about dogs:

> I love inseeing. Can you imagine with me how glorious it is to insee, for example, a dog as one passes by. *Insee* (I don't mean in-spect, which is only a kind of human gymnastic, by means of which one immediately comes out again on the other side of the dog, regarding it merely, so to speak, as a window upon the humanity lying behind it, not that.)—but to let oneself precisely into the dog's very center, the point from which it becomes a dog, the place in it where God, as it were, would have sat down for a moment when the dog was finished, in order to watch it under the influence of its first embarrassments and inspirations and to know that it was good, that nothing was lacking, that it could have not been better made. . . . Laugh though you may, dear confidant, if I am to tell you *where* my all-greatest feeling, my world-feeling, my earthly bliss was to be found, I must confess to you: it was to be found time and again, here and there, in such timeless moments of this divine inseeing.
>
> Rainer Maria Rilke, *New Poems,* translated by J. B. Leishman (Berkeley, Calif.: North Point Press, 1977)

At the time I became acquainted with this quote and the concept of inseeing, I had been appointed head trainer of the monastery German Shepherd Dogs and began boarding and training recalcitrants of all breeds dumped off at the monastery kennels for "rehabilitation." I had only been training for about one year. I hardly even knew what I was looking at when I encountered criminal canine behavior. I certainly didn't know how to see it for what it was, truly observe it, memorize what I had observed and write up a program to help a distraught owner eliminate the behavior. Inseeing, I thought, was truly a distant, and maybe even an unreachable, goal. But at least I knew there *was* a goal to strive for. Now you do, too.

I started to do daily exercises, such as the one we've discussed in this chapter, with the monastery dogs and with inanimate objects out in the woods. Slowly my perceptional abilities developed. With a little practice yours will, too. So don't feel frustrated if you can only inspect and not insee. In fact, even perfecting your ability to inspect your dog's actions will help you to set up sterling set-ups. Inseeing will most probably be reserved for more contemplative, quiet, nondemanding times with your dog. Those "timeless moments of inseeing" Rilke mentioned will deepen your relationship with your dog and balance off those times when you have to inspect its behavior and stage a set-up to change it. But it all starts with *you* and your ability to look, see, observe, memorize and insee.

You might wonder if your dog needs to perfect *its* ability to truly see *you*. Trust me—your dog watches you more closely than you'll ever watch it. After all, it's got little else to do except eat, behave, or misbehave, play with its toys, go for walks—and watch your every move. It's *we* who don't see, not them!

9

RRRR:
A Radical Regimen
for Recalcitrant Rovers

$\mathbf{Y}$OU KNOW that presiding over every wolf pack there is a leader, or Alpha wolf, who keeps order within the pack. This wolf informs other wolves about their status on a particular day, about how well they are doing and about how poorly they are doing. Depending on the Alpha's style of leadership, its role might be that of a dictator or a guide, or the Alpha might adopt either of these roles at different times. All subordinate wolves look to this Alpha for leadership and direction.

You also know that domestication has not nullified in the dog this ardent need to lead or be led. While dogs are light-years distant from wolves in some respects, in other matters they still resemble wolves closely—especially in their need for an Alpha figure to guide them, and failing the presence of such a guide, the desire to assume the position themselves. For your dog, there should be absolutely no question as to who is the Alpha figure in its life. You are, or more accurately, you'd better be!

Trainers often express these theories of Alpha leadership to their class and private clients in crude ways that accentuate the "control" the owner must gain to be the "boss." Trainers will often say, "Let him know who's boss!" and then hand out a few folklore corrections to whatever problem is at hand.

Trouble is, just applying those few corrections—even if they do seem to address the behavior problem at hand—will not by itself elevate the wimpy owner to anything approximating Alpha status in the naughty dog's mind. In fact, the dog might rebel fiercely, getting into a dominance fight with the owner, or simply correcting itself on one set of problems (say, destructive chewing) and substituting another (soiling in the house instead of chewing). A few folklore corrections down the pike and the owner is *still* not Alpha.

Often a more holistic approach to bad behavior is called for—a hit list of changes that are imposed on the dog in order to rattle its brains, disturb the status quo and slot the owner in the starring role as Ms. or Mr. Alpha once and for all. Little things add up. Just as it was probably a plethora of little infractions, little slips, little forms of naughtiness that allowed the situation between dog and owner to deteriorate, it will be a series of little changes and renovations that will bring the relationship back into sync and stop the problem behavior. The *specific* problem areas can be restructured via set-ups, but more on that later.

No Quick Fixes

If you are the owner of a problem dog, please reflect on the above comments before reading on. You probably would prefer a quick-fix solution from this book—just one or two techniques that will cancel whatever behavior problem you are now putting up with from your dog. I must say to you: It's not that easy or simple. With few exceptions, your problems with your dog, at root, are *relational.* The dog probably fancies itself as the Alpha. Or it doesn't know who is or doesn't care or doesn't want to know. Whatever the case, you're not it! You might be regarded as a friend, as a companion, as a littermate, as a lover or as all of the above, but you're not regarded, at least not fully, as the Alpha. To grab that role, you have to take a radical approach to your problem dog. I am going to suggest twenty different ruses you can pull to convince your pushy dog that you are the boss.

This more holistic approach is rather new in dealing with dog behavior problems, but not totally new. Until rather recently, trainers tended to hand out 1-2-3 remedies to behavioral inquiries, without addressing the underlying malaise that affects the owner/dog relationship. Lately, there have been some heartening efforts toward a more all-encompassing approach that help owners to identify problems, solve them *and* restructure their relationship with the dog. Carol Lea Benjamin's "Alpha Primer" (*American Kennel Gazette,* November 1986) is an excellent example of this, as is the chapter on behavior problems in *Training Your Dog* by Joachim Volhard and Gail Tamases Fisher (Howell Book House, 1983). Both programs are designed to help you up your Alpha status. My RRRR program—Radical Regimen for Recalcitrant Rovers—is similar, with my own personal flourishes, gathered from too many years of experience with too many problem dogs and too many problem owners. I offer my RRRR program to you with my sympathy and support.

Have your dog hold one thirty-minute down each day. These can be done during dinner. If your dog doesn't yet know a long down, sit on the leash, measuring out just as much as the dog needs to "crash." *Judy Emmert/Dealing with Dogs/TV Ontario*

Should your dog sleep on the bed? Not if it needs the RRRR—problem dogs do not belong on their owners' beds. You'll look like littermates. *Judy Emmert/Dealing with Dogs/TV Ontario*

Some final tips before the hit list: Don't modify the program until the behavior problem stops. Obviously, act on the behavior problem itself using sensible and humane set-ups, but add the RRRR program if you are experiencing any of the following:

Housetraining problems
Destructive chewing
Digging
Chasing people
Chasing cars
Jumping up
Overbarking
Aggression
Biting
Fighting with other dogs
Not coming when called
Predation

These are all *major* behavioral problems and they call for a *radical* approach. Apply the following program for the dog who is exhibiting any of the above problems and apply it for *one solid month.*

1. Give your dog two obedience sessions a day practicing whatever exercises the dog knows. These sessions should be ten to twenty minutes long. Do not praise physically during this session. Use only verbal praise and keep the session moving. Give commands quickly, dazzle the dog.

2. Have two formal eye-contact sessions with your dog each day. Problem dogs look at their owners only when they feel like it. Up the eye contact. Practice formally. Put a leash on. Sit the dog. Step around in front and animate the dog, saying, "Watch me. I want your attention *right now,*" in a low growling tone of voice. Do not yell. You want three to five seconds (*not* minutes) of locked, sealed eye contact. Once you get this moment, end with light *verbal* praise. See "Bitch Basics" for more details on eye contact.

3. Have your dog hold one thirty-minute down each day. This is very important. These downs can be done during television shows, dinner, reading or any time that works for you. Enforce it! If your dog doesn't know the down, teach it immediately, as well as the stay command. For now, sit on the leash and measure out only as much as the dog needs to hit the dust. If the dog jumps up on you, whip the leash down hard with a "No!" If the dog stress-whines, give the dog a slap under the chin and say "No!" If the dog bites the leash, whip it diagonally out of its mouth. During this time no petting, no toys, no soothing, no *nothing.* Long downs make you look Alpha. Consult chapter 13 concerning teaching the "long down."

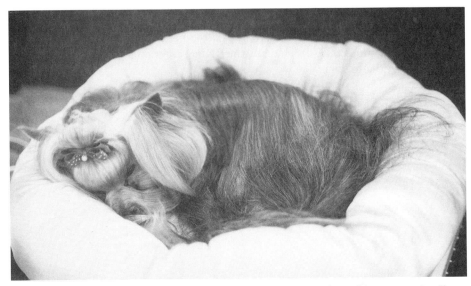

But don't demote your dog from the bedroom altogether. Instead, provide your pooch with comfortable sleeping accommodations of its own.   *Kevin Smith*

Enough exercise is essential! How much is enough? Consult point number five in RRRR. Dogs that aren't exercised enough often resemble hummingbirds in the house.   *Kevin Smith*

4. Move your dog into the bedroom for overnight sleeping. Read the chapter "Where Is Your Dog This Evening?" in *How to Be Your Dog's Best Friend* by the Monks of New Skete. This simple step has tremendous bonding effects. Remember, in the bedroom, *off the bed*. Problem dogs do not belong on beds. You'll look like littermates—but you want to look Alpha, remember? If the dog jumps up on the bed, tie the dog to the foot of the bed.

5. Exercise is very important. Problem dogs usually don't get enough *aerobic, sustained* exercise, which is what they need to calm them down. Putting the dog out in the backyard for three hours is no solution—it isn't exercising, it's exercising and resting, or just resting, period. Use a leash and jog or run with your dog. Sometimes the dog can be made to run alongside a bike. Keep moving. A good guide: for a small dog, ¼ mile, no stopping, four times a week; for a medium-size dog, ½ mile, no stopping, four times a week; for a large dog, 1 mile, no stopping, four times a week. I'm not even asking you to run with your dog every day. And a mile can go by quite quickly. Obviously, if your veterinarian advises against exercise for your particular dog, you'll have to skip this step.

6. Whenever you leave home, leave the radio on—easy-listening music, not rock or talk shows. Stressed tones of voice usually keep dogs on edge, and talk shows feature people who call in with problems and stresses.

7. Feed two times a day, if possible in the early morning and the early afternoon. Place the food down and leave it ten to fifteen minutes. Leave the dog and the food alone in a quiet room. Then return and pick up the food even if the dog hasn't finished. Do not make a thing out of the dog not eating—you may be engaging in faulty paralanguage and encouraging the dog *not* to eat even as you try to get it *to* eat (see "Nutrition Notes"). This method of feeding keeps food in the dog's stomach during its waking hours, eliminating hunger tension and giving you more of a chance for a calmer dog.

8. Reevaluate the diet. In my opinion high-quality meat-meal-based rations surpass soy-based rations. Drop all people food from the dog's diet. Your dog knows it was your food and sharing it with him doesn't make you look Alpha. When your dog doesn't have problems, you can slip in some people food, but not now. Remember, little things add up—usually to big problems. And never, ever add anything to the food after you've placed it down—not because you forgot an ingredient, not because you want to encourage the dog to eat. The dog will simply learn to wait until something yummy is added, and again, you won't look Alpha.

9. Give absolutely no food treats for one month. Yes, that's right, zero treats! Owners often place themselves in a subordinate position vis-à-vis the dog by giving too many treats or giving them in the wrong way.

Tighten food controls if your dog is on the Radical Regimen. Stop all treats for one month, drop all people food from the diet and insist on a short sit-stay before the gang chows down.

Judy Emmert/ Dealing with Dogs/ TV Ontario

Tug-of-war is taboo! It is not "cute." You're teaching your dog it's OK to bite down hard. Here, the Cocker is learning that the leash—which it should consider a symbol of the owner's authority—is really just a plaything. *Judy Emmert/Dealing with Dogs/TV Ontario*

Stop for one month. If your dog's problems clear up and the month has passed, give one treat a day only if the dog sits. Never give a free treat carte blanche—make the dog do something for the treat. But nothing for one month. For more nutrition nuggets, see "Nutrition Notes."

10. Stop petting, stroking or fondling your problem dog for minutes, not to mention hours, at a time. Get your hands off the dog and pet for only seven to ten seconds and only if you've told the dog to sit or down. I know you love your dog, but love isn't enough. If it were, you wouldn't be having the behavior problem you're having. What your dog needs from you now to help it out of its behavioral jam is scratch-type petting, quick and light, not seductive stroking. It would shock most dog owners, but problem dogs are often pooped from petting, yet they oblige and stay for it because they're addicted to it.

11. Don't allow the dog to go before you in or out of a door. Make the dog wait by giving the stay command or at least go together. If you allow the dog to barge in or out of the door before you, you're telling it something pretty powerful about who controls the territory. The dog will say, "I do. After all, I always go *first*, and that wimp goes second." If this happens three or four times a day, the dog really gets to stake a claim to the territory it enters first, with ensuing problems. Some examples: The dog is allowed to barge out onto the street and has a problem fighting other dogs. Aren't you setting the stage for the fighting by allowing the barge? The dog chews destructively when the owner is not home. If you routinely let the dog crash into the house before you, aren't you telegraphing to it that the home is its territory—to chew up, to trash, to rearrange at whim? Don't allow the dog to go before you in or out of territory! Again, little things add up, usually to big problems. If that phrase is beginning to sound like a mantra in this chapter, I'm getting through.

12. Pick up all the dog's toys and leave one, perhaps its favorite, out. That's all the dog gets for one month. When a month passes and the problems clear, add one toy a week.

13. Stop playing any and all tug-of-war games. When you let go you look subordinate, and you're teaching the dog to bite down hard while in your presence. You're OKing serious mouth play. A no-no for a problem dog. Play only fetch and if the dog doesn't bring the object back to you and release it, get up and walk away.

14. If you have to have the dog move because it is in the way, make the dog *move*. Don't refrain from doing something or step over the dog because you don't want to bother it. If you're Alpha, you can go where you want when you want. Even if you want to change the channels and the dog is in front of the TV, make it move. Believe me, if you don't, the dog will notice. Little things add up.

15. Resolve to stop yelling at your dog and instead speak in a low tone of voice. If you yell, the dog will learn to wait for you to yell. Change your tonality, not your volume. Most problem dogs are yelled and screamed at. Most have tuned their owners out and learn to wait for louder and louder yelling until they finally don't hear their owners at all. If you've been tuned out, don't yell, change your tonality. You'll probably find you have to couple a physical correction with your lowered tone of voice to get the dog to tune back to your station on the dial—radio station Alpha. So don't hesitate to use a shake, a swat under the chin or a leash correction if necessary. But stop yelling.

16. If your dog knows the down command—really knows it—pull a surprise down on this problem dog once a week. For instance, you're in the kitchen doing dishes and you hear Rover waltz in. Wheel on him, give both the hand and vocal signal and command for *down!* Recalcitrant Rover will probably look shocked, and then do it. If not, you'll have to enforce it. The surprise element is the key. Remember, just once a week. Each down is a notch on your Alpha belt, and combined with your daily long downs you'll look like Evita Peron—which is how your dog needs to see you right now.

17. If your dog is aggressive, immediately employ a private trainer to work with you in your home. Please don't wait. One session can work wonders. The situation could get out of control. It certainly won't get better without training. Your dog is just growling, you say? You're in trouble—big trouble. *A growl is a bite that just hasn't connected yet.* Don't delude yourself. Call a trainer—yesterday! Institute RRRR immediately, even before the trainer gets there to tell you what to do specifically for the aggression. You'll make his or her task easier if the RRRR is on a roll. Read over my "open letter" later in this book in "Aggressive Advice."

18. If you have a shy or aggressive dog, neuter the dog right away. Male or female. Right away. Don't even think of breeding the dog. The problem could be partially genetic. The spay or neuter operation could help calm the dog and, in my experience, is a card you should play regardless of the age of the dog. The only exception is a very old dog who cannot risk the surgery. Otherwise, in my opinion, this step is merited and could be of great help.

19. Whatever the problem is, be sure you understand the *specific* corrections for it outlined by your trainer or in this book. Apply these techniques as well as the RRRR. You'll find that instituting the RRRR rarely interferes with specific corrective techniques and almost always aids their effect. I've had many clients who did nothing about specific problems such as chewing or aggression (usually because they were too busy, too tired or too scared to act on the problem itself) but *did* begin the RRRR program, and the problem

lessened and in some cases disappeared. I won't promise you that, but you will find the RRRR will greatly aid your specific corrections for whatever problem plagues your dog.

20. Finally, to balance the harshness of the RRRR program, create a little jingle for your dog. This jingle can be based on a popular television ad, and should be light, lilting and friendly—sometimes just substituting your dog's name where the product name was in the jingle will achieve the desired effect. Sing the jingle to your dog once a day—even from afar. I've used jingles from a variety of ads. Just sing it out to your dog once a day—and make eye contact. And don't go over ten seconds. It's a jingle not an aria. Your dog will know, and it's your way of saying, "Yes, you bratty boob, I still love you, even though for now you're living under this Radical Regimen for a Recalcitrant Rover!"

The Frito Filcher gets an advance warning with a distinctive phrase and a couple of taps on the "centering spot."

Kevin Smith

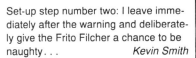

Set-up step number two: I leave immediately after the warning and deliberately give the Frito Filcher a chance to be naughty...   *Kevin Smith*

... and of course the Frito Filcher readily obliges.

Kevin Smith

10

Setting Up Set-ups

IF YOU READ the RRRR and winced, you might go into catatonic shock after this chapter. Sit down and take a deep breath. Set yourself up to learn about set-ups. Still there? Let's go.

Remember the Iran-Contra affair? Remember Abscam? Remember Watergate? All these events were set-ups, sting operations of one sort or another designed to achieve a secret or not-so-secret goal. You don't have to be a politician to set up a set-up. You can simply be a frustrated dog owner using your superior thinking ability and creative powers.

What's a set-up? A set-up is a deliberately concocted event in which a given bad behavior is elicited from the dog. The difference between a set-up and real life is that the owner is physically, psychologically and environmentally prepared to correct the dog. Read the above sentence again. This sentence is the core of this book. Remember, you are smarter than your dog, and if you understand what a set-up is, you can outsmart your dog and eliminate problems. The steps of a set-up are

1. Issue an advance warning.
2. Deliberately give the dog a chance to be naughty.
3. Deliver verbal and/or physical discipline.
4. Reissue the warning phrase.
5. Give the dog another chance to be naughty.

Let's go over the steps in detail using a sample behavior problem.

1. *Issue an Advance Warning*

Advance warnings are very important. Unfortunately most people don't think enough in advance to give one. For instance, an owner might know darn well that when Fritos are left out on the coffee table Fido will filch them. Yet this owner will consistently place a bowl of Fritos on said coffee table and leave the room to shower in preparation for a party, hoping against hope that maybe, just *maybe* Fido won't steal the Fritos just this time. Of course Fido *does*. If you want to do a set-up for a Frito freak you must realize that every time you have put Fritos out and then left the room without saying anything you were *training*. You were training Fido that Fritos would be put out and nothing would be said. You were overtrusting and unintentionally training your dog to steal Fritos.

Now all that's going to change. Your days of saying nothing are over. Take a bowl of Fritos and get your dog's undivided attention. Use eye contact and as you place the Fritos down on the coffee table stare your dog down and issue an advance warning in a low, growling tone. Emphasize a few select phonics in your phrase ("OK, *Fido,* you *filch* those *Fritos* and you'll *fry*"). Don't worry about the words of your sentence. Other than its own name, which should be included, the words won't matter much to the dog. The phonics do. Emphasizing key phonetical sounds strengthens the sentence and helps the dog to remember the warning. This is important because you will use this same sentence later on in the set-up. Again, don't get hung up on the literal meaning of the words of warning. The sentence in this case could just as easily be, "OK, *Fido,* mushrooms, mushrooms, *mush* rooms, *Fritos, mush* rooms." But do emphasize three or four phonetical sounds in the warning.

2. *Deliberately Give the Dog a Chance to Be Naughty*

Now you leave the room to shower. Remember, there is no law that says you are not allowed to stop at the doorway just before you disappear from sight, stare down Fido and issue your advance warning again. You are going to give your dog a chance to steal the Fritos. Of course you're not really going to go take a shower. But it may be necessary to have your bathrobe on and a towel flung over your shoulder to trick the dog into thinking that you are. Instead, you simply go around the corner or two doors down the hall (whatever distance is necessary to convince the dog the coast is clear) and wait to hear the crunch of corn chips. This step is usually easy, but can involve fine points of trickery in order to elicit the bad behavior. Be creative! If you think long and hard enough it's usually possible to get the dog to misbehave.

3. *Deliver Verbal and/or Physical Discipline*

As soon as you hear Fido eating the Fritos or, worse, hear the bowl crash to the floor, you charge, and I mean *charge* back into the room, grab Fido,

I'm hiding out at the top of the stairs. When I hear the first crunch of corn chips I head downstairs, *pronto*. "Oh, my God, he's coming *back*! I'm caught!" *Kevin Smith*

The Filcher is focused on the Fritos . . . *Kevin Smith*

. . . and humanely disciplined with a swat under the chin. *Kevin Smith*

87

sit Fido, brandish some Fritos in front of Fido's face and give a firm swat under the chin, or in the case of a puppy a simple shake correction. This sounds easier than it may turn out to be if you haven't thought out this step of your set-up in advance. In anticipation of the chase that will probably ensue after you charge back into the room, you will certainly want to have put a collar or even a short tab leash on the dog so that the dog can be immediately retrieved if it dives under the buffet or runs to a corner. Of course, you've closed off the rest of the house to lessen the dog's options and eliminate all avenues of escape. Remember, chases cheapen owners. Even if you catch your dog after a prolonged chase, your physical correction might be lost on the dog because it is too delayed. So think this step out in advance so that you are environmentally prepared to act as Alpha—a quick, fully in control Alpha.

"Environmental preparation" is important. It is amazing how many owners will perform the first two steps of a set-up nicely enough but fail to think out this step. Think out the set-up in advance. What are the possible ways the dog can elude you and your correction? What do you have to do to prepare the environment so that you come out as top dog?

4. *Reissue the Warning Phrase*

You've caught your canine criminal in the act and disciplined said criminal. Now you haul out the same phrase you used in step number one, emphasizing the *same* phonics. Very often step number four will need to be teamed simultaneously with step number three. In our case of the Frito fracas this means that the warning phrase needs to be delivered at the same time the dog is shaken or swatted. Remember, no screaming, no whining and no laughing. A low, serious growllike tone is what you want. Remember to punch out those phonics. "OK, *Fido,* you *filch* those *Fritos* and you'll *fry.*" By reissuing the phrase you help your dog to understand you meant business when you used the phrase the *first* time. The whole point of a set-up is to get your dog to the point where warning phrases alone stop bad behavior. You can get to the point where you can even shorten the phrase as time goes by, simply saying, for instance, "Fritos, *fry,*" when you leave the room the first time. Further along, the dog should internalize the correction and give up Frito filching completely, even if no warning is issued. Great goal, eh?

5. *Give the Dog Another Chance to Be Naughty*

Guess what? We're not done with our set-up quite yet. We want to truly test the dog. So, after steps three and four are executed, go back to step one and again deliver the warning phrase. Now leave the room again. Move! You want to leave again while the correction is still fresh in the dog's mind. Reissue your warning and go into hiding again. If the dog filches Fritos again, go back to step three.

Maybe all you can gain with a first-time set-up of this sort is one or two

Set-up step number four: The same warning I gave in advance of the wrong-doing is repeated as I depart. *Kevin Smith*

Another sample set-up: The problem is that the dog jumps and barks when the intercom signals the arrival of guests. Downstairs, a decoy "guest" buzzes once every thirty seconds five to ten times. *Levon Mark*

Meanwhile, instead of hurrying to admit the guest, I discipline the squealer and only then buzz the guest in. The guest knows there might be a wait because all of this is prearranged. *Kevin Smith*

The dog is placed on a sit-stay, and instead of watching the entering guest, I watch the dog—ready to promptly correct the barking with the shake or swat correction and the jumping up with the three-part jumping correction.

Kevin Smith

The guests are admitted and stay for a few minutes. They then leave but return a few minutes later and repeat the whole set-up. *Kevin Smith*

minutes during which the dog doesn't steal any more Fritos. That's progress. Tomorrow is another day and you can try another set-up. You will gain more time with each set-up until the dog understands that items, even food, placed on the coffee table belong to *you.*

Frequency and Fairness

How often do you try a set-up? My usual answer to clients is "until one works." However, some owner discretion is necessary. Some harsh, blamer owners will do thirty set-ups in one day. In the above case, the owner of the Frito freak, in an attempt to proof the set-up even more, might go to the ridiculous extreme of "setting the dog up" to not even *look* at Fritos when taken into the corner deli! The owner might sit the dog at the deli door, deliver the warning phrase, trot the dog inside, deliberately glide the dog past the Fritos and rudely yank the dog away. This is taking the idea of a set-up too far. The dog stole Fritos only at home, not in the store. I mean, really, let's be fair.

But there are some owners who worry about whether the whole idea behind set-ups is fair to the dog. Of course, there will always be instances of possible overkill, like the one mentioned above. But, in general, set-ups are much more fair to your dog than the pressure the dog feels from being constantly nagged, cajoled or overtrusted. It is more humane to stage one successful set-up than to constantly browbeat your dog about bad behavior.

Sometimes the concepts of frequency and fairness are intertwined. Just as it's unfair to overuse set-ups, it is also unfair to underutilize them by not staging enough set-ups. Don't think your dog is rehabilitated after one set-up. Staging the same set-up thirty times in one day might be appropriate for a rare dog. But for most dogs one set-up a day is the limit.

Now using what we've learned here, look over the following worksheets. Included are the set-up steps and another sample behavior problem. Just get acquainted with the worksheets for now. Then go on to the next chapter, "Why Set-ups Sometimes Foul Up." If you're skipping around in this book and were attracted by the worksheets, my advice is to go back to the beginning of the text rather than risk staging a poor set-up because of lack of information. Then if future problems crop up, you will find you will be able to go directly to the worksheets to script your set-ups. Use a pencil so that you can use the worksheets over and over again.

People, Pooches & Problems
Worksheet 1

Use a pencil when filling out the form as you may want to erase and rework the form later for additional or new problems that may arise. Better yet, make copies of the worksheets. If you do not have a specific problem in mind, make one up. Remember, practice makes perfect. The more experience you have in thinking about set-ups, the better you will be at implementing them. Good luck!

My problem pooch has the following problem: (Briefly outline the problem behavior, e.g., My dog attacks other dogs it passes on the street.)

_____

_____

_____

_____

Pause now and review the steps in a set-up. They are:

1. *Issue an advance warning,* using eye contact if possible and a distinctive phrase, e.g., *"Tippy,* you *touch* that other *dog* and you're *DEAD."* Be sure to include the dog's name in the phrase.
2. *Deliberately give the dog a chance to be naughty,* e.g., glide Tippy right into the path of another dog, loosen the leash and pray that Tippy will start a fight.
3. *Deliver verbal and/or physical discipline,* e.g., Tippy gets a firm swat under the chin.
4. *Reissue the warning phrase,* e.g., "Well, excuuuuuuse me, *Tippy,* I said you *touch* that other *dog* and you're *dead!"*
5. *Give the dog another chance to be naughty,* e.g., you hang a wheelie as you complete step 4 and catch up with the dog Tippy just molested and glide Tippy past the dog again.

Now, using the following worksheet, notate the steps of your set-up for your problem. If you made copies you can place them side by side if you need to refer back to the steps or example.

People, Pooches & Problems

Worksheet 2

My Set-up:

1. _____

_____

_____

_____

2. _____

_____

_____

_____

3. _____

_____

_____

_____

4. _____

_____

_____

_____

5. _____

_____

_____

_____

Will you put your problem pooch on the RRRR for one month? __yes __no

If not, why not?_____

Is there a reason a set-up won't work? __yes __no

If yes, why? No evidence to facilitate discipline after the fact; corrections cannot be given quickly enough; firm enough corrections cannot be given; dog is stupid, etc. See next chapter.

_____

_____

_____

_____

_____

_____

_____

_____

_____

_____

_____

_____

_____

_____

_____

_____

People, Pooches & Problems
Worksheet 3

If for any reason you cannot figure out how to set up a set-up on your own, you need to pick a partner. It's preferable to pick someone who does not live with you or your dog as he or she will be more objective and exact in designing a set-up. However, in a crunch, a family member, spouse, boyfriend, girlfriend or significant other will do. Have this person read the chapters "RRRR" and "Setting Up Set-ups."

This worksheet is for your partner to use to critique your set-up. Partners: Be frank and helpful in your comments. Point out any gaps in the five steps. Look carefully to any stated reasons why the set-up won't work and decide whether you agree or disagree as to whether the dog should or should not be put on the RRRR. Good luck! Remember, two heads are better than one.

Partner critique: _____

_____

_____

_____

_____

_____

_____

_____

_____

_____

_____

_____

_____

_____

_____

_____

11

Why Set-ups
Sometimes Foul Up

W E'VE SAID A LOT about set-ups so far, and you might think that they are miraculously fail-safe and, well, "set." But no set-up is perfect. No sting operation *always* stings. And doing one set-up doesn't necessarily mean that your dog will never act up again.

Let's review some of the reasons set-ups sometimes foul up. You can refer back to this section if your set-up goes awry. Remember, though, not to use the following complications as excuses not to correct your canine criminal. You'll see in most instances these qualifications don't foul up the set-up irredeemably. These flukes force you to fine-tune your set-up just as the FBI has to fine-tune sting operations. Remember, Abscam took a lot of thought and planning. (For that matter so did Watergate!) Trickery, however well intended, isn't easy. You owe it to your dog to put as much time into designing, and if necessary redesigning, your set-up as the cops put into Abscam and the criminals put into Watergate. Here are the potential areas where set-ups foul up.

The dog is just too young for set-ups. In this case you might have to wait things out. Practice "creative avoidance" by using confinement or a crate and give the dog more time until your canine Dorothy makes it out of Oz. This potential foul-up occurs most frequently when owners try to set up very young dogs for chewing or housebreaking problems and the puppy is simply too young to assimilate the information imparted in a set-up. You certainly should not be setting up, for instance, a three- or four-month-old puppy to destructively chew or soil. The puppy is too young, the set-up is unfair and you should simply confine, confine, confine the puppy or have it under your direct supervision. Be fair to the young.

The correction is too soft. For wimpy owners with dominant dogs, this is far and away the most common reason their set-ups foul up. Some examples: The owner of an aggressive dog might simply *restrain* the dog from lunging, charging or biting when what Jack the Ripper really needs is a good strong slap under the chin. Or, the owner of a lunatic lunger may simply give ineffective jerks on the training collar, or even not have one on the dog, rather than giving an effective pop and snap on the collar. In my years of dog training I find that the running themes marking ineffective physical correction are, in a nutshell: The owner will *restrain* the dog instead of correcting it, or the owner will simply *reposition* the dog instead of correcting it. Double-check your set-up for this foul-up and be honest with yourself: Are you sure you were correcting your dog firmly enough? Are you restraining the dog or repositioning it instead of correcting it?

The correction is too slow. After youth and lack of force, owner slowness tops the hit parade of excuses and potential foul-ups. Examples include using the shake correction when the swat could be delivered more quickly. Another form of owner slowness is simply verbally *nagging* the dog to "be good" and *then* finally delivering a physical correction that unfortunately might as well be five years late. There will always be owners who, because of lack of physical dexterity or coordination, cannot deliver corrections quickly enough. Their timing will be forever off and the dog will always explode, cheat, chew, lie or steal faster than they can correct, or so they think. These souls need help in the form of a private trainer. But let me tell you something: It's a lot cheaper to try to speed yourself up and weed this foul-up out of your set-up than to pay a high training bill. I sympathize with you—I used to be one of the slowpokes, but with coaching from my training mentors, I learned just how *fast* "fast" really is. Often, one session with a professional trainer will help you to duplicate the correct speed for the set-up.

The owner is too loud. Even if the dog is old enough, and the owner fast enough and forceful enough, some set-ups still foul up because the owner becomes a screaming banshee. This will often happen during part four of the set-up (when the owner is supposed to repeat the warning phrase), and the owner (in an attempt to make sure that he or she "got through" to the dog) will bellow so loudly that the set-up fouls up. If you yell, the dog then focuses on the *correction* rather than the *connection* that you want it to make. For instance, if you find an "accident" and scream at your dog—even if you are properly executing discipline after the fact—your screaming will simply make the dog focus on *you* instead of its shame. Be sure to read chapter 6, "Do Dogs Feel Guilt or Shame?" for more on this. Screaming makes any shame the dog might feel turn into pure fear and the desire to flee. If your set-ups make your dog freeze or take flight, the chances are you're too loud. Your voice can be hard and firm but you mustn't yell or shriek. Remember the gentle growl of the bitch directed at a naughty puppy: *Grrrrrrrrrrrrrrrrrrrrr.* Growl softly and carry no big sticks! And please, no rolled-up newspapers: first-class folklore—no bitch ever disciplined a puppy with a rolled-up newspaper!

There is no proof and some proof is needed to shame the dog. An example is the theft of food, when the theft includes complete digestion of the desired "proof." Another example is destructive chewing. Perhaps you don't even know *what's* been chewed—until days later when you miss it or need it. But, by then, the object of the dog's desire has been completely ingested. There is no proof to justify discipline after the fact. In fact, you might have to wait for the elimination stage of the digestive process before you recognize what you're missing. What can you do when proof is needed and you can't get any proof to convict the dog? You can think, and think hard. After all, we are supposed to be smarter than them. Is there any way you can trick the dog into leaving a trail or even a smidgen of evidence?

I once had a client who had a devious Dalmatian that inhaled whatever it could find on the kitchen counter. The Dalmatian had also learned to open the refrigerator, which it investigated when the counters were bare. Of course, the dog did all of these things when the owner wasn't home. The owner finally got tired of counter climbing and refrigerator raids and devised a set-up under my guidance. The dog was "invited" to steal peanut butter mounded on a dinner plate. Dogs tend to ingest peanut butter rather slowly. My perverse sense of humor found this quite satisfying. So, some of the peanut butter would be left stuck to the plate. We would have the proof we needed. We came back after a short stroll. The dinner plate was smashed on the kitchen floor with just enough proof stuck to it to give the Dalmatian a correction with a connection. The dog was walking around trying to scrape the peanut butter off the roof of its mouth, and was brought to the evidence, disciplined and isolated. Score: Humans, 1, Dalmatians, 0. By the way, use creamy not chunky. It sticks to the plate better.

The stimulus cannot be repeated, it is too specific. This is often the situation in cases of aggression. You need to get the dog grouchy, but often the stimulus or stimuli that set the dog off cannot be reproduced in order to secure a set-up. For instance, if your dog growls at other dogs when passing them, it might not be easy to get the cooperation of another owner and have them glide their dog past yours so that you can correct your dog. After all, people may not want to cooperate, no matter how badly *you* want to do your set-up. The solution may have to be using people and their dogs without them knowing they are being used. This might demand your securing the services of a professional. A professional will have the timing to make sure no other person or dog gets hurt.

Sometimes owners will claim they cannot give an advance warning, or even do a set-up at all, because the dog "just explodes." Or they will claim that they don't even know what the stimulus *is* that sets off the dog. But unprovoked, unexplainable and unannounced attacks by dogs are very rare. Usually the dog is responding to a given stimulus, and *is* announcing way in advance its intentions. The owner simply cannot read the dog's signals. For more on this, see chapter 17, "Aggressive Advice," and try to find a way to read the signs of aggression more quickly and repeat the stimulus.

The dog cannot give up his Alpha status so quickly. In this case the owner might be trying to do set-ups too soon. Instead of doing set-ups for specific problems, wait awhile and let the Radical Regimen for Recalcitrant Rovers kick in. Follow point ten *strictly* and give only earned praise. See what develops, wait and pray. Go two weeks like this and then try set-ups again. The RRRR will change your relationship with the dog and quite possibly soften your problem pooch, preparing the dog to accept set-ups.

The dog is mentally or genetically defective. Don't laugh—it does happen. But it is very rare. Occasionally there are dogs that are so "stupid" that they can't figure out the five parts of the set-up. This is not to be confused with *owners* who cannot comprehend the five steps of a set-up! There are also dogs who will rather stupidly fight through the correction step of the set-ups. Check yourself: Are you being too loud, too soft, too slow or too hard in your corrections? Remember, if you are too hard some dogs with active defense reflexes will simply go completely on the defensive and fight the correction. This is not the same as stupidity. Usually these dogs are quite smart. They just fake stupidity.

Dogs that are genetically defective are another matter. Sometimes genetic defects predetermine not only the physical health of the dog, but the dog's mental health as well. This is sometimes the case with "puppy mill" produce or dogs from "backyard breeders." In my opinion, even a genetically defective dog is worth working with, and worth staging set-ups for, because the alternatives are pretty grim. Of course, if you don't yet have a dog, my advice is to procure one only after being *interviewed* by a reputable breeder who uses Puppy Aptitude Testing (PAT) to evaluate temperament. That's the only sure way to skirt genetic behavioral defects, and even this method isn't 100 percent effective.

Set-ups that foul up usually mean that the owner is too slow, too loud, too soft or too hard. Or perhaps the stimuli can't be repeated and really needs to be repeated for that particular dog, or the dog is too bossy, too stupid or too genetically weak to assimilate the information and discipline.

In my experience—and my records show this—80 percent of the time the set-up doesn't "take" because of *owner softness or slowness.* When skills improve, the set-up usually kicks in successfully. Remember, part of owner slowness is simply not doing enough set-ups over a long period of time.

If you think your set-ups foul up because of disciplinary softness on your part, remember, while you should always go for the softest correction possible, if continual failed set-ups are happening the dog is probably informing you that you can get tougher. Heed the message. Get tougher.

My records show that 5 percent of the aggressive dogs I've worked with will simply not relinquish their Alpha status. The bond between themselves and their owners is so corrupted, so out of kilter, so entangled with the owner as a submissive party that the dog cannot be corrected or shamed any longer. These dogs usually bite their owners or other family members and will continue to do so even after training is attempted. They usually have to be euthanized. My records also show that another 5 percent of aggressive dogs are too slow, too stupid or genetically defective, thus preventing them from understanding the corrective and informational content of set-ups. But in 90 percent of cases of canine aggression I have found that if a dog is smart enough to have the organizational and mental skills required to run a human household via dominance, canine stupidity usually is *not* the issue. Human stupidity, lack of education and lack of motivation usually *are* the issues. Once in a while, everyone, dogs and humans alike, need some time out to make set-ups work out. As I always urge, read on.

12

Creative Avoidance

$\mathbf{T}$IME OUT! This is a phrase you've probably yelled when in the midst of a heated argument with someone. Perhaps you felt you just needed a breather so that a criticism could sink in, or needed time to think over a response. Sometimes in canine/human relations similar time-outs are necessary. A given canine conundrum can become so complicated and convoluted that both owner and dog feel lost at sea. It is sometimes necessary to simply let some time go by so that a particular form of bad behavior is simply *avoided,* not allowed to happen, somehow circumvented, *before* trying to correct the naughtiness. This is what I call "creative avoidance." By simply avoiding triggering the dog's bad behavior, sometimes an atmosphere is created in which the dog will accept correction. Many times this will entail simply establishing a moratorium period on a given bad behavior so that it just can't take place at all. Some examples:

• Mary Kratzmiller had a Labrador Retriever who was in the habit of not coming when called. This behavior had been going on for at least one year. The routine was this: Mary would routinely let the dog out in the morning to relieve itself, which the dog promptly did. But the Lab would then encircle the house three times, like clockwork, and disappear into the neighboring woods. Mary would helplessly call the Labrador from her porch, standing in her bathrobe and fluffy slippers. Sometimes her Lab would even grant her the favor of glancing back at her for two seconds and would then, of course, gallivant off into the woods. The behavior had become so patterned in that even immediate training for the recall would not turn the situation around. A moratorium period had to be put into place—some creative avoidance practiced—while at the same time the dog entered formal obedience training. We had to buy some time to let the dog forget about the morning ritual of running away and begin to teach the word "come." "Does that mean that I'll have to take him out on a leash every morning to let him do his business?" Mary asked. "I guess so," I answered, "or you'll have to get an aerial runner chain and string it between the house and a tree and hook him onto that. Or maybe one of the kids will have to walk him. But under no circumstances can this dog be allowed to run away from you." Every time in the past Mary had said the word "come" and the dog had disobeyed, Mary was *training* the dog that the word "come" meant "Stay where you are or run the other way." It takes a *long time* for a dog to forget such mistraining and apply a new meaning to an old word. I usually recommend a moratorium period of six weeks for dogs who do not come when called. For more on this, see chapter 18, "To Come or Not to Come."

• Twinkles was an unaltered Yorkshire Terrier. He had a habit of leg-lifting every place he desired, including on the sides of the sofa, the bed and even his owner's leg. While it was easy enough to stage a set-up for such behavior (and we did), I recommended that Twinkles first be neutered and then strictly confined to a crate whenever the owner was not home. The bulk of the sprinkling that went on occurred at that time. But the owner wanted to start work on the problem right away and was enthusiastic about the idea of set-ups and discipline after the fact—perhaps *too* enthusiastic. Because the behavior was long-standing, and because it would take a few weeks for the benefits of the neutering to kick in, some creative avoidance was in order. We set it up so that Twinkles resided in a crate so small he would have to lie in his own urine if he let loose. He refrained, and after two weeks of strict confinement (and the neutering operation) the owner staged a set-up. She left the house with an advance warning, returned, disciplined if Twinkles had urinated and then repeated the process. Twinkles tightened up after just one set-up. It was probably the combination of neutering, crating and the actual set-up that helped Twinkles become a little star. But creative avoidance also played a role in this success story.

No Cop-out

Twinkles' owner asked me at one point, "Aren't we just *avoiding* the problem by neutering and crating him?" I replied, "Yes, in a sense we are, but we need to let a little time pass during which Twinkles adjusts to the hormonal changes of the neutering and to strict crating. He has to learn to correct himself, so to speak, from within, by simply learning to hold his own urine." This owner was gung-ho on discipline. So the idea of "setting Twinkles up" was a genuine thrill. But she had been using the classic folklore technique of striking Twinkles on the rump with a rolled-up newspaper. I explained that no bitch would use a rolled-up newspaper as an implement for discipline, and demonstrated correct discipline techniques. The owner was still ready to really go to town on Twinkles. But it was still too soon. Instead, creative avoidance was employed and success achieved.

I'm a strong advocate of getting on your dog's case if it is flubbing up behaviorally. But you should also know that often stalling correction is OK as well—as long as during the stall period the dog simply cannot do whatever naughty thing it was doing. Creative avoidance does *not* mean that you let bad behavior go on unchecked. It simply means that you structure the dog's environment, schedule or exposure to suggestive stimuli to avoid triggering the bad behavior you will later correct.

Creative avoidance is not a cop-out. Some hard-line trainers may say it is more productive to go after all problem behaviors immediately, but this presents several problems. Some strong, dominant dogs will not accept immediate correction for specific faults. They will often retaliate against their owners. Softer dogs might simply crumple under discipline and begin to submissively urinate, nervously shake or simply avoid their owners by hiding from them. A structured waiting period during which the problem behavior is avoided gives owner and dog a cooling-off period. Trainers who go after problem behavior with heavy corrections without giving a second thought to the benefits of creative avoidance often wind up treating only the symptoms and not the cause of the problem. For more on this, see chapter 4, "A Worthy Cause."

Often, if set-ups continually fail, it is an indication that a little creative avoidance is in order. Back off, refrain from disciplining and try to think out some ways that you can simply avoid triggering the bad behavior. During this period of time, I'd suggest putting your dog on my Radical Regimen for Recalcitrant Rovers for one month. This will begin to change the relationship between you and your dog and make the dog more open to correction for a specific problem—if only because it forgets old behavior patterns.

Creative Avoidance Forever?

Some *permanent* forms of creative avoidance are frankly necessary and inevitable for most dog owners. For instance, no matter how well-trained your dog may be, it's probably unwise to leave a pot roast cooling on the edge of the kitchen counter with your dog in the kitchen unattended. The temptation is simply too great, and most owners learn to avoid such a challenge. I *suppose* you could stage a set-up and trick the dog into stealing the roast, but why waste the time (and the roast) when it's just as easy to place the roast on top of the refrigerator or simply leave it in the oven? Some owners with several dogs simply have to use crates as tools of creative avoidance, so that individual dogs can get special attention or proper nutrition, or just to avoid tripping over too many dogs. This form of avoidance is fine as long as the dogs do not live out their entire lives in crates, and as long as the crates are not used as a cop-out or a way of avoiding correcting bad behavior.

Finally, the break provided by a period of creative avoidance gives the emotionally upset, distraught owner a chance to think out how to concoct a perfectly structured, nonhysterical, instructive set-up to stop bad behavior. Domineering owners might feel that a waiting period prevents them from reforming their dogs pronto, but it is precisely these owners who will tend to get too loud and too bossy when they attempt corrections. Just because, by reading this book, you have the knowledge of how to set-up and correct your dog does not mean that you have to *use* that knowledge right away. Unless the problem behavior is a threat to life and limb, time is probably on your side. If you find repeated corrections fail, try creative avoidance for one to three weeks and then stage a sterling set-up. During this time-out period, begin to teach, or *reteach,* your dog essential words that will help you to stage set-ups—words your dog can live by.

13

Words Dogs Live By

EVERY GOOD DOG needs to know the words "heel," "sit," "stay," "come" and "down" to function reasonably in human society. Of course, a well-trained dog can learn to understand forty words or more, but if your dog doesn't know at least these five basic words you should consider it a functional illiterate. The difference between canine illiteracy and the human version is that your dog is hardly responsible for its own lack of knowledge. Bluntly, it's your fault. It is every owner's responsibility to teach the dog these five basic words, either at home with the aid of a book or the help of a private trainer or in obedience class.

Magical Thinking

Teaching your dog words will, however, be useless unless those words are usable in real-life situations. Please don't assume that your dog knows a command if it only obeys the command some of the time. For instance, if your dog comes to you when you happen to call its name while you're fixing its morning meal or sees you brandishing a treat, but disobeys the same command when it is running around a baseball field and you call, I'm sorry to inform you, but your dog simply doesn't know how to come when called. The dog might have an acquaintance with the word, but it does not *know* the word. It is not a word the dog lives by. Yet, many dog owners caught in just such a jam would swear to high heaven that their dog *does* know how to come when called. I note this misperception on the part of dog owners because this magical thinking is one of the most common reasons that dog training doesn't take with some dogs. The misguided owner thinks that the dog already knows certain words when the dog just *doesn't.*

The problem with this lack of education—again, purely the fault of owner negligence—is that many set-ups involve the use of one, two or even three command words in order to succeed. For instance, let's say your dog has a problem shying away from children. You decide to follow the five steps outlined in the set-up chapter to conquer, or at least lessen, this problem. First, bravo to you for going even this far in your efforts!

So, following the set-up scenario, you arrange for a trip to the local playground at recess time. You know you can trick probably half a dozen or, more likely, one zillion kids into attempting to relate with Shy Sam. You park yourselves on the fringes of the playground and, sure enough, children start to approach to solicit attention from Sam. Naturally (big surprise), Sam backs away behind you to hide from his young admirers. You haul Sam forward out into "reality" every time he does. You warn him, following the set-up scenario, and at one point realizing that even shyness can be disciplined, you give him a good shake, tap his centering spot and start the set-up process again. But Sam keeps retreating. What's wrong here? What's crucial, and what's missing, is the issuance of, and obedience to, the command word "stay." Each time the kids approach, the word and signal for stay should be given to the dog. Technically, if Sam really, truly *knows* the word, he will not be able to retreat behind you—if only because he fears being reprimanded for disobeying the stay command. But since Sam doesn't know stay, he can't be given the command, and the set-up fouls up. When your dog has no words to live by, it can quite literally be doomed.

When you first introduce a word, teach it in a quiet environment. This is what Sam's owner had to do before a set-up succeeded. If you can't practice at home try to find a quiet nook outside in which to teach each word. Graduate to more hectic areas. You will see your dog begin to comprehend each word. A light will go on in your dog's eyes—that special light of recognition and obedience. As soon as you see that "light" that's your signal to up-scale your training environment to one that will have more distractions to throw your dog off the word. It's important to "proof" each word as fully as possible, especially for shy or aggressive dogs.

Equipment

I prefer a metal collar with pounded, flat links. If the links are pounded flat and not rounded, the action of the collar tends to be quicker. Just run your hand across the collar after laying it flat on the store counter. Form your hand into a fist and pass the collar over it. Snap it on your wrist. Is the action quick, clean? Nylon collars are fine, too, but they tend to stretch with use and are harder to locate on the neck of a speeding dog who is taking you on a goose chase. The tighter the collar rides on the dog's neck, the more effective it usually is—but even properly fitted collars tend to sink down the dog's neck.

When a training collar is placed on your dog properly it will look like the letter P turned sideways.
Charles Hornek

The solution might be to purchase a nylon "snap-around" collar that is clipped high on your pet's neck, yet still has training collar action and speed. It might take some searching to locate such collars. Try your speciality pet store or a dog-ware catalog. I have used such snap-around collars on dogs who would otherwise have needed a prong collar and have had good results. The secret, of course, is that the collar stays hiked up on the dog's neck, which makes even small corrections or restraints more effective.

Some owners are enamored of harnesses. I think, at least in most cases, harnesses belong on horses. Occasionally there is a dog with a trachea problem or other medical malady that simply makes the use of any kind of neck collar impossible. But many owners simply use harnesses because Fifi fidgeted once when a neck collar was put on. Usually the harnessed dog just spins around like a yo-yo at the end of the leash, and it becomes impossible to give quick corrections—and possible only to restrain the dog from getting in trouble.

When a training collar is placed on your dog properly, it will look like the letter P turned sideways. Stand with your dog on your left side, make your collar into a P shape and pass it over the dog's head. There should be only two or three inches of extension when the collar is pulled tight. If you are using a snap-around collar, there will, of course, be less extension, but you should be able to run your index finger all the way around the inside of the collar in a smooth motion.

Lastly, you need a good leash, one that fits comfortably in your palm yet is not so wide that you cannot manipulate it with your fingers. Chain leashes are hard on the hands, and the weight of the leash decimates the corrective tug by the time it reaches the dog's neck. I prefer a leash of braided construction made of leather with no sewn parts. With this kind of leash, there is nothing to break, and strong corrections can be given without worry.

Heeling

Set-ups for dogs who lunge at other dogs, snarf up garbage or simply pull ahead are next to impossible to concoct with any success unless your dog has an acquaintance with the word "heel." This is the word your dog must live by if your set-up is to succeed. The word "heel" means pretty much what it says—that your dog should be at your heel, precisely with its withers (shoulders) at your left heel. Why the left? There is probably no absolute reason except that many people are right-handed and all dogs are creatures of habit and prefer predictability.

As for the word "heel" it's a somewhat funny word to many people. At first they feel somewhat uncomfortable saying it to a dog because they've never said it before. In fact, most trainers don't know why we use this particular word. The reason is that phonetically "heel" simply doesn't sound like any of the other five command words. Take a moment and say all of the five basic words aloud and you'll see that they each sound very different. In fact, if you place your fingers over your mouth and clearly pronounce heel, sit, stay, come

In heeling, the dog is on your left side. Keep your hands palm down on the leash—you will then have full power of your forearm to "check" the dog toward your thigh if the dog breaks the heel.

Judy Emmert/
Dealing with Dogs/TV Ontario

Step off with your left foot so that the dog can see that you're leaving.

Charles Hornek

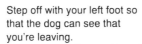

This is the proper heeling position. Settle for nothing less. Remember, you might have to use heeling someday in a set-up so you'll want to teach it right and teach it *tight* from the beginning.

Dealing with Dogs/
TV Ontario

and down you can feel in your own fingers the difference between the words. Proper enunciation of the words is important and, as we've discussed before, screeching commands is absolutely forbidden. Just as chases cheapen owners, there is no quicker way to cheapen yourself in a dog's eyes than to scream command words or reprimands.

Remember the tips concerning vocalizations in the RRRR: When giving a command or reprimanding the dog, change your tonality by lowering it but do not change the volume of your voice. If the command is for an active exercise, pitch your voice slightly higher (heel, come) or slightly lower for static commands (down, stay, sit). Simply put, just remember if the word involves movement, up your voice. If it doesn't, lower your voice.

In heeling, the dog is at your left-hand side. Keep your hands palm down on the leash so that you will have the full power of your forearm to tug the dog in toward your thigh for a correction. You will find that the inside portion of your left wrist does a lot of slapping against your outer left thigh; after years of training I have a permanent bruise on mine to prove this. Keep the collar up high around the dog's neck with the rounded rings of the collar rotated underneath the ear closest to you. Step off with your left foot, saying, "Rascal, heel." Try to remember to use your left foot so that your dog can see that you're leaving. If the dog lags or lunges ahead give a sharp correction in toward your left thigh. Make this a smart snap, not a restrained choking action. Snap that leash! Pop that training collar! Zip that dog in toward your thigh—that's the key to good heeling. Restraining your dog by keeping tension on the lead will only result in a standoff. Use plenty of praise as you strut, and when you stop, sit your dog next to you by simultaneously pulling up on the leash in and up toward your chest, and if necessary push down on the dog's rump. You'll find that in time just a slight snap of the leash up and slightly in toward you will telegraph a sit through your dog's backbone.

The Automatic Sit

Part of the heeling process—and one that is essential for successful set-ups—is drilling your dog in the automatic sit. This means that when you stop for any reason, at any time, rain or shine, your dog is to sit smartly alongside your left leg. This technique can be trained in when you are teaching the heel. Many dogs just sit naturally when the owner stops and if yours does, you're lucky—you were just spared a slipped disk. But if yours doesn't, pull up slightly on the training collar one or two seconds before you actually stop. If necessary, transfer your right hand to the base of the leash. Then your left hand will be free to guide the dog's bottom into a sit as your right hand jerks the collar up. If you don't make this hand transfer you'll find that your arms crisscross, forming an uncomfortable X. You will probably not be able to execute the maneuver.

Drill your dog. Take five steps ahead and then insist on a sit. Take another five steps. Sit the dog again, and so on. Don't say the word "sit"—just get the dog into the position. If you say the word continually the dog will simply learn to wait for you to say the command word. The dog will think that it should remain standing until you say "sit." You will then be condemned to saying "sit" every time you stop. But, especially if you own a problem dog who is a hooligan on heel, you will want the assurance that the automatic sit is subliminally solid in the dog's brain. That way, if your lunatic lunger suddenly comes upon another dog, squirrel, pigeon or other distraction, you can rest assured that as you screech to a stop the dog's training dictates "sit" before its instincts dictate "score!" Insist on the automatic sit—it is not simply ornamental. You will feel so relieved knowing that your dog glides into a solid sit when you stop—so that you do not have to be dragged or pulled about. Be careful about double commands like "sit down" or "c'mon, heel" while practicing heeling. Remember, "down" and "sit" will very shortly be distinct words meaning desired actions. Don't confuse your dog. Use "let's go" as a term of encouragement instead.

OK

"OK" is used when you want to release your dog from strict heeling to relieve itself, to play with another dog, to sniff around or as part of a set-up to trick the dog into bad behavior. I simply don't believe that a dog should pull you to where it likes to eliminate, play or sniff. Dogs that yank their owners around are displaying dominance. Instead, I believe in an either/or proposition, which means that *you* heel your dog where you want it to engage in any of these activities, and then *you* release the dog from the heel command with a clearly pronounced "OK!" Your palms will be flat down on the leash, but at this point, turn your hand around and dramatically push the leash forward, clearly indicating that the loose lead means that your dog gets more freedom. For instance, let's say that your dog is on heel and you want to do a set-up for garbaging. Garbaging, of course, means that your dog likes to snarf up objects on the street and perceives itself to be a vacuum cleaner. When you pass a particularly attractive gob of garbage you simply issue the OK command, issue an advance warning and push the leash out to release your dog from the heel. If you are really lucky, the dog begins to gobble garbage, at which point you reprimand your dog, repeat the warning and double back over the same gob of garbage. If your dog dips its head again, you repeat the set-up steps again.

Finally, remember that it is absolutely essential for problem dogs and problem owners to begin the heeling process *indoors.* You cannot allow your dog to yank you out of the front door, yank you across the front yard, yank you into the car, yank you out of the car and then ask your dog to heel down the smartest avenue in town. If you consistently allow a dog to precede you in or out of territory you are telling the dog a whole heck of a lot about who owns the territory. Your dog will simply surmise, "I do. After all, I go first. The dummy I'm dragging goes second."

Please remember that dogs do not think in terms of addresses, street names, your reputation or—for that matter—what you may be trying to accomplish via a set-up. Instead they think in primitive terms of *territory*—and who owns the territory is dictated by who gets to go first. City owners encounter particular problems involving heeling because their dogs live—at least outdoors—almost exclusively on leash. Urban owners will find a lengthy explanation of the intricacies of city heeling—probably the fullest explanation in print—in *The Evans Guide for Civilized City Canines.*

Sit and Stay

You might find that you've taught the word sit at the same time you were teaching the heel just by tightening up on the lead. If you're not so lucky, or if you've decided to teach "sit" first, which is perfectly OK, use three fingers pressed together in a curved motion over the dog's head as you say "sit." The dog's rump will sink as it follows the motion of your hand.

Attach a leash to teach the sit command. Start from the heel position, with the dog on your left. Keep the leash absolutely straight up and down. There should be a slight amount of tension on the lead. Hold the taut lead with your left hand and bring your right hand down in front of the dog's face with your hand just slightly cupped closed. Now, as your hand nears the dog's eyes, flash it open, fingers closed, and say "stay." Step in front of the dog. If the dog moves, give a zip on the leash and repeat. If the dog stays, praise and return to the heel position. Now go halfway around your dog, return and go all the way around. Say "stay" each time you leave and flash the stay signal in your dog's face. Now loosen the tension on the lead and widen the distance you go away from the dog. Repeat the above steps until you can walk completely around your dog using a six-foot leash with the dog not moving.

That little "flash flourish" to your stay signal is very important. It makes the signal more dramatic and makes more of an impression on the dog. While most trainers use a flattened hand with no flashing movement, I prefer the sudden burst of fingers. I picked up this training technique by watching old clips of Diana Ross and the Supremes singing "Stop! In the Name of Love" and flashing their hands at the audience in their dynamic dance routines. It was effective for audiences then and it's effective for dogs now. Dogs do stop and stay in place!—if not in the name of love, then in the name of obedience.

Proofing the Sit-Stay

I like a proofing method found in *Training Your Dog: The Step-by-Step Manual* by Joachim Volhard and Gail Tamases Fisher (Howell Book House, 1983). They suggest the following to get the sit-stay tight and superreliable, and a supertight sit-stay is essential in staging many set-ups. From the heel position, signal and command "stay." Walk three feet in front of your dog and turn to face it. Your left hand is at your midsection and the right hand is ready

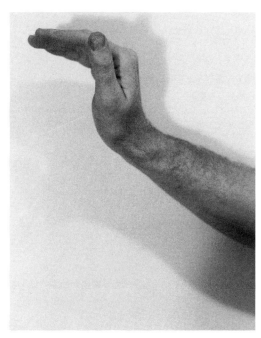

Use a "flash flourish" when giving the hand signal for "stay." Cup your hand slightly. . .

Charles Hornek

. . . and then open your hand. Keep your fingers together.

Charles Hornek

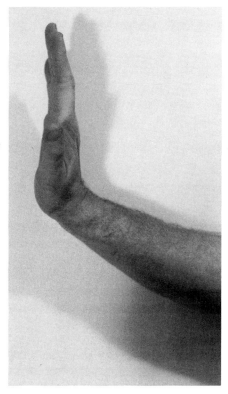

Teach a solid stay for successful set-ups! From the heel position, signal and command "stay."

Judy Emmert/
Dealing with Dogs/
TV Ontario

Walk in front of your dog and be ready with your left hand to "zip" the dog if it breaks the stay.

Judy Emmert/
Dealing with Dogs/
TV Ontario

Loosen the tension on the lead and widen the distance you go away from the dog.

Judy Emmert/
Dealing with Dogs/
TV Ontario

The tug test: Gently pull the dog toward you while reissuing the verbal and visual commands. *Dealing with Dogs/TV Ontario*

to reinforce the stay. With as little body or hand motion as possible, apply slight pressure toward you on the collar. This is accomplished by folding a few more inches of the leash into your left hand. If the dog begins to come to you, reinforce the command by slapping the leash with your right hand, repeating "stay." This "tug test," as I've dubbed it, forces the dog to give primacy to the word and the signal and not the distraction of your pulling toward you. It really forces the dog into a mode of deductive reasoning, making it think out, indeed, that words mean what they say in spite of distractions. In this case the distraction emanates from you via the slight tug (don't go over three to five seconds of slight pressure) but out on the streets of Metropolis, the distractions will assault you from all sides without your being able to control them. Better to proof the exercise inside first, and then hit the streets for these progressions to a solid sit-stay. By the way, be sure to keep your fingers closed when flashing your "Supremes" signal. The air holes in an open hand make a slight difference to the dog in terms of the overall blocking effect. Don't use your dog's name while teaching the sit-stay and don't praise physically until the tug test is successfully completed. You'll just break the flow of the progressions and switch the dog into a play mode when you want it in a work mode.

At first the sit-stay looks rather frivolous. Heeling and the down look far more important and many an owner considers the sit-stay marginally valuable. Besides, with all that flashing of signals and saying of "stay" it's boring to teach—and what if I hardly use it anyway? I sympathize, but I disagree. I agree that the sit-stay can be boring to teach and that the progressions can appear Sesame Street-ish and even exasperating. But they are necessary. I once confessed this to a client with whom I was discussing the sit-stay exercise. I used the term "Sesame Street-ish" to describe the steps involved in teaching a good sit-stay. The client turned out to be the originator of the children's show *Sesame Street.* It was not my first taste of shoe leather, even though the series' creator thought it quite funny. You'll need sit-stays for successful set-ups and to successfully socialize your dog.

Welcoming the Wanderers

The fact is, there are a myriad of uses for the sit-stay. The first and most obvious is greeting people when they come to your home. This is where all hell often breaks loose. First the admittance bell is intoned from the street or by the doorman or concierge or the doorbell rings. This primes the dog that someone is going to come through the door momentarily. The dog then begins organizing its welcome, usually by spinning around the house or apartment at full speed, yapping its head off, chasing its tail and generally going nuts. The owner screams, "No! No! No!" but to no avail.

By the time the person actually arrives at the door the dog has entered the Twilight Zone. The neighbors upstairs and downstairs are phoning or pounding on the floor or ceiling. "Shut that @#$%#!#@! mutt up or we'll have you evicted!" You hurry to open the door and admit your guest, hoping

Another way to "proof" the sit-stay is to jump up and down and clap in front of the dog—correct *quickly* if necessary.
Dealing with Dogs/
TV Ontario

The jinx for jumping: a nifty three-part correction that can be used whether the dog jumps on yourself *or* others.   *Kevin Smith*

that once he or she is inside and settled, Screechy will shut up. And sometimes the dog does (but sometimes it doesn't). The pounding on the ceiling stops and all is peaceful and serene again.

Not quite. Although the barking, yapping and yodeling have subsided your dog is now scaling your guest's body in ardent passion. If you are *really* a spaced-out owner, unconcerned with what your dog is doing to others, you will make the usual excuses:

- "He's just friendly!"
- "That's funny, he's never done that before."
- "Just let him jump on you for a while and maybe he'll calm down."
- "He just wants a little love."
- "He only bites if you push him down."
- "Don't worry, his paws are clean."

Well, my God in Heaven above, my friend, how very rude of you! You wouldn't allow your child to behave this way toward a guest, so why are you allowing such behavior in your dog? Did you really invite your friend over for a mauling? Do you really expect the grocery clerk to keep delivering foodstuffs to a house where he is molested by a dog? What about Aunt Matilda's best nylons, now torn to shreds? When you've worked for Calvin Klein, as I have, you learn that not everybody likes to be jumped on when he or she is wearing fine clothing, especially not by a dog that just came in from the rainy streets. Stop all excuses. Your salvation is a solid sit-stay.

The Jinx for Jumping

Here's your correction for jumping; in shorthand, then I'll elaborate.

1. Whip down *hard* on the collar, tab leash or leash and say *no.*
2. Pull on the collar, tab or leash, say *sit.*
3. Flash the stay signal in your dog's face, say *stay.*

You should understand that refusal to sit or stay or spring-jumping on guests is not just love, it is canine dominance. Attempts to seek love can indeed be exercises in dominance; ask anyone who has suffered a relationship that went down the tubes. So don't put up with jumping, no matter how cute you think it is, no matter how small your dog is and no matter how much guests tell you *they* think the jumping is cute. I can assure you, they are lying. Outside they are saying, "Oh, how cute, he likes me," and inside they are saying, "Get this creature off me this instant." Since they will most probably not administer the correction it is up to you to step in from behind and remove the canine clinger from your guest's body. Snap the collar up smartly and issue your verbal stay command and the stay flash. Now, have the guest pet the dog again, right away. If the dog jumps again, readminister the correction.

The best ruse you can pull on your dog to teach it to greet guests is to stage a set-up in which a family member and then a less familiar guest show up at the door. The difference between a set-up and real life is that you will be prepared to correct your dog. Attach a short tab leash for your set-ups so that you will have more than flying fur to grab if the dog breaks the sit-stay. Quite obviously, you will issue the stay command to your dog *before* you open the door. It's perfectly OK, during the set-up, to slam the door in the "guest's" face (he or she will understand this is a set-up) and correct your dog. The point you want your dog to get is that persons are not admitted until the dog is seated and under control.

I'm not saying that guests arriving is easy for most dogs—but set-ups pave the way to success. You might try a dry-run set-up without any person at the door. Put your dog on leash and station it at least four feet from the door. Issue your advance warning. Don't let the dog crowd the door. You will need that space for admitting your guest. Get your dog into a sit and deliver the stay command. Open the door halfway. Correct your dog with an upward snap if it moves. Close the door. Reissue the command and open the door all the way. Close it. Reissue the command and open the door all the way and ring the doorbell or buzzer. If the dog breaks the stay (and believe me this is Waterloo for many dogs that have been unintentionally trained to freak out when the doorbell rings), stage a set-up as a peopleless dry run. You can gradually build up to a set-up with a real person, and then really real people!

The above teaching techniques and corrections apply equally to meetings on the street or in a lobby. Passersby often make it difficult, especially on owners of smaller cute breeds. They will greet the dog and then, when it jumps up, actually hold the dog up on its hind legs, supporting the paws. Very few if any will ask your dog to sit before petting it, and of course, every time the dog jumps up on someone and is supported, the behavior is OKed. So since you can't train the people you meet in chance encounters not to hold your dog up, you must train your dog. If the dog is jumping up on someone who does not know or will not use the three-part correction outlined above, then *you* will have to step in from behind and grasp the leash to yank your dog off firmly, sit the dog and flash the stay. Remember, only three words should come out of your mouth when you administer the jump correction: no, sit and stay. Recapping:

Verbal sequence: no, sit, stay.
Physical sequence: pull down, pull up, flash stay signal.

What too often transpires is a ton of verbiage that just confuses the dog: "*No! Off,* Tippy. Gosh darn you bad dog get the @#$% *off* that man. Oh, I'm sorry. Tippy, *off,* down, no! Stop!" No dog can make sense of such oververbalization, so remember just three words coupled with the physical sequence of the correction. Don't say *anything* else. It should now be obvious that the words "sit" and "stay" are not at all ornamental but essential words for your dog to live by.

Long Stays

Teach your dog to hold the stay for longer and longer periods of time. Issue the command and let out the extension of your lead. Turn sideways and count to sixty. Return and praise. Correct with a "No!" and a snap of the lead if your dog breaks the stay during that time period. Now turn your back to your dog and watch your dog in a mirror. Keep a hand cupped under your leash ready to snap it up if the dog moves. The purpose of this exercise is to teach your dog to hold the sit-stay even when you appear unable to correct the dog if it breaks.

Now take it to the streets. Go window-shopping using a display window that features mirrors or reflects the dog's image nicely. Set your dog up on the sidewalk (leave room for passersby) and issue the command. Window-shop, but watch your dog in the reflection. The faster you correct breaks, the faster your dog is going to learn a rock-steady sit-stay. A technique I often use with my canine students is to set the dog up facing a restaurant window. Most restaurants display both the menu and their reviews in the window. Simply pretend to read the menu or the review or both, but of course, really watch your canine student's sit-stay in the reflection.

Sometimes I really *do* read the menu, and while I'm reading a rave review or drooling over reports of an establishment's perfect chateaubriand, duckling, baby lamb chops (I could go on and on, but I won't), my dog will be wandering around aimlessly, having broken the stay who knows how long ago. Pick badly rated restaurants that get boring reviews!

Try to build up to five to ten minutes on your long stays. The time period can seem like an eternity, so pick a place where you can read a review, take in a view or window-shop to proof your dog. Remember, the lesson for your dog is very important here. You are teaching it that it has to do what you say, when you say it, for *as long* as you say it. This is invaluable practice in teaching your dog to be patient in stores and on the street and also prepares the dog to hold the long down.

Recently I was helping a client proof her dog's store-stays in a drugstore and we wandered into an area of the store with large cardboard boxes. I assumed they were baby diapers and after putting the dog on a sit-stay began to read the instructions on the box aloud as a distraction to the dog. Suffice it to say that the box contained not diapers but another paper product used by women. Another taste of shoe leather for the naive ex-monk.

Stoop and Scoop Sit-Stays: Elimination without Exhaustion

It can be very difficult to stoop and scoop the feces of a dog that is dragging you away from or even *into* the very excrement you are attempting to remove. No wonder so many dog owners cheat on the laws of their locales and run away from elimination sites. The solution, again, is a solid sit-stay.

Wait until your dog has eliminated fully, and then place it in a firm sit-stay. Stoop and scoop. It helps if you have previously staged a fake stoop-and-scoop session during which you are picking up a stone, gravel, garbage or even nothing, in order to proof the dog's sit-stay. So your set-up sequence would be: Sit your dog after elimination; issue a warning, "Sam, don't move, stay!"; now stoop, scoop. If Sam breaks, correct immediately, reissue the same warning emphasizing the phonetic sounds—"I said, *Sam, stay,* and I *mean* it!"—and stoop and scoop again. Remember, when you bend over, your body language looks pretty subservient and inviting, and your dog doesn't necessarily know that you are obeying the city law and retrieving waste. Truth be told, your dog could care less. All it sees is a bending human who *appears* to be inviting the dog to come, play, cavort or even stomp on the very feces you are trying to remove.

It's never surprising to me why this type of set-up is readily agreed to by my city clients, whereas they might object to other set-ups they see as "too strict." The fact is, picking up after your pet, while the law of the land, might not be the thrill of your life, but a lunging maniac pulling you into and through elimination won't increase your desire to perform this task. You don't have to be played the fool—you can obey the law and perform this essential service without losing a shred of your, or your dog's, dignity. Practice and teach a solid stoop and scoop sit-stay. Then do a few set-ups. You'll be soon home free.

Down

The down is also taught from the heel position, with the dog already seated. There is a sensitive spot on your dog's back that is analogous to the spot behind your knees. Pressure here can fold the dog into the down position. Put your left hand on the dog's shoulder blades (properly called the scapula) and with your thumb and index finger trace down the scapula to where the spinal column begins. You will find an indentation there into which your thumb and finger will fit readily. For those more experienced with canine anatomy, the "secret spot" is the upper thoracic vertebrae. Push gently forward and down on this spot. Most dogs will go down readily, but if there is resistance, lift one or both front legs and say "down." Add a hand signal as you say "down," with your finger (right hand) pointing to the ground.

The Long Down or "Coma on Command"

For a trained canine a good, solid down is the essence of being civilized. Now that you've got your dog going down on command, getting into the actual physical position of all fours flat on the floor, you are at a very critical and important juncture in your training efforts. The reason this moment is so important is that you can royally goof up right now and train your dog to give you only short minidowns unless you *insist* on a long down. Insist? Yes, as in i-n-s-i-s-t!

How long? Well, I'm going to ask you to go for the big time: thirty minutes. OK—I hear you screaming with laughter. "Thirty *minutes?*" you might be saying. "My sweet monster has never hit the dust for longer than thirty *seconds!*" Or you might be not just a Doubting Thomas but also a Sympathetic Sam, who feels thirty minutes is too lo-o-o-ng of a down. After all, what if your dog has to amuse, feed or relieve itself during those thirty minutes? Too bad! There are twenty-three-and-a-half hours left in the day for your dog to pursue those activities. Right now, *you* need some quiet time, too—and the long down is your way to get it. Besides, there are hidden benefits to this exercise your dog doesn't have to even know about.

Don't expect to get much coaching about long downs if you are taking your dog to the typical obedience class. Unfortunately, long downs are rarely taught in classes. What *is* taught are three- to five-minute minidowns because these are all that are needed for the obedience trial competition. Not withstanding, a three-minute down is next to useless in real life. You can *do* something with thirty minutes and the dog can be easily convinced to extend the time once it's passed the thirty-minute threshold.

Don't attempt a thirty-minute down until your dog goes into a down reliably without your touching the special spot and/or offering paw assistance. When you are getting the down response to just your finger signal, and when you can flash a "Supremes" stay signal in your dog's face, rise and walk slowly around your dog (keep a hand cocked over the dog's back to correct it if it rises), *then,* and only then, are you ready to try out thirty minutes. I stress again, though, don't train-in too many short downs, releasing the dog with praise, because you may never get the long down.

Don't Tread on Me!

Where you position your dog when you ask for a thirty-minute down is important. I'd advise you to avoid placing the dog directly underfoot or in passageways. Directly underfoot is a bad choice because if you so much as cross your legs with an inexperienced dog trying to hold a long down at your feet, the dog will probably interpret the movement as a threat or as permission to move. Also, with your dog camped out at your feet, you cannot make effective eye contact to correct the dog if it breaks from the down, and probably more important, you are going to find your hand stroking your dog, which will only make it more difficult for the dog to stay down and not rise and solicit more praise. Be fair to your dog. I'm not saying that your dog can *never* lie at your feet, but if you are counting on a canine to commit itself to a long down it's better to *recess the dog from your body.*

For committed long downs always think in terms of centrifugal force— put the dog against the wall and out of a passageway. Dogs do not like to be told to lie down and stay in a passageway. They know that passageways are where the humans walk and they are worried about getting stepped on. Little dogs really fret about this (cats are almost phobic about passageways). All dogs psyche out the passageways in a room the minute they enter it, and when they

Teach the down from the heel position with the dog seated. Pressure on the "special spot" on your dog's back will help ease it down. Give the hand signal simultaneously. The spot is usually easily located on larger dogs.
Dealing with Dogs/TV Ontario

On smaller dogs the spot may only need pressure with your thumb and index finger.
Charles Hornek

If there is resistance, lift one or both legs and ease the dog down. *Judy Emmert/ Dealing with Dogs/ TV Ontario*

123

want a silent snooze will often select a spot against a wall or at least in an out-of-the-way area. Sometimes dominant, bratty, bossy dogs will deliberately plop themselves in passageways to make their owners step over them. If you own this type of dictator, it's even *more* important that you place your dog on long downs out of the mainstream of traffic. Wherever you go with your dog for the lifetime of your pet—even if you are in unfamiliar surroundings—check out the room from the point of view of the dog in terms of where the passageways are. See why this exercise if often not taught in a class setting? You need a real room to train real long downs, but even if this exercise wasn't introduced in class or in the books you've read, select your spot and read on.

Tough-Love Corrections

Got your dog positioned in a proper spot? OK—attach your six-foot leash and string it out from your dog's side toward wherever you'll be sitting. Now down your dog. Flash your stay signal in your dog's face. Stroll to your seat—that's it, keep a strict eye on your pooch and immediately wheel on the dog and say, "No! Down! Stay!" if the dog rises. Remember, no screaming. Just darken your voice; change your tonality, not your volume. You did get to your seat and the dog didn't break down? Great. Have a seat, but *as you sit* flash another courtesy stay at your dog just so it doesn't misread your body language and think that your sinking down is permission to come. Don't look at the dog, but keep an eye on it. Staring will invite the dog to negotiate with your eyes—which are full of weakness and worry at this point because you really, really *don't* believe that the dog is going to stay there for thirty whole minutes, do you?

Well, it is. You are going to make it. You're going to make the dog stay because you know that even though this exercise looks like a terrible limitation on the dog's freedom right now, this long down will really be its liberation if the two of you really get this exercise, well, down. Why? Because you will be able to take your dog many more places because you will know that you can, in essence, park it. So you have to be strict.

Here's your corrective sequence if your dog breaks down (and believe me they all do).

- *At the first break,* say, "No. Down. Stay!" On the word "no" raise your finger up as in a warning, on "down" throw that raised finger down dramatically and on "stay" flash the stay signal at your dog. No excess verbiage. No screaming. If the dog hits the dust again, fine—but don't say "good." Say nothing. The dog isn't doing anything good—it's correcting a command issued a while ago that it goofed up. If the dog tries to bolt out of the room, step on the leash and reposition the dog in the exact same spot.
- *At the second break,* repeat the above sequence, but even if the dog drops back into place go and give the dog the shake or the swat

correction. Strict? Yes, but totally humane and in the dog's best inter-ests—if you do not get physical, the dog will simply continue to rise and fall, rise and fall, with your rising from your seat to reposition the dog. Some dogs will actually come to enjoy being shoved down again and again and making you get up and sit down, get up and sit down—a sort of canine musical chairs.

- *At the third break,* repeat the verbal correction and the physical one, and then in silence tie your dog to an immovable object like a chair leg. Tie your tether tightly and *short*—so short the dog cannot rise to sit. Do this in silence. Return to your seat, complete the thirty-minute down.

Through this corrective sequence you tell your dog how important this exercise is to you, and that you will not give in and let it walk around at will, nor will you give in and use your crate as a cop-out or throw the dog in another room or cheapen yourself by yelling and screaming until finally, finally, the dog leaves you alone. You are through with yelling and screeching. You are through with avoidance, casting your dog off to another room. You are teach-ing, not tolerating your dog.

Review these long-down rules:

1. Don't place your dog underfoot.
2. Don't place your dog in a passageway.
3. Leave the leash *on* in case the dog decides to split—at least until you are confident it won't.
4. Don't look at the dog during the long down—but keep an eye peeled on it.

Proofing the Long Down

Proofing means weeding the kinks out of an obedience exercise so the dog knows that the word really means what it says. Proofing means upsetting situations in which the dog is tempted to break its down and decides not to or gets corrected if it does. Proofing means tying the long down into the structure of real life. Proofing means letting the dog know that it has to do *what* you say *when* you say it for *as long* as you say it—whatever "it" is. Including "down."

Proof your long down against four distractions: movement, going out of sight, food and friends. Here's how:

- To proof against movement, flash a courtesy stay from your seat and move to another chair, adding a second courtesy stay as you sit again. I call these extra flash stays "courtesy stays" because they are just that—forms of politeness to the dog so that it doesn't think the stay is over. You'll find you need fewer and fewer courtesy stays because the dog will settle into the down (especially if you do one or more thirty-minute downs each day). But at first they will be necessary. Try throwing a magazine up in the air and saying and flashing "stay" just as you do. Or "accidentally" spill a dish of candy on the floor with an accompanying "stay." You get the idea. Be creative.

- Snap a set of keys on your dog's collar (just use the bolt of the leash). Return to your seat. Now rise and flash a courtesy stay. Leave the room and flash one more courtesy stay just as you disappear from sight. Listen carefully. If the keys jingle, your dog is cheating. From the room you exited to, say, "No. Down. Stay." If the keys stop, your dog listened. If they keep rattling, the dog is still moving. Return and replace the dog in its spot. Repeat going out of the room and follow the same corrective sequence outlined earlier. Crafty, aren't we?

- Don't try to do your first thirty-minute down during Thanksgiving dinner. The canine mind goes nutzola around food, so start with a glass of water and a cracker at the dining room table with your dog properly positioned on the down. But eat the cracker *slowly,* savoring every bite. Slurp the water. Get ready to go through your corrective sequence. Remember, at some point you are going to have noisy eaters as guests, if not already in residence. Proof that long down! Don't forget the alfresco dining situation. Proof these by simply ordering a drink or an appetizer at an outdoor restaurant. Be sure to check in advance if dogs are admitted—often they are, at least in the outdoor portion of the establishment.

- Finally, most dogs, even dogs who have performed spectacular long downs and resisted movement, food and disappearing owners, will fail miserably to stay parked in the presence of your friends. The dog just senses that you are not going to be as strict in front of your friends and that all bets are off. Since you'll really want to use the long down when friends come over—especially friends who may not appreciate being mauled by your Malamute or nuzzled by your Newfoundland—proof the down by inviting over an understanding friend who will sit in total silence as you correct your dog. It usually takes one or two proofings but, believe me, most dogs then reason: *"Everyone* is in on this long down business. The only way I get in on things that happen around here is come in, say hello, find the nearest wall and plop myself."

Your release word for a long down is simply pronounced "OK!" Don't say "come," because we don't want the dog resting on the down but inwardly thinking any minute you'll say "come" and this stupid exercise will be over. Praise your dog nicely after a successful long down. Make it know how very pleased you are that it's done the greatest obedience exercise of all—the one that shows its deepest respect for you as leader, the one that allows you to take it to baseball games, dog shows, libraries, outdoor restaurants, even, in some cases, church—the hard-to-achieve but blessed-to-have long down!

The long down is the culmination of all of the other exercises. It produces deep dignity in the dog, respect for the owner in the dog and reverence for the dog in the owner. It is the crowning achievement that elevates mere obedience training to the level of etiquette and manners. While you must be strict in teaching it, don't deprive your dog of learning the long down.

A praise problem: Excessive stroking and fondling sometimes backfire when the dog comes to expect longer and longer stroke sessions. *Kevin Smith*

14

Praise Problems

DOGS LOVE PRAISE so much that you wouldn't think it could conceivably be any problem for them. But sometimes it is, mainly because we humans misunderstand its use. Praise is *absolutely essential* to a healthy dog/owner relationship. Any book concentrating on problem behavior will inevitably put more emphasis on corrective techniques and discipline than on praise. Indeed, some problem dogs deserving radical therapy need to earn *all* of their praise simply because they have become accustomed to "stealing" large amounts of it from their owners. Once an owner realizes that dishing out praise for nothing can backfire and result in problem behavior, the owner often tightens up and goes to another extreme: "OK—no praise for you, Bozo!"

Antipraise owners have an ambivalent relationship with the concept of praise. They may feel it is unnecessary and will spoil the dog. The real problem, of course, has very little to do with the dog and everything to do with an uptight owner. If you are the type of person who is basically a sad sack and finds it difficult to give encouragement and praise, you should rethink dog ownership.

On the other hand, you might be an owner who simply gives too much praise or gives it at the wrong time. One problem with praise results when it is too high-powered, too bombastic or too sweet and whiney in tonality. Placating owners especially have to guard against whimpering praise at their dogs. Rather than feeling congratulated the dog simply feels placated. Blamer owners have to be wary of praise that is too loud because it can actually frighten the dog.

I've seen placaters, for instance, call their dogs and then fawn over them in such whimpering tones that the dogs will simply collapse at their feet and, sometimes, squat or even flip over and submissively urinate. Then there is the dog that looks truly bewildered and somewhat berated as its owner bellows out "GOOD BOY" because the dog obeyed some simple command. Praise that is too high-powered or too bellicose often makes a dog switch out of the "work" mode and snap into a "play" mode. If this happens the dog can lose concentration and certainly doesn't remember what specific action it is being praised for.

Bubbles Belong in Champagne

When I began training dogs I received contradictory information regarding the intensity and vivaciousness that should accompany praise. One trainer who tutored me insisted on using a lot of what she called "bubbles" while training. What this meant was that one flitted around the training area constantly singing praise to the dog, even for the smallest positive actions. Training sessions with this trainer resembled the opening moments of *The Lawrence Welk Show*. So I tried her technique. My perception was that the dogs saw through my "act" and seemed more puzzled than pleased by this type of praise. The bubbles went flat quickly. My main mentor, Brother Thomas, certainly believed in praise, but used it in a more constructive way. He would, for instance, praise with just the words "good boy" or "good girl" and he pronounced those phrases in a way similar to that of a sergeant telling a soldier "at ease." The dogs seemed to respond more quickly and efficiently. Training sessions went more smoothly. Because the dogs were not distracted by the praise, they learned more in a shorter period of time. I think, therefore, that parceling out praise is best during actual training sessions.

Meanwhile, off the training field, just hanging around the house with the dogs, Brother Thomas would toss out praise to them constantly. He had a personal jingle for almost every dog, which he would sing when the dog was doing nothing but being itself. This use of praise—which on the surface can seem like a misuse—kept all of the monastery dogs in a friendly frame of mind toward Brother Thomas. While overtly "good" actions, such as obeyed commands, received simple and succinct praise and praise during actual training sessions seemed parsimoniously doled out, the balancing factor was the joy and affection expressed in the silly jingles and personalized songs during other parts of the day. The philosophy I learned from this was that when actually training a dog, it's not good to overload the dog's circuits with praise that borders on frivolity, but during the bulk of the day other types of praise should be used to make the dog feel welcome and appreciated. This philosophy has stood me in good stead. Often, even during an initial training session, I will parcel out praise. I train as though the dog already knows the exercise. This type of praise challenges the dog and at the same time rewards it.

Getting Physical

Physicality in praise is, of course, also important. Very often praise that includes an excessive amount of stroking or fondling backfires when the dog comes to expect longer and longer "stroke sessions." I like to concentrate physical praise on the centering spot on the dog's forehead. Often the lightest touch of your index finger, a gentle massage with your thumb or even a kiss planted on the centering spot will have an almost magical effect. Because this spot is so important to so many dogs, *where* the physical praise is given intensifies its effect. Yet, how many times have you seen a trainer *kiss* a dog's forehead as a form of physical praise? Not many times, I'm willing to bet. Contrary to the lyrics of the famous song, a kiss is not always "just a kiss."

Another super stroke spot is the sternum—that protruding breast bone that juts out especially when your dog is sitting. A brief stroke or scratch on or around the sternum keeps the dog happy yet "on" to the learning task at hand. From the heel position it's easy with many dogs to, with your left hand, deliver praise to this sensitive spot.

Inappropriate Praise

Another praise problem is the misuse of praise in which the dog is praised for simply refraining from bad behavior. This is a source of great confusion for many lay owners. A typical situation: Let's say you're reading quietly in the living room and suddenly you notice that your four-month-old chocolate Labrador Retriever has started to munch on the cable TV wire. You haul out your best "bitchy," growllike sentence and quietly pronounce, "Rascal, get your mouth off that right now and I *mean* it." Bravo for you. You didn't yell. You didn't scream. Rascal stops chewing on the TV cord. But now you blow it. You turn to Rascal and in the sweetest possible tones coo, "Gooooood boy. Now, don't touch that wire again, pleeeeeeeaze." To complicate matters, you go over to Rascal and give him a chew toy while continuing the praise. What's wrong here?

What's wrong is that Rascal doesn't deserve or need any praise for simply refraining from doing something bad. It would be far better to say nothing after the reprimand and simply return to your reading. If Rascal were to resume chewing the cable wire, sterner action, such as a shake correction, is warranted. The idea of giving the dog an appropriate chew item sounds like a worthy one, but this too could backfire. If Rascal always has something appropriate shoved in his mouth whenever he chews on something inappropriate, what will happen when Rascal chews destructively and the owner is not home to pull off the switch? Bite your tongue if necessary, but make it a cardinal rule to never praise your dog for simply refraining from unacceptable behavior—most especially if it's engaged in such behavior time and again. Considerable canine confusion can result.

I am a cheerleader for crates—but constant or careless crating is a cop-out.
Lionel Shenken/Visual Productions

15

The Crate as Cop-out

I'VE ALWAYS been a cheerleader for crates. I've used them when housetraining my own dogs and recommended them to others for myriad reasons. There is absolutely nothing wrong with crating your puppy or older dog. Most dogs accept crating because they are, at heart, den animals. Wolf progeny are born in a den, a cave or some similar shelter. The mother keeps the den clean by consuming all the body wastes produced by her children. When wolf pups grow older she starts to send them outside for defecation and urination. The youngsters soon learn that it is important to keep their enclosed area clean. Otherwise, they will quickly incur the wrath of their mother and this they do not wish to do. Using a crate, then, is historically and scientifically valid because the crate environment simply replaces the den environment.

Crates are manufactured in different styles, such as a pressed fiberglass model used by the airlines and wire models, available at most pet stores. I usually suggest that owners invest in an airline crate because it can be used in the back of a car or on a plane if it becomes necessary to travel with your dog. Sometimes behavorial difficulties make this model the best choice. If you have a chronic leg lifter, avoid the wire crate because your dog can simply aim its urine outside the crate. An airline crate is better because then Squirt will have to sit and simmer in his own urine. On the other hand, if your dog has a severe problem with destructive chewing stemming from severe anxiety at the prospect of being separated from you, the wire model might be a better choice because the dog doesn't feel so cut off from you and shunted away. The dog can see you leave and simply resign itself to the fact. There are crate rental services in many cities so you can try both models.

The Crate Craze

There's been a real revolution in the dog training community in terms of the use of crates. Twenty-five years ago they were hardly mentioned in dog training literature. Now it is *de rigueur* to recommend them for everything from housetraining to much more complex behavior problems. I find some problems in this emphasis on crating. I guess I wonder what dog owners did to control their dogs prior to today's crate craze. For instance, if the dog is getting in your hair, simply driving you nuts, it's extremely tempting and convenient to crate the dog—and this is routinely recommended by trainers. Old-timers who grew up in the fancy, not using crates at all or using them on a very limited basis, would solve this problem by training the dog to go to its place, lie down and stay. If every time your dog bothers you, you simply pop the dog into a crate, what, I ask, are you *teaching* the dog? Are you not teaching it that whenever it starts driving you bananas it will be confined in its private quarters? Aren't you also communicating to the dog that you have no way to control it except by confinement? Further, could you actually be *rewarding* the dog for bad behavior—especially if it adores its crate?

Many crate connoisseurs will readily admit that if, in a moment when the dog is engaged in frenetic activity, they were to say, "OK, Conrad, go to your place and lie down and stay," Conrad would simply stare at them as if they were out of their minds—and of course continue whirling around the house. So then, it's off to the crate. What is really needed for dog *and* owner is instruction in, and insistence on, a long down. What will these owners do if they ever need to anchor their dogs in a crateless situation? They will be in a real bind, forced to simply restrain or reposition their dogs. Many dogs sense this loss of control. They can see that the handy, dandy crate is nowhere to be seen. This is a perfect example of the "rewards" reaped when the crate is used as a cop-out.

If you *do* use a crate make sure you've also taught your dog good, solid obedience commands. Remember, use the crate when you *are* at home; do not simply deposit the dog in it when you leave. If you crate the dog only when you are gone this can lead to separation anxiety, whining in the crate and clawing at the metal grating to achieve escape. It's a good idea to teach your dog to go to its crate, lie down in it and stay there while leaving the crate door *open.* When you release the dog from the crate, just ignore it for a few moments. If you are too enthusiastic when releasing it from the crate you might be unintentionally training the dog to badger you for earlier and earlier release. This can lead to barking and stress whining when you are away.

Special Crate Conundrums

A small number of dogs absolutely *refuse* to be crated. They will urinate and/or defecate on themselves while in their crates. They lie in their refuse and seem to enjoy it. There are others who will become absolutely crazed when confined to a crate and will even bend the metal bars of the crate with their teeth to try to get out. Often these dogs simply need to be decrated but still confined. They do better in a larger area.

If the problem concerning crating has to do with soiling, the crate is probably too big. You'll have to get a smaller crate or shrink the area by loading up half of the crate with an indestructible yet safe object. Remember, though, some pet store puppies are used to sitting in their own wastes. Shrinking the crate won't matter, so in this instance you should decrate the puppy or older dog and use baby gates to confine the dog to one room.

Crate That Crate!

Frankly, my idea of how to use a crate in dog training consists of employing it as a tool during the housetraining process, and then folding it up and putting it away in a closet or the rear of the car so that the dog can travel in it. I think the crate gets used as an excuse by many owners who do not want to invest the time in training good, solid sit-stays and down-stays. I do not think it is anthropomorphic to suggest that the dog senses a lack of control on the part of the owner when no crate is available for confinement. The desire to stay still in one place is first instilled in the dog by teaching command words, such as "sit," "down" and "stay." These words can then be strung together and the concept of *place* added to the command, as in, "Go to your *place* and lie *down* and *stay.*" If the dog only stays still when confronted by the three walls and grate of a crate this desire will never flow from *within* the dog. Yes, by not using the crate as a cop-out and by making your dog do one or two thirty-minute downs a day, your dog will begin to "sense" when to go away and plant itself, sometimes before you even issue a command. Trained dogs seem to develop a sixth sense of when you want to be left alone. They come to know that if they don't make the decision to lie down on their own, you will probably tell them to do it anyway. These dogs start to realize that they are never crated, yelled at, tethered or banished to another room if they simply take their place in the family circle and lie down quietly. This is no less than we would expect from a well-behaved child. It is not wrong to ask and expect as much from your dog. Teach a good, solid long down using the techniques in this book. If crating is abused your dog will never learn to think out its downs for itself. The crate then becomes a cop-out and the joy of owning a well-trained dog is greatly diminished. Train, don't just crate and complain. You want to be your dog's leader and friend, not its warden.

16

Our Own "Urine Analysis"

NOW, I'M GOING TO TALK about urine. Shocked? Don't be. Doctors regularly run urinalysis tests on their human patients, so it's about time a dog trainer analyzed the role of urine analysis for dogs and their owners. Many owners simply do not realize the overwhelming power of dog urine as a tool of dominance. The novelist J. R. Ackerly wrote, "Dogs see with their noses and write their history in urine." I can only agree. If you have a dog that is leg-lifting, anointing your couch or squatting on your bed, you have a dominant dog trying to write his personal history on your personal stationery. With the possible exception of submissive urination (more on that later) inappropriate urination is almost always, in my experience, an expression of dominance by the dog—an attempt to gain or regain Alpha status in the household. You see, dogs have an easy life—if they see it, they sniff it, if they like it, they lick it and sometimes if they love it, they wet on it. That's the truth, short and not so sweet.

It's helpful to know a bit about the composition of urine itself. While urine may look clear or just sport a simple yellowish hue, it is a complicated substance. It is made up of water, proteins, uric acid, urea, amino acids, salts, several inorganic compounds and—guess what—ammonia. That's why it is foolish to clean up urine with ammonia or any dog cleaner that contains it. And, believe me, almost 75 percent of the cleaners I've researched contain a healthy dose of ammonia. Ammonia is a compound of urine: You will be compounding your problem, adding, in essence, urine over urine if you use ammonia to clean up housetraining accidents or other urine deposits.

Why then, do so many doggie cleaners contain ammonia? Well, I figure it this way. Maybe either the manufacturers of such products know that the product will backfire on the owners who use it and just don't care, or they ascribe to the more-is-better theory that pervades the American consciousness. You know what I'm talking about—the doctor told you to take one pill a day, so you take *two* figuring you'll get better faster. So the owner uses *twice* as much ammonia doggie cleaner thinking that it will stop Yuri from urinating once and for all. Yuri then urinates ubiquitously. Solution? Go buy *more* of the same ammonia-based "cure." A classic catch-22. I like catch-22's in novels, not in dog training!

There are scent substances called *pheromones* in the dog's urine—they are also present in feces—and these substances tell the dog that it's OK to eliminate in that same area again. The best way to kill off these naughty pheromones is to *acidify* them out of existence. The cleaning fluid I've always used is 50 percent white vinegar and 50 percent water. You can cut the vinegar to 25 percent if you're worried about whitening out a colored carpet, but one caution: Do *not* sponge with vinegar on marble floors, as the vinegar will discolor the marble. So what should you do if you have marble floors and your dog lays a load or places a puddle on the floor? Simply clean with a *swipe* of vinegar and then *immediately* clean up the vinegar with water. Frankly, if you can afford marble floors you probably have a maid who needs this information more than you do.

Bed Wetters

My clients often call ranting and raving because their pooch has wet the bed—not its bed, theirs. I've had clients so disgusted with this practice that they were ready to hang the dog at high noon, feeling that the dog was morally depraved and perverted to do such a thing. I always assure these souls that there are pooch perversions far worse than this one and the dog isn't acting in a morally deficient way, anyway. It's just marking territory—probably territory it wants from *you*. It often begins by having the dog up on the bed, or even under the covers, and never informing the dog that getting on the bed is a *privilege* you grant, not a *right* it holds, and that you can elevate the dog or demote it from the bed on whim.

Many dogs urinate on things they are trying to claim from another dog or person. Male dogs especially do this, but I've known plenty of bitches who do it, too. Remember what I said about the use of urine as a tool of dominance? If you think of urine here as a canine attempt to gain the bed, you've got the right idea. My advice, then, is to teach your dog that the bed is a place it gets invited up to, not a landing platform that it can hurdle itself onto whenever it wants.

If you have a bed wetter, immediately demote the dog from the bed for one month. If necessary tie the dog to the foot of the bed or to the table nearest you. You'll then be able to reach down and pet the dog if you'd like, and you can yank the leash, *hard,* if it pipes up to protest being demoted—which it probably will. After one month, you can begin teaching your dog the difference between having the privilege of being on the bed and seeing it as an inalienable right. Put a tab leash on and leave your dog free. As soon as it hurls itself onto the bed, grab the tab and send the dog *sailing* off the bed. Don't let go of the tab. When the dog lands, give it a good shakedown and scold firmly—but not loudly. Release the tab and if the dog tries it again, repeat the process. This time use a swat to cap off your correction. Remember, if you don't cap off the correction with the shake or the swat you have *not* corrected your dog, you have simply *repositioned* it. And many dogs will make repositioning into a game—forcing you to reposition and reposition until you are about to go nuts. So be sure to give the shake or swat correction after the first repositioning. Chuckles is to stay off the bed for one month. If he's lost his "chuckle"—too bad. He'll rediscover it, on the floor.

After demoting Chuckles from the bed (remember, for one month) you pull a fast one. One night while you are quietly reading in bed or watching TV, call Chuckles (who is now snoozing on the rug, resigned to being on the floor) and say, "Hey Chuckles, *come up here* on the bed." Emphasize the words "come" and "up here" as these are the new commands you're teaching. Pat the bed invitingly. At this point Chuckles will look at you with a perplexed look. The dog doesn't know this new command, and certainly doesn't trust your invitation even if it *does* understand your meaning. So repeat the command and again pat the bed encouragingly. Most probably the dog will approach the bed hesitantly and then place one paw up. Encourage the dog. There are some brazen pooches who, even after being demoted for one month, will hurl themselves up on the bed readily. Whatever happens, praise your dog once it hits the bed. Let the dog quiet down for a few minutes. Now, pointing your index finger toward the ground, announce, "Chuckles, get *off* the bed." At this point Chuckles will look at you like you're out of your mind.

But of course you're not. So *gently,* not too forcefully this time, guide Chuckles off the bed, repeating the command phrase and emphasizing the word "off." Now repeat all of the above until you have Chuckles jumping on or off the bed at your command. Congratulations, you've just taught your dog that being on the bed is a privilege you grant, not its supreme right. If you had a bed wetter I am willing to bet that the problem will never reoccur. And if you have a lover or spouse, they may be extremely happy. Also, whether you know it or not, you just staged a stealing set-up.

If your dog wets its *own* bed, and believe me this is not uncommon behavior, simply take the bed away for two weeks and let the dog sleep on the floor or provide a towel. Clean the bed with vinegar and water, if you can. Many dogs will wet their own beds. I usually advise owners not to invest big bucks in elaborate beds at first. Buy a simple bean-bag style bed instead or just use a towel or a rug until Fido proves trustworthy. The Louis XIV canopy bed can wait.

Illegal Leg-lifting

Do you recall when I mentioned that urine is the "ink" that dogs use to write their history? If you have a leg-lifter you have a dog who is a very active historian; it is writing a book! Follow the step-by-step approach for disciplining inappropriate urination outlined in the chapter "Do Dogs Feel Guilt or Shame?" Illegal leg-lifting can often be disciplined even after the fact because the pheromones still "stink" to the dog. Visually, the dog can often still see the stain. If you have a shred of proof I would give discipline after the fact a try.

Remember, leg-lifting is almost always an attempt on the part of the dog to dominate the owner. First, have your veterinarian rule out any medical problems. Put the dog on the Radical Regimen for Recalcitrant Rovers (RRRR) right away. In most cases leg-lifters need to be neutered. Put aside any emotional qualms or anthropomorphic projections you may have concerning neutering. Simply have the operation performed. You'll be doing your dog a big favor. If I seem blunt or curt in my advice to neuter the chronic leg-lifter you'll have to understand that after seventeen years of patiently explaining the benefits of neutering to clients who appear to think the operation will be performed on *them* and not the dog, I'm just bone tired. Every single behavioral and medical study clearly indicates that neutering is in order and can help ease or eliminate this problem. If you want to cheat, and not neuter, and only want to discipline your dog and put it on the RRRR, I certainly can't stop you. It's a free country and you're welcome to do as you like—but don't blame me if your dog continues to squirt the staircase or baptize your bedroom.

Tighten the Controls

Besides neutering, there are a few other aspects of your leg-lifter's behavior you'll have to control. Don't let Squirt spray the neighborhood. Some leg-lifters are unintentionally trained that urinating in the house is OK when owners allow them to leg-lift ten, twenty, even thirty times during each walk—and, of course, heartily praise each outdoor spray. Limit your dog to only three or four urinations by using the methods detailed in the section on heeling in chapter 13. City owners might also consult my book *The Evans Guide for Civilized City Canines,* which has an extremely well-detailed section on city heeling. Rather than letting the dog pull you from pillar to post, *you* release the dog from heel for urination.

Second, limit your dog's water intake by simply offering water three or four times a day rather than leaving it down all the time. Remember, what goes in, must come out, and if your dog tanks up after each walk it's more difficult for it to exercise control. If you have to leave a leg-lifter alone, leave a bowl full of ice cubes instead of water. They will melt down gradually and "ration out" the water. Some chronic leg-lifters will not agree with discipline and will need to be crated. But some recalcitrants, if crated in open-air crates, will simply squirt their urine outside the crate. What these dogs need, as unpleasant as it might sound, is to sit and stew in their own you-know-what. Get an enclosed airline crate so that if the dog lifts its leg, the urine will drip down and the dog will have to sit in it—something most dogs prefer not to do.

You can check with your veterinarian about drugs that might help Squirt stop squirting. Progestin therapy can sometimes be useful for dogs with this problem, and the veterinarian may have other drugs in his or her arsenal that you should consider. But remember, you will have to train the behavior out by doing set-ups during the period of time that you are using a given drug. If the problem is behavioral, drugs alone won't cure it.

Concocting a set-up to limit leg-lifting is really quite simple. You simply pretend to leave the house, issuing an advance warning. Hide so the dog can't see you but you can see it. The moment the "lift" commences, charge, and I mean *charge,* to your leg-lifter, discipline, repeat the warning and leave again. If it's not possible to position yourself so you can catch the dog right in the act, simply leave for as long a period as you think it will take for Squirt to leave some proof. Use your worksheets to design a set-up, and remember to seal off as much of the house as possible so that when you administer discipline you will not be cheapened by a chase.

Submissive Urination

Submissive urination is a completely different matter. It occurs when the dog is highly excited and feels that the owner is dominant. It is often an attempt on the part of the dog to *please* the owner. The response is out of the dog's control and usually corrects with maturity.

If you are having a problem with a submissive wetter *don't punish the dog.* This will only worsen the problem. It is still possible to do a set-up, skipping the discipline step. The first thing to identify in setting up this kind of set-up is *when* the behavior tends to occur. The most frequent times that submissive urination occur are

- When the owner arrives home and greets the dog too effusively
- When the owner disciplines the dog
- When the owner catches the dog after a chase
- When the owner argues with another human—even on the phone
- When friends greet the dog after coming onto the owner's territory

If the problem occurs when greeting the dog it's important that you do *not* touch the dog. Avoid eye contact during these times and pass the dog as if it does not exist. Try to avoid approaching the dog directly and instead pass the dog on its side. Don't hover over the dog when saying hello or good-bye. It's also a good idea to take this type of dog to obedience school. Here the dog will learn the words "sit" and "stay" and you can use these words in your set-ups. Obedience training will also instill a certain confidence that will help the submissive dog.

Staging Set-ups for Submissive Squatters

If your dog has a problem with submissive urination and tends to exhibit the behavior when you come home from work and overaffectionately greet the dog, your set-up would be scripted as follows:

You might think you have to skip step one, the advance warning, because you won't be home to issue any warning since you will be coming back from being away. Not so. You can gently, and I mean *gently,* issue the warning as you *enter* the house, without making eye contact or touching the dog. When the dog squats, which you'll be looking for out of the corner of your eye, softly repeat the warning without physically disciplining the dog. Then, immediately hang a wheelie and leave the house again, coming back perhaps five or ten minutes later and repeating all of the above.

The next time you do a set-up perhaps you would touch one finger to the dog's forehead, bending your knees to reach down to the dog, not hovering over the dog. You would still avoid eye contact and perhaps just say "Hello," and then give the warning phrase. In future set-ups, increase the physical contact.

You can also dry your dog out for the set-up by limiting water beforehand. This might give you an edge for success. Submissive urination is no picnic, but it can be treated by carefully staged set-ups. Again, I urge you to use your worksheets to script the set-up. Especially for this problem, a set-up has to be finely tuned.

Finally, I must stress again that my records and consultations clearly show that various urination infractions are the number one "closet" problem among dog owners. Owners often fail to connect urination problems with other ongoing difficulties the dog may be having, such as aggression and destructive chewing. But in reading this "urine analysis" I hope you now clearly see the importance of correcting your dog for all forms of illegal urination. Please don't think that occasional "mistakes" can be ignored or tolerated because "It really isn't much of a problem." It *is* a problem, and one that is often intimately connected with whatever "big problem" the dog is having. If you don't eradicate illegal urination you won't eradicate that big problem either. By illegally urinating, your dog is writing its history, and part of that history is what the dog thinks of *you.* Your dog is sending you a message when it inappropriately urinates and (with the exception of submissive urination) that message could be, "P___ on you." Fill in the blanks.

17

Aggressive Advice: An Open Letter to the Owners of Canine Terrorists

Dear beleaguered friend,

If you are living with a canine terrorist who lunges, growls, snaps, snarls or bites other humans or other dogs, this letter is for you. You must know the frustration experienced by government officials, security personnel and airline pilots. As with human manifestations of terrorism, canine attacks often seem to come out of nowhere. The aggression often appears to be totally unprovoked and unexplainable. Just as an airliner can be suddenly taken over by a thug, some canine terrorists seem to take over a household and hold their owners hostage.

What you should know is that, just as governments with good intelligence agencies often detect signs of impending terrorist action, a skilled trainer and an educated owner *can* decipher the signs of upcoming aggression from a dog. In fact, even while the dog is being aggressive correction *is* possible. Remember Entebbe? Israel essentially concocted a set-up, a sting operation to save its citizens held hostage in Uganda. President Carter tried and failed to rescue U.S. hostages from Iran; the set-up fouled up, but at least he tried. You *can* stage set-ups to stop your canine terrorist and rescue innocent human hostages. The first step is to get out of denial and into action by setting up a plan of action. You need to reason out the context of your dog's aggression.

In fact, very few incidents of canine aggression are unexplainable or unprovoked. Aggression is almost always *context specific*. That means that when your dog flies off the handle it has a *reason* for doing so. The dog has probably been placed in a specific context of psychological and environmental influences that trigger the aggression. You need to find out what these influences are. But first, some background.

In this open letter to you, the troubled owner of an aggressive dog, I need to deliver up-front aggressive advice. I'd like to share with you my thoughts about what society thinks of aggressive dogs and what you yourself must do to spare yourself society's wrath. You see, people have pretty much *had it* with aggressive dogs. You only have to look at the incredible number of city and state "dangerous dog" laws that have been enacted over the last ten years, the Pit-Bull controversy and the enactment of legislation banning certain breeds from certain places to realize that there is *zero* public sympathy left for aggressive dogs and their unfortunate owners. There are an estimated 3.5 million dog bites each year in the United States. Most of these bites occur in the spring or summer, but the seasonal differences disappear in states like Hawaii or Florida where the weather is more temperate all year. Children ages five to fourteen are most likely to be bitten, and boys between those ages are twice as likely as girls to suffer injury. Such a statistic readily shows that there is no small amount of cultural conditioning—especially macho cultural training foisted on young boys—behind some of the bites. In short, young boys often tease aggressive dogs and get themselves nailed in the process. We can't necessarily do anything to change the way youngsters are culturally conditioned, and because a child teases your dog it still does not justify your dog biting that child. You must do your best to train your dog to be better behaved than some children! Again, remember the trend in society is definitely away from any kind of support or sympathy for you and your grouchy dog. Stop blaming society, "unfair" laws and teasing kids. Train, don't complain.

A Dreamworld of Denial

Now that you realize that you won't win any popularity contests, and that a large number of people would just as soon see your canine Jack the Ripper imprisoned or even eliminated, instead of pouting because nobody likes you or your dog, engage in an examination of conscience. Owners of aggressive dogs often live in a dreamworld of denial, a twilight zone of rationalizations and excuses for their dog's bad behavior. They are often afraid of the dog themselves, terrified that the dog may turn on them next and feel powerless and hopeless. Perhaps you feel that there is not much you can do about the aggressive behavior except avoid the instances that trigger it—and so you structure your life around skirting situations that will make your dog angry and you unpopular. It's a difficult task to break out of this dreamworld of denial and stop your tendency to avoid rather than confront your dog's aggression, but it *is* possible to do so, but only, I repeat *only*, if you are sufficiently *motivated* to do so.

It is more difficult to motivate someone in print than in person, but I'll give it a try. Let me talk to you in the same way I have spoken with hundreds of clients with aggressive dogs over the last nineteen years. As a first step let's take a fearless, honest look at exactly what alternatives you have with the dog. Here are the four options that I know of for the owner of an aggressive dog.

1. Live with the behavior the way that it is.
2. Try to train the behavior out of the dog.
3. Give the dog to somebody else.
4. Euthanize the dog.

Options, Options, Options

Now let's take a look at each one of these options individually. By virtue of the fact that you are reading this book and this specific chapter, something tells me that probably option number one is not a possibility for you any longer. You probably don't want to live with the behavior the way it is. Perhaps you have visible evidence of this choice in the form of a bite mark on yourself or someone in your family. To "live with the behavior the way it is" might also be something you've been doing for several months or even years, hoping that the dog's aggression was just a phase it was going through and would outgrow. But as the days and months have gone by you've come to see that the aggression only gets worse, not better. Your excuses for it have grown more numerous, but sound, even to yourself, more and more hollow and evasive. You know that you have to break out of that dreamworld of denial. So this option is not viable for you. Now, as corny as this sounds, I want you to take a pencil and cross out option number one on the list. Go ahead, cross it out.

Alternative number two, trying to train the behavior out, might leave you excited, hopeful, skeptical or all of the above. When I discuss this option with my clients excitement is often the initial response. They ask me, "Is it really possible to stop the aggression?" My reply to them and to you is a qualified "yes." Many aggressive dogs *can* be rehabilitated, but only with the cooperation of a motivated owner, sufficiently committed to the task. The rehabilitation will consist of placing the dog on the Radical Regimen for Recalcitrant Rovers, and I ask my clients to read over the regimen right at this point. That's not a bad idea for you either. Just stop reading here and flip back to chapter 9. Read over all twenty points of the regimen, and ask yourself whether you are committed to following it completely. Adherence to the

RRRR will mean major life-style changes for your dog and possibly for you. The Radical Regimen will be the *platform* on which you will stage set-ups to rehabilitate your recalcitrant. If you honestly can't see yourself following the RRRR, get your pencil and cross out number two in the list above. Go ahead, flip to the RRRR, read it over, determine whether you can "obey" the twenty points and then cross out or leave standing option number two.

Option number three, giving the dog to somebody else, might seem mighty attractive. "After all," you might reason, "if it only had a country home where it could run and play and get all that energy out of its system maybe the dog would be so *tired* it wouldn't have the *energy* to bite anyone." Magical thinking. As if energy or lack of it ever determined who gets bit when. Or you might reason that if your dog just didn't have to see so many black people, white people or purple people perhaps it would never growl at another member of those groups again. Or maybe your dog growls and lunges at people who wear funny hats or cheap perfume. If you could find it a hatless home with unscented owners maybe it wouldn't get so grouchy. Maybe, maybe, maybe. Maybe if . . . If only . . . A dreamworld of denial. A twilight zone of excuses for excuses for excuses. See the syndrome?

Trouble is, life in a country home, even if the dog gets a Jane Fonda workout each day, might also include the possibility of visits from black, white or purple people in funny hats wearing cheap perfume. Sooner or later the stimulus that sets your dog snarling is bound to appear. An added difficulty is that the new owner won't necessarily know all the different people, places and things to avoid in order not to trigger the aggression. There is a strong likelihood that the new owner will unwarily walk right into a dangerous situation. The result can be injury to that person and others. I'm sure you wouldn't want that on your conscience. So it becomes increasingly obvious why giving the dog to somebody else is not a viable alternative. In most cases it would be far better for *you* to keep the dog, try training and walk into situations that might set off an aggressive response fully aware that you are setting the dog up to misbehave and fully prepared to discipline it. Once again: Stage set-ups. Train, don't complain.

There is another problem in giving your aggressive dog—or any problem dog—to a new owner. It's one you might not have thought about yet. The second owner and the dog will be new to each other. They will not have had the time to bond and feel deeply about each other. In short, the new owner will not be in love with the dog the way that you most probably are—or at least once were. Tolerance often flows out of love. Love for another can be the birthplace for motivation. The new owner will have little tolerance or sympathy for the dog's bad behavior and scant motivation to try to modify it through training. Most probably the new owner will simply transfer the dog to yet another owner. Or take option number four. We'll discuss that option next, but if you see the insanity of taking option number three (unless you know a hermit in Antarctica who wants a dog) go back and cross out option number three from the list.

Option number four, euthanize the dog, is a prospect that horrifies many owners. However, there is a small number of owners, especially those enduring life with an unpredictable, violent dog, who will see euthanizing the dog as a viable option. While most owners really want to give training a try, hoping that the behavior can be eliminated, there are some owners who have simply had it with the dog. These owners often try to get professionals such as veterinarians or trainers to support them in their decision to put the dog to sleep. I suppose this is understandable, but no trainer or veterinarian can ethically indicate that this alternative is the only one to be followed without a full discussion of the other three alternatives. In fact, the American Veterinary Medical Association has published ethical standards dealing with this question. It is not the veterinarian's mission to decide anything in this area for the client. Whatever is done is, after all, your decision, and the ultimate authority to make that decision rests with you.

I *never* indicate euthanasia as the desired option, but rather lead the client to examine *all* the alternatives and take responsibility for the final decision. Sometimes an owner simply euthanizes an aggressive dog without any attempt at training the behavior out or, if that isn't possible, at least educating themselves as to what they might have done wrong with the dog that helped set the stage for the aggression. Very often what then happens is these owners procure another dog and repeat the whole sad process again. Sometimes the second dog is even *more* aggressive than the dog that preceded it. It's sad to say, but often the trauma of the decision to euthanize the dog helps the inadequate owner face personality difficulties and lack of leadership skills more squarely. If this is done honestly, even if the dog is beyond repair, frequently the second owner/dog relationship is much better.

That said, it's far more common that owners do *not* want to play this final card and will readily cross this option off the list. If you've made the decision that option number four is *verboten,* turn back and cross it out. Still, it's a good idea to look at this alternative because it *is* a possibility. Just looking at the option can be cathartic in and of itself. If you decide it is not a viable possibility you can look back at our list of four alternatives and see that probably your only option is to try training. There may still come a time when you are forced to accept option number four and put your dog to sleep because perhaps training doesn't work. But at least if that sad day comes you can assure yourself that you did everything in your power to change your dog's behavior through training, and correct any handling errors on your own part. I know that's not much of a consolation, but some consolation is better than no consolation at all. At least you will be able to say that you yanked yourself out of self-pity and denial and really tried to reeducate your dog. There are some people who think that self-pity is better than none, but they probably aren't reading this open letter.

To sum up: Most probably you have crossed out options number one and three and are left with options two or four. You've decided you cannot live with the behavior the way it is any longer and that it is impractical, unethical and unthinkable to simply transfer the dog to somebody else. You are left with the options of either training your dog or euthanizing your dog. In short, train the dog or kill the dog. That's blunt, and perhaps even hurtful to some of you, but it's probably accurate—and again, as much as it may hurt to hear such a statement, it's a lot better than denial and despair. Right? Whoever lived richly, fully in denial or despair? Not you. So, let's gear up for action.

Going into Action

If you've decided to try training, great! You've chosen option number two. The first thing you must realize is that there is the strong possibility that you might need the help of a private trainer. Do not take the aggressive dog to a dog training class. Such dogs don't belong in class but rather need private, in-home training. Place your dog on the Radical Regimen for Recalcitrant Rovers right away, following all twenty points *to the letter.* This program will begin to change your relationship with your dog and set the stage for successful set-ups.

If it's absolutely *impossible* to hire a private trainer—and you've checked with your veterinarian for a referral and come up with no leads—you can try the following program on your own. However, I must add that I can in no way take responsibility for your personal safety or the safety of others if you opt to try to train your aggressive dog all alone. Working with an aggressive dog, even if it is a personal pet, can be potentially dangerous. This book can only give you a skeleton plan at best. It's simply not possible for me to diagnose in print what type of aggressive behavior your dog exhibits. If you do want to wing it the first step is to try to get an idea of what type or types of aggression your dog displays. Aggressive behavior can fall under any of the following classifications, or it may fall under several. Here's a checklist:

Fear-induced
Learned
Pain-induced
Territorial
Interspecies (dog fighting)
A response to teasing (by children *or* adults)
Genetically predisposed
Jealousy related
The result of brain disorders (petite or grand mal seizures, biochemical, lesions, infections, etc.)
A response to medications
Focused on other animals (predation on chickens, cows, deer, etc.)

It should be obvious that your first stop with any aggressive dog is the veterinary office. Make sure, absolutely sure, that there are no neurological problems that may be contributing to the aggression. Get a second opinion if necessary.

Fear-induced and territorial aggression are by far the most common and easiest to categorize. They are often also the easiest to stage set-ups for because they are so predictable. A good way to figure out which categories of aggression your dog exhibits is to simply write down in short paragraph form everything you can remember about the last growling, lunging or biting incident. Take the time to do this now before going any further in this chapter. Just write down who was involved in the incident, where and when it happened and how long the "action" lasted. Don't try to justify or explain the dog's behavior. Just write down here the bare bones of what happened.

_____

_____

_____

_____

_____

_____

_____

_____

Now, reading over your description and looking over the checklist, try to classify the aggression. If you're truly baffled show somebody who does not know the dog your description and the above listing of aggression categories. You want to get a handle on the *type* of aggression because this information will help you to design set-ups.

If writing a description of the last episode doesn't seem to help, try this: Sit down and write as full a description as you can of a typical day with your dog. Begin from the time you get up in the morning until the dog is snoozing at night. Again, don't try to diagnose or justify the dog's behavior. Just write down everything it does during the day—good and bad. If you have a problem dog, the description of the day might be weighted on the negative end, but that's OK. The important thing for right now is to simply get the description down.

Well, I get up in the morning and_____

_____

_____

_____

_____

_____

_____

_____

Here's a sample description written by one of my clients describing the typical day of King, a one-and-a-half-year-old unneutered Doberman male:

Well, when I get up in the morning I have to get up very carefully. Why? Well I don't want to wake up King because he'll growl at me if he doesn't get to sleep until at least eight-thirty. King sleeps between me and my husband in bed. I get out of bed quietly and get dressed quickly. I go downstairs and eat breakfast in a hurry because he'll be up any minute and it's impossible to keep food on the table when he's around. He just takes whatever he wants from the table. I have to make sure the bathroom door is shut because otherwise he takes the end of the toilet paper and starts running around the house with it and wraps it around everything.

Also I have to have his food dish down and ready when he gets downstairs because for some reason he doesn't like me offering him his food. He doesn't like anyone near his food dish. I have to watch the kids carefully because if they let him out when they run for the bus stop he'll terrorize all the kids at the stop. So I let one kid out at a time, and I throw a hunk of meat into the next room to distract King. He doesn't like to be brushed either, so usually there is a lot of vacuuming to be done around here. But that's a problem, too, because King attacks the vacuum cleaner. I had to rent a post office box rather than have the "scene" with the mailman every day. He's already bitten him once. I go to the drugstore to get the daily paper rather than risk the life of that poor paperboy. It has to be a fast trip because King gets lonely easily and will rip up the house if I'm gone for more than a half hour. So you see, I've had to make a few adjustments in order to live with this dog.

If you've read the chapters leading up to this one and are getting the point of this book, as you read the above description you were probably ticking off various set-ups that could be staged to correct King's terrorist ways. Of course you were also saying to yourself, "Oh, that's disgusting." Or, "I would never let a dog of _mine_ do that." But if you _aren't_ getting the point of this book, astonishment and amazement might have been your only reactions. Readers who are in tune with my message will not waste time being surprised at King's shenanigans, but instead will be anxious to go into action to modify his behavior. I mention this because many owners of problem dogs seem to almost _enjoy_ being astonished at just how bad their dog can be. A stupid waste of time and energy. Train, don't complain!

Easy Set-ups First

Let's work on King's problems. Your battle plan should be to stage the easiest set-ups first. From the description given above it's obvious that there are over fifteen possible set-ups that can be staged. The easiest ones are, of course, the set-ups where it would be most difficult for King to retaliate physically. In short, set-ups we won't get bit staging! Put on your thinking cap and think along with me. What are the easy set-ups that can be staged right away? Try these:

- Get King out of the bed! This is accomplished easily enough and doesn't have to involve a fight with the dog. Simply tether King to the foot of the bed without giving him enough lead extension to hurl himself on top of it. Another solution would be to use a crate in the bedroom. Remember that part of the RRRR is to let the dog sleep in the bedroom but not in the bed. Because the in-bedroom sleep increases or preserves owner/dog bonding, we don't want to demote King from the bedroom completely, but rather teach him his place in it.
- For food stealing and toilet paper unraveling, mousetraps can be used. A mousetrap can be placed strategically on the toilet paper so that it goes off when King investigates. However, King should *not* see his owner set the trap. A fake plate for breakfast can be set for a fictitious child, perhaps complete with muffin and mousetrap. Remember, we are trying to stage the easy set-ups first and for a dog of this type, that means avoiding getting bit. It is not "cheating" to practice some creative avoidance or use mousetraps so that the environment itself appears to discipline the dog.
- King's problem with having his food offered to him or barging out the door for the bus stop can be remedied by beginning to teach a good, solid sit-stay. A set-up can be staged dramatizing a fake school day morning, perhaps on a Saturday, during which the children could be employed to run for the bus stop while King practices his stays and gets corrected if he fails to stay.
- A simple set-up will vanquish the vacuum cleaner vexations. Place King on a sit and stay (or hold some upper tension on the lead to hold him in place if he doesn't know the sit-stay) and issue your warning phrase. "OK, King, you *touch* this vacuum and you're *dead.*" Now follow out the traditional steps for a set-up. Flick the switch of the vacuum on for just two seconds. Of course King will probably break his sit-stay and lunge for the vacuum. You know what to do. Grab King and give him a firm shake correction, a swat under the chin. If neither of these is possible because of a chance of physical injury from the dog, give him a firm collar correction. Repeat the warning and the stimulus, this time turning the vacuum on for perhaps three seconds. Repeat the correction if necessary, but if King decides to refrain from

attacking the vacuum, end the set-up for now. *Do not praise the dog for not attacking the vacuum.* He isn't doing anything good, he is simply refraining from being bad. There's a difference, and he knows it. You've just had a success, if only a three-second one. Remember, every time in the past the vacuum has been attacked has been a failure. Nothing succeeds like success, and nothing fails like failure. So take your small success for today and build on it tomorrow. You can try for five seconds then, until you are vacuuming in peace.

Similar set-ups can be concocted to solve the problems of grooming King or leaving him alone and coming home to destruction. For the latter problem it's probably OK to try discipline after the fact as outlined in the chapter "Do Dogs Feel Guilt or Shame?" It's my opinion that a dog like King is probably quite capable of understanding discipline after the fact if it is correctly administered. After all, this is a dog who has a good enough memory that he can remember to sleep until eight-thirty and still make it downstairs in time to essentially run all the morning activities of the household. This is a dog with organizational skills galore, a *smart* animal, a whiz, in fact, although his owner considered him stupid.

Save the Worst for Last

The more difficult set-ups will have to wait awhile. In this case we had to wait two weeks for the RRRR to kick in and begin to change the owner/dog relationship. Needless to say, several points of the RRRR directly addressed the overall situation between King and his owner. The dog was on the bed, there was too much indulgent petting, too many treats, but too little obedience training, earned praise and respect for the owner. If you have a dog like King, a strong, large, dominant dog, I'd advise you to practice creative avoidance, institute the RRRR and then start the simpler set-ups.

On the other hand, if you're working with a professional trainer or if your particular canine monster is cooperating fabulously on the easier set-ups, you can go for broke and try some harder ones. Looking back at the earlier description of King's behavior, there are several more difficult set-ups.

King's malevolence toward the mailman will need a carefully concocted set-up. It will take owner motivation, speed and stamina. It will also take a considerable amount of environmental preparation. Needless to say, such a set-up needs to be thought out and even *written out* in advance, in much the same way a director would plot out a crucial scene in his directorial notes. I've always suggested that my clients write out a script for the harder set-ups in advance. Here's what King's owner came up with.

> One of King's problems is barking at the mailman, and if he has access to him, charging at him. I now realize that every time in the past King has done this and the mailman runs away it reinforces the bad behavior. King thinks that he is chasing the mailman away. Also, every time in the past I have not issued an

advance warning to King, and instead hope against hope that maybe, just maybe, today he won't bark at or chase the mailman, I have been party to unintentionally training him to do just that. I am happy to announce that those days are over. Instead, I will do a set-up with the mailman. I'll speak with him a few houses away and ask him to pause for a few moments after delivering the mail. I will have the house closed off in advance so that King cannot run away from me. I'll attach a short tab leash to his collar so that I can grab him and discipline him when he even *looks hard* at the mailman. I will not wait until he disappears into that never-never land of crazed barking. If I can catch King's eyes growing serious and "hard" as he stares down the mailman I'll issue an advance warning *then.*

Another difficult set-up is, of course, the situation concerning newspaper delivery. This gambit would involve careful preparation because we would not want the newspaper boy to be injured. King may have to be on a twenty-foot rope or leash, and an adult might have to play newspaper boy. Of course it's understandable that when a stranger throws an object like a newspaper into a dominant dog's territory, the dog exhibits territorial aggression. Understandable, but not acceptable. Some owners might decide to stage all of the above set-ups and continue to pick up the daily paper at the drugstore. That sounds like an OK compromise to me—an acceptable form of creative avoidance.

My tendency as a trainer, however, would be to go for the gold and reform King's bad behavior from A to Z. However, I stress again that too many set-ups staged too quickly will force some dogs to retaliate, with the risk of personal injury to their owners or others. Further, often after the RRRR is put into play and set-ups begin, sometimes the behavior of the dog will become *worse*—at least for a while. Clients are often amazed at this phenomena, especially because they themselves are suddenly so motivated and dedicated to correcting bad behavior.

But there's nothing really strange about this bad behavior backlash. From the dog's point of view it is a perfectly natural response to a changing situation. What the dog is saying to the owner in colloquial terms is

> OK, *bimbo* . . . look here: Whether you knew it or not we had things set up around here so that I was the head honcho. I ran the household, I slept where I wanted, I ate what I wanted, I chased, growled and lunged at who I wanted—when I wanted. When I said "move" you moved. Now you're telling me all that is changed? That I'm not sleeping on the bed anymore, I have to obey words you say like "stay," I have to earn all my praise and I can't touch the toilet paper, any food that's not mine, the vacuum cleaner, the grooming brush, the mailman or the paperboy. *Well, don't expect me to buy it, Bimbo!*"

It's quite natural and normal for the dog to fight through some initial corrections. This is a phase you'll have to live through with the dog. But if you're going it alone in your training efforts, following the RRRR and the advice in this chapter, and the backlash period lasts longer than one week, it is clearly indicated that you need the help of a trainer. Get one. However, many dogs do not experience any backlash reaction at all and are happy to give up their dominant role in the household.

In Search of Sinister Signs

It should be obvious that in order to stage a sterling set-up it's necessary to be able to decode what the dog is feeling in order to issue an advance warning or deliver a well-timed correction. Many owners simply are not acquainted with or cannot see the signs of impending aggression. A rundown is in order. The following signs of aggression must be *memorized* in advance and watched for extra carefully, otherwise the set-up will foul up because of delays.

- *Hackles:* A dog makes itself look larger by raising hair along the back of its neck and spine, called hackles. There are muscles underneath these hairs that the dog can use to make them stand up dramatically. This is a first-class sign of imminent aggression. Unless the dog is a trained employee of a police force or the military—which I'm willing to bet your dog isn't—in my opinion a dog with raised hackles is exhibiting aggression and should be *disciplined.* Yet I've seen owners who are deep in denial simply try to smooth the hackles down by petting them! The aggressive dog is thus *rewarded* for its belligerence, and the behavior is trained *in,* good and tight. You should *never* bring a hand in contact with an aggressive dog when it is exhibiting aggression unless it is with the intent to discipline the dog. Any other contact, even the slightest touch, can be misinterpreted by the dog as a reward.
- *Ears:* A dog will also sometimes prick its ears forward, as if listening intently for something, when it is feeling aggressive. This is another classic sign of belligerence.
- *Legs:* Some dogs will tighten their front and back legs, firming up their overall stance, seemingly bracing themselves for an attack.
- *Tail:* The tail-set of the dog will often change so that the tail is held straight out from the rump rather than drooped down or held high. It is quite possible that the straight-out tail will also be wagging. This confuses many lay owners because lay dog wisdom has indoctrinated the public with the idea that a wagging tail indicates a happy dog. It can be easy to misread a signal. Why would a dog raise its hackles, prick its ears forward, firm up its stance, growl and at the same time wag its tail? Probably because it *likes* the reactions it is getting and is *enjoying* itself in its aggressive display.
- *Vocalization:* Obviously any growl, even a low, barely audible one, is an indicator of escalating aggression. Pronounced barking and snarling are even worse. Dogs emitting such sounds should, in my opinion, be sent to the stars with a firm swat under the chin, or, if that's not possible, a superstern collar correction.
- *Eyes:* Watching the dog's eyes is probably the best way to decode aggression because changes in the eyes often *precede* some or all of the above signs. Specifically, the dog's eyes will get "hard." Sometimes the eyes will glaze over and sometimes not, but the general look will be serious, fixed and unblinking. Do not stare at a dog who looks like this.

Watch for sinister signs of aggression. This Cocker is defending its bone, which the cat happened to walk over. A vigilant owner would issue a warning *now*.

Judy Emmert/Dealing with Dogs/TV Ontario

Instead, the dog chases the cat into another room and corners it. Now he *really* needs to be corrected.

Judy Emmert/Dealing with Dogs/TV Ontario

Simply try to get a moment of eye contact and then launch into the steps of your set-up. If you cannot understand what I mean by "the look" and you own an aggressive dog, please find a trainer or other professional who can indicate it to you in person. Occasionally, depending on breed type or the personality of a given dog, the *only* sign of imminent insanity will be this slight change from softness to hardness in the dog's eyes. This is why it is so important to read your dog's eyes, or find someone who can.

Breed Idiosyncrasies

Sometimes because of the "design" of a particular breed you will be deprived of seeing one or more of the above signs. For instance, if you're dealing with an aggressive Rhodesian Ridgeback, it's senseless to watch for raised hackles because the hackles are always raised. If the canine criminal is a Pembroke Welsh Corgi, it's silly to watch for a straightened out tail because this is a tailless breed. Some breeds, like Old English Sheepdogs, Australian Shepherds and some Benji-type mixes will not prick their ears forward, at least not in a way noticeable to laymen. An aggressive Irish Setter or Golden Retriever may sport so much feathering on the legs that any stiffening of the limbs will be difficult to see. Finally, some dogs simply growl so inaudibly (or not at all) that even a concert microphone wouldn't pick up the sound. All of this points to the absolute necessity of being able to read your grouchy dog's *eyes,* while at the same time mentally cataloging all of the other signs and then warning and/or correcting the dog speedily. Obviously, it is essential that any hair covering the eyes be clipped off or groomed and held back. Experienced trainers know that sometimes all of the above manifestations of aggression appear within *two* to *three seconds,* and that response time is critical. The point here is, don't feel guilty or stupid if your layperson's eye is not as quick as a professional's eye.

Does It Have to Be a Dog-Eat-Dog World?

Interspecies aggression—dogs fighting other dogs—is probably the most misunderstood form of canine combat. Owners make several mistakes. They try to decide who started a given fight and often discipline the *wrong* dog. The dog who exhibits overt aggression, such as a growl or an attack, gets clobbered. However, it takes two to tango. Very often, the more silent dog "began" the fight by casting a hard look toward the second dog. The owner then explodes into the room and wails on the dog who responded with a growl, snap or lunge. This teaches dog number one to perfect its hard stares to trigger increasingly quicker reactions from the more vocal dog. Sometimes the dog with the hard stare is comforted.

Things become even more complicated when the two fighters are separated, even if both are disciplined. This plays right into the dogs' paws! They

It doesn't have to be a dog-eat-dog world. There are friendly or neutral interactions like this one . . .
Levon Mark

. . . or there are interactions that go overboard—when even the "submissive" dog exhibits aggression. If they live in the same household, both dogs should be disciplined, not separated, and placed on a long down.
Judy Emmert/ Dealing with Dogs/ TV Ontario

By ditching denial, elevating your Alpha status and concocting set-ups that demonstrate that you are "top dog," even arch enemies can sometimes become kissing cousins.
Kevin Smith

156

wanted to get at each other, but failing that, they'd like to be separated from each other. Owners cooperate beautifully by hauling off the fighters into separate corners, or worse, completely separate portions of the house. This is understandable because, after all, if the dogs are left in the same room, they will simply resume fighting, right? Wrong. Not if you remain and make each dog hold a long down. If the dogs don't know the down, tether them *tight* a few feet apart and make them stay in your presence for thirty minutes.

The message one dog is giving the other is: "Look *you,* I don't like your *ugly* face. Maybe I like you sometimes, some days, but right now, for reasons of my own, I don't like your mug. And the best thing that could happen is for me to rip it apart. Failing that, at least get your ugly mug off my territory and out of here." And of course in trots the owner and separates the dogs. The dogs still win.

Instead the message the dogs should receive from the owner is: "Look you two (or three, or four, whatever the number of fighters is), you may not like each other and you don't have to. But you must tolerate each other, and if you fight, I will discipline you—harshly. In fact, I'll even set you up to fight, and if you do, you'll still have me to answer to. Think of it this way, guys: The fleeting, momentary rush you'll get from fighting with each other will be so miniscule compared to the horrendous price you'll have to pay from me, that it just doesn't seem worth the fight, now does it?"

Faced with that ultimatum, most dogs start to inhibit their aggression toward each other, if only to avoid incurring the wrath of the owner. If you have a house full of scrappers, immediately put all resident dogs on the RRRR. That's right—*all* of the dogs. The dogs who are seemingly innocent of starting fights (remember, you could be dead wrong in this assumption) will simply have to pay a price for the more overt fighters. It's simply not practical to place only one or two dogs on the Radical Regimen since it is an overall life program—and placing one dog on it and not another could well inspire jealousy. Look over the twenty points and you'll see why the program must be leveled on all resident pooches.

If the fighting is really out of control, practice creative avoidance for a few weeks until the RRRR starts to kick in. Then try a set-up with the help of an assistant. Be sure to have the gladiators wearing tab leashes in advance, so that you will have a way to separate them and discipline them if a scrap ensues. It's nearly impossible to discipline two dogs at once, so you may have to reprimand one while stepping on the leash of the other until you can get to it. If the fighting is so intense that the dogs turn on *you* if you try to intervene with discipline, your problem is indeed serious and you need the help of a professional trainer, *in* your household. But get ready—some trainers will advise you to discipline only the dominant dog, without spending enough time to see just who is being dominant in which ways. Other trainers may suggest letting the dogs work it out—to the tune of a walloping vet bill due to injuries they inflict on each other, and possibly you.

My experience comes from eleven years living in a household, New Skete

Monastery, with twenty to twenty-five in-house German Shepherd Dogs—all of whom got along, including, yes, males. The dogs knew the rules about fighting. They would have us to answer to if they even looked cross-eyed at each other! I also take my cue from my parents. I come from a large family—eleven children. Yes, it was a big litter. My psychologist father and my savvy mother usually ended fights over an object by removing the desired object from both the children fighting over it—without wasting one second to see who "rightfully" deserved it. Instead we were *both* reprimanded and sent to the kitchen to scrub the floor or clean the cupboards. In silence. The point was, of course, to substitute a productive, creative activity for the destructive and definitely uncreative one we had been engaged in. We had the cleanest kitchen floor and cupboards in the state of Michigan. The training took. All eleven of us are extremely close with each other. We fought, but we don't *fight.*

Drugs

A word about the use of drugs with aggressive dogs. Sometimes they can be quite useful if the right drug and the right dosage are used. Some behaviorists like to use tranquilizing drugs such as Valium or Librium to calm the dog. I do not. Since these drugs depress the central nervous system it is more difficult for a dog under their influence to think out the steps of a set-up. These drugs can wear out in effectiveness or, occasionally, be so effective that the owner will complain of a drugged dog, no longer aggressive but one that more closely resembles a possum than the dog they once knew.

The drug that I have had the most success with is megestrol acetate, commonly dispensed as Ovaban. This hormonal drug was originally developed to control estrus (heat) in females, but given in higher or varied doses seems to have a calming effect, without tranquilizing, on some aggressive dogs. Veterinarians and behaviorists have reported amazing results using this drug in treating behavior problems, *as long as the drug is administered concurrently with ongoing behavior modification training.* In other words, a good veterinarian will not prescribe Ovaban, or any drug meant to effect aggressive behavior, without at the same time prescribing a good trainer or specialist.

Ovaban and similar drugs are not cure-alls. If they were, there would be no aggressive dogs left to bother anybody. Progestins are currently the single most effective chemical therapeutic agent for problem behavior in dogs. The problems that are most responsive to the medication are

- Attacking other males without obvious provocation
- Urine marking in the house when the behavior is clearly not a reflection of inadequate housetraining
- Mounting of other dogs, people or inanimate objects when the mounting is not a reflection of puppy play
- Roaming

Notice that fear-induced and territorial aggression are not listed, but my experience with these forms of aggression has been that set-ups sometimes go more smoothly when Ovaban is used. My professional criteria for using or not using a drug is this: If I can concoct and stage a successful set-up and begin to rehabilitate the dog, but the owner cannot, whether because of lack of motivation, stamina or long-standing subordinate status in the dog's eyes, drug therapy is worth a try. The effect of the drug might mellow the dog sufficiently to think out the set-up and accept the correction. If on the other hand, a professional cannot attempt to educate the dog without being injured, usually the only possibility is to prescribe the RRRR for a while, avoid triggering the dog's aggression, wait and see what develops and try set-ups at a later time. The dosage I suggest for Ovaban is the one suggested by the manufacturer, Schering, for behavior problem management. Some behaviorists use very high doses, but there can be side effects. Consult your veterinarian if you think drug therapy will help you in training your dog.

Finally, I know this letter may have been rough reading for some of you, especially those who own and still love a grouchy dog. But after years of dealing with owners of aggressive dogs, and several bites down the line, I have the battle scars to prove that bluntness pays off. I have seen many aggressive dogs who have been rehabilitated go on to lead happy lives and give great pleasure to their owners. Good luck in your training efforts and your attempts to lead your dog from grouchiness to graciousness.

My very best,

Job Michael Evans

18

To Come or Not to Come

NEXT TO HAVING a grouchy, aggressive dog, there is nothing worse than owning a dog who will not come when called. Owners of such vagabonds have to live in constant fear that they will lose control over their dog, that the dog will get hit by a car, lost or stolen. It's a supreme difficulty to live life with such an animal. As usual, my sympathy and now my advice.

Of course I have to immediately jump to the defense of the dog. First, has the dog ever really been *taught* the recall? Some owners simply assume that the dog knows how to come when called, when they have never spent one iota of time teaching the dog the actual word. When the dog was a puppy, the owner reasons, it seemed to always come when called. But now that the dog is older, it doesn't anymore. This is delusionary thinking. Puppies have a natural tendency to *follow* their owners. This tag-along propensity can last up to the fourth or even fifth month, when the puppy becomes more mature and independent and begins to go its own way, responding less and less to the word "come." Perhaps during the following phase the owner just happened to say the word "come" in an animated tone. The puppy hugged the owners leg closely. This certainly looked like a valid come to many lay owners. But all the puppy was doing was following. When a dog gets older it has to learn the word "come" through formal training. Here's how:

- First, teach a good solid sit-stay. Be sure your dog knows how to sit and stay in one place before you begin teaching the recall. Start from the heel position. Attach a twenty-foot leash to your dog, issue the stay command and signal and, holding one end of the leash in your left hand, walk directly out from the dog the extension of the lead.
- Walk away from the dog, don't back away. This will only make you look hesitant and make the dog break its sit-stay. Keep an eye peeled over your shoulder and if the dog breaks the stay command, spin around quickly, flash the stay signal again and scold, "No, *stay!*" If the dog doesn't replant itself, get the dog and take it back to the *exact same spot* where it broke the sit-stay. Repeat the above process.
- When you reach the end of the twenty-foot lead, turn smoothly, genuflect, fling open your arms wide, smile and clearly command, "Rascal, *come.*" If the dog doesn't start toward you, give a pop on the leash to get it started. If it does start toward you, start to praise in a higher-pitched, but not whiney, voice. It doesn't matter much *what* you say, as long as it is genuine praise. However, *don't* say the slang term "c'mon" within your praise phrases, because you will be repeating a command the dog is already obeying.
- For owners of young puppies or older, "green" dogs who have never formally learned the recall, I usually suggest seven such recalls a day, building up to off-leash trustworthiness.

A Running Away Remedy

Of course preventative training as described above is easier than corrective action, but if your dog has been schooled in the recall and is simply running away or staring at you when you say the word "come," it probably does not perceive you as its leader. Sound blunt? Well, sometimes the truth hurts. Recall problems are, in my experience, most frequently *relational* problems. Something is wrong in the relationship between the dog and the owner. Specifically, the dog does not view the owner as Alpha. You see, the dog is coming to *somebody,* and you'd better *be* somebody to that dog if you want it to come to you. Makes sense, doesn't it? If you're viewed by the dog as an insignificant presence, a casual friend or, worse yet, a complete nothing, then there is no underlying reason for the dog to obey the command. In short, the underpinning for the recall is the relationship.

I mention this right at the beginning of our discussion because very frequently owners do not think of recall difficulties as *relational* but rather *mechanical.* Such owners drill, drill, drill their dogs in the recall in a mechanistic fashion, often making the dog hate the command in the process. Meanwhile, nothing is done to change the dog's perception of the owner. The dog still looks for the first opportunity to split, and when it does, the owner becomes even more enraged.

If this scenario sounds familiar, and you have the humility to admit that,

During the six-week moratorium on any off-leash freedom, you can "umbilical cord" the dog to your body to keep it near. This exercise also has bonding benefits—which you can cash in on later.

Dealing with Dogs/
TV Ontario

During the moratorium, practice formal recalls. Issue the stay and walk out unfurling a twenty-foot leash.   *Charles Hornek*

162

just perhaps, your dog refuses the recall because of relational problems, I offer again my sympathy and the following advice:

- Immediately, as in *yesterday,* put the dog on the RRRR program for one month. You will see the dog grow in respect for you during this month.
- On the same day that you institute the RRRR begin a six-week moratorium on any and all off-leash freedom. That's right, six *weeks.* Under no circumstances should you say the word "come" to your dog and not be in position to correct your dog if it doesn't obey the command. Remember, every time in the past you said the word "come" and your dog either stopped and stared at you or ran the other way, you were *training.* Whether you knew it or not, you were unintentionally training the dog that the word "come" meant to stand and stare at you or to run the other way. It takes a dog a *long time* to forget that kind of unintentional training and ascribe a new meaning, the *correct* meaning, to an abused word. Don't worry, though, the dog *can* relearn the word. It simply needs this moratorium period to forget the bad associations attached to it.
- Remember also that dogs that run away usually have some place to go. If your runaway is an "overnighter" that disappears for hours on end, or even all night, there is a very strong chance that the dog has memorized a route it follows. It will take six weeks for the dog to forget its itinerary and for the scent substances called *pheromones,* which are found in urine and feces and were left to mark the route, to die off. So don't cheat on the six-week period. Arrange your dog's life so that it simply does not hear the word "come" without having to obey it. The six-week moratorium period is not a punishment for you or your dog. Instead, it's a beneficial period for both of you.
- During the six-week moratorium period, practice seven formal recalls a day in an enclosed area. Leave a twenty-foot leash on the dog in order to get it if it bounds off, then graduate on week two to a six-foot leash. These are formal recalls in which you place the dog on a sit-stay, walk away and use a full complement of positive body language, positive tone of voice and positive eye contact. Do all seven recalls one right after the other, and make your praise short and snappy in between each recall. Don't overpraise. The dog will tend to focus on praise that interrupts the flow of recalls. All seven recalls should only take fourteen minutes.
- Remember positive body language! Lower one knee completely to the ground, balancing yourself with your other leg. Open your arms extra wide to funnel the dog in toward you. Sometimes, while holding your arms outstretched, pointing your index finger in toward your chest helps to orient the dog to come directly to you. The top portion of your body should be erect. Under no circumstances should you stand and

Positive body language! Lower one knee to the ground—Catholic or not, *genuflect*. Open your arms wide. Use another dog or person as a distraction.   *Levon Mark*

If you are ring-bound get ring ready by "straightening up" your body language in some sessions. Don't forget to employ a decoy person.
Dealing with Dogs/
TV Ontario

Graduate to free-lance recalls. Spring a recall on your dog when it's distracted. Be sure the leash is in your favor so you can correct quickly.
Levon Mark

simply bend over at the waist. This stance does not give the full impact of the "genuflection." When I use that term, I am not trying to be funny. Think it over: Catholics genuflect in church to honor a spiritual friend they want to have "come" to them. Your dog will also read these sentiments in your body language.

- Your tone of voice is important. Cough out the word "come" with an emphasis on the *co* portion of the word. Place your dog's name before the command. Remember also light, lilting praise as your dog proceeds toward you, but *do not* say "c'mon" as an encouragement word.
- Your eye contact should be gentle and encouraging. You should look at your dog throughout the recall. As the dog arrives in front of you, rise slowly so that you are fully erect. This will tend to make the dog sit in front of you because your height is imposing. The dog will cast its eyes upward to meet yours. Make sure that you are looking down to meet its glance at this point. Your four eyeballs should *lock*. In this meeting of eyes there is also a meeting of minds. There will be a sense of completion to the recall process, which, from the dog's point of view, includes the launch, the transition toward you and the arrival at your feet. Each of these segments demands sustained eye contact.

Free-lance Recalls

After two weeks practicing seven formal recalls as described above, you and your dog are ready to free-lance. Take your dog to the *same* enclosed area you have been using to practice the more rigid recalls. Take along a paperback book as well and a twenty-foot leash or rope. Take your dog to the middle of the area, tell the dog to sit, but *do not* say "stay." Guess what? You are now going to stage a set-up to see if your dog has begun to relearn the word "come."

Please don't simply detach the leash and let your dog run around the area. Instead, leave the leash on, sit your dog, tap the centering spot and issue a serious, but not scolding, warning. "OK, Tippy, I want you to *come* when I *call.*" Tap the centering spot lightly on the words "come" and "call." Now, without issuing a stay command, and after making one last check to make sure that the area you are working in is fully enclosed, drop the leash. Turn, walk ten feet away from your dog. Turn halfway back around to your dog. Pretend to ignore the dog, but keep an eye on it. Hoist your paperback toward your face and pretend to read. If you'd like, you can begin to stroll around randomly. Keep one eye peeled on your dog.

You might see some amazing reactions. Many dogs will simply sit stock-still, thinking that you simply forgot to say the word "stay." They will be afraid to move in one direction or another because they are not quite sure what you are up to. Besides, many dogs are also still in a state of shock from practicing seven formal recalls and living under the RRRR for the last week. Don't worry, though, if you saunter about long enough and pretend to read your book long enough your dog will begin to move about.

You are going to spring a recall on your dog. Wait for a moment until the position of the leash is in your favor. When your dog starts to move around, either following you or going away from you, try to position yourself so that the dog is facing away from you but the end of the twenty-foot leash is at your feet. This might involve walking swiftly toward the end of the leash if the dog is moving away from you. If the dog is hugging close and following you, you can suddenly go into reverse and start walking backward. Hopefully your follower will forge ahead. The end of the leash will wind up at your feet, in short, in your favor.

"In your favor" for what, you might ask? For delivering a correction, of course. If you've mastered the steps of a set-up, you can see that we are now on step number two. We are giving the dog a chance to be naughty and *not* come, but we are fully prepared to correct. So, now, in your most animated voice, issue the come command. "Tippy, *come!*" If Tippy voluntarily turns toward you and starts in your direction, begin your praise chant and complete the recall by rising and making eye contact as you did when practicing formally. When the dog arrives, praise for just a few seconds, release your dog again, do not say "stay" and continue sauntering about and reading. Try once again to get the leash in your favor, and spring another free-lance recall on your dog. If you're on a roll, do seven such recalls and then call it a day.

If the dog does not come to you, grab the end of the twenty-foot leash and *propel* the dog toward you with a firm jerk on the leash, simultaneously repeating the command. Make the dog finish out the recall even if you have to reel it in like a fish. Give very little praise. Instead, sit the dog, don't say "stay," reissue your warning phrase. Drop the leash and try another free-lance recall. For the dog who does not voluntarily come and ignores you or tries to run the other way, further free-lance recalls should be practiced. The elements of surprise and timing are essential. With the leash in your favor, try to spring the recall command on the dog, especially when it is fully involved sniffing leaves or socializing with another dog. You must teach the dog that it must listen for the come command and obey it *even* when it is distracted. The dog must learn that the word "come" applies at all times, in every place. Some dogs who have been drilled on only formal recalls never learn this. Practicing free-lance recalls helps change the dog's perception. *Always,* dog, *everywhere.*

Risk Taking

After one week of free-lance recalls using the twenty-foot leash, begin one week of free-lance recalls using a six-foot leash. You will now be on week four of the program (see the chart on page 170). You should still be working in enclosed areas, but they do not have to be the same ones you were using before. Getting the leash in your favor will now be much more difficult, simply because it is so short. Don't forget: Don't say "stay," issue your warning, including tapping the centering spot. You will have to surmise for yourself how your dog is doing. You will also have to be quick on your feet in order to get up behind the shortened leash, or at least within striking distance of it in order to give corrections. Most dogs at this point will be voluntarily turning toward their owners when they hear their name and the command. After all, this *is* week four of the RRRR. Many recalls have been practiced, both formal and free-lance style. The dog has begun, through the RRRR and practicing recalls, to regard you as a somebody worth coming to.

If the dog is crafty enough to sense that you cannot control it as easily on the six-foot leash as on the twenty-foot leash, and returns to its old ways, go back to week one of practicing seven formal recalls a day. Don't be disappointed if this happens. Perhaps you goldbricked in practicing recalls earlier, or perhaps your dog just needs more time. Perhaps the RRRR wasn't followed to the letter. Check and double-check.

But, if you *have* been successful with six-foot-leash free-lance recalls, you know what tactic comes next. You've got it—put your dog on a short *tab* leash and practice free-lance recalls as described above. Again, don't forget your advance warning! At this point the tab is simply for safety's sake and to enable you to give some sort of correction if the dog does not return to you. You will have to go and get your dog because there will be no leash to use for correction. If you must do this, the dog should be given a firm shake. Place the dog on a stay and snap on the twenty-foot leash, which you've brought along just for this occasion. Make the dog do seven formal recalls. You'd be wise to return to week number three at this point and practice free-lance recalls for one more week using a twenty-foot leash. On the other hand, if everything goes smoothly, and your dog returns to you on command, tab leash gaily flapping in the wind, go on to the finals.

Reaping Recall Rewards

When five weeks of the six-week moratorium have been completed, you're ready for the big league. Unless it is illegal to do so, take your completely leashless and tabless dog to a large, unenclosed area that is as free of distractions as possible. Sit your dog, give your advance warning and release your dog. Say a prayer, rub your lucky charm and call your dog. Remember, stoop and smile! Get those arms open wide to receive your friend. Praise heartily as your dog bounds in toward you. Positive body language! Positive tone of voice! Positive eye contact!

But if by chance your dog does not come at this juncture, you must have a battle plan. Memorize these steps in advance of releasing your leashless, tabless dog in an unenclosed area. You will have to have each step firmly in mind in case the dog does not come:

- If you've genuflected once and you have called your dog and it has not responded, rise and wait for another moment of eye contact from your dog. Sink to the ground again *just as the dog looks at you* and simultaneously call the dog. Your command and your genuflection should be timed as exactly as possible with the first moment the dog looks at you. Don't stoop down before the dog makes eye contact with you because this may make you look submissive, and don't genuflect too late because the dog will have looked away already. Hit the moment just right. There is a powerful, orienting effect on the dog that hearkens back to previous training.

- If your dog still does not come, try genuflecting again. But, if your dog *still* doesn't come after the second attempt, you have a decision to make. If you think you can get your dog, *go and get it.* You might have to chase the dog down, corner it or have an assistant trap it. Once you get the dog, deliver the shake correction, the swat correction, shove it into a sit, repeat the warning phrase, snap on a six-foot leash (or use your arm for a leash) and put the dog through seven formal recalls. Do not drop the leash and do not praise. The reason for this strict discipline is that your dog has just goofed royally. After all the practicing you've both done, after weeks on the Radical Regimen, the dog has committed a major gaffe. Go back to week two and resume practice on the twenty-foot lead.

- Let's say that the dog has not come after two attempts at the recall. But you also realize that you cannot possibly get to the dog to discipline it. Perhaps the area is too large. Or perhaps the dog is too fast and you are too slow. Whatever the case, you have another decision to make. It's possible to get the dog to *follow* you. Wait for a third moment of eye contact. Instead of stooping down and calling the dog, swivel around dramatically and begin to walk *away* slowly. Hunch your shoulders humbly toward the ground, hang your head and look depressed. You will be anyway. If the dog follows you, calculate your chances of grabbing it. Perhaps you can get it to follow you into an enclosed area. Perhaps it follows closely enough that you can lunge and grab it. If you think you have a chance, make the attempt. Once you've got your recalcitrant, shove the dog into a sit, give the shake and swat and practice seven formal recalls on the spot. Go back to practicing on a twenty-foot leash. Don't worry about justifying discipline for a dog who *followed* you. It's perfectly allowable because the dog *didn't* come to you. It followed you. There is a difference, and the dog knows it. After all, the way you have been teaching the recall, both on a formal and a free-lance level, for so many weeks dictated that the dog present itself in *front* of you and make eye contact, *not* follow behind you.

- Let's say the situation is really bad. After two attempts at the recall your dog will not come to you. You have also determined that you cannot trap or capture it. Attempts at tricking the dog into following you have failed. Well, my friend, you just have to get your dog however you have to get it. Enlist the help of friends, open your car or your house door, use a butterfly net—whatever you have to do, but under no circumstances should such a dog be trusted again. Go *all the way back* to week one of this program, reinstitute the RRRR and begin again.

So, that's it, my answer to the ongoing query in the heart of every dog, "To come or not to come?" If some of the numerical prescriptions suggested in this chapter, such as one week for this, two weeks for that, sound arbitrary, trust me. Over the years I've fiddled with this program and fine-tuned it. I sincerely want you to have a dog that comes when called. I want you to live with the peace and security you deserve. I also want your dog to be able to enjoy its life fully. For most dogs, unless it is legally proscribed, that enjoyment includes rip-roaring times gallivanting about in open fields, on the beach or in the woods. I know the absolute thrill I get watching my Dalmatian, Sport, chase down waves on the beach or wildly chasing his tennis ball in a city playground. These are the times when he really gets to be himself, and he is a real fun-loving character. But I also have the security, and so does he, that when I open my arms and say his name, he faithfully returns. Through training, he has answered *for himself* the question "To come or not to come?" and his answer is *yes!*

Running Away Remedy Chart

	Moratorium on any off-leash freedom?	Formal and/or free-lance recalls?	How many recalls?	Where?
Week one	Yes, strict	Formal	Seven each day	In enclosed environment, using 20-foot leash.
Week two	Yes, strict	Formal	Seven each day	In enclosed area, using 6-foot leash. Vary locations.
Week three	Yes, except for practice	Formal *and* free-lance	Seven of each type, each day	Same enclosed areas, using 20-foot leash.
Week four	Yes, except for practice	Formal *and* free-lance	Seven of each type, each day	*New* enclosed areas, using 6-foot leash.
Week five	Yes, except for practice	Formal *and* free-lance	Seven of each type, each day	Same enclosed areas as in week four; *tab* leash on the dog.
Week six	No, unless necessary to backtrack because of goofs	Free-lance	Seven each day	Unenclosed but safe area (unless illegal), leashless, tabless dog.

End Program

Live Life Securely
with a Dog That Comes Reliably

19

Nutrition Notes

I HAVE already written extensively about nutrition in my other books—some say too extensively. I am deeply concerned about how nutrition affects behavior. Dr. Paul Pemberton, an Australian veterinarian, did a study in which he showed that in order for a dog to be successfully trained a nutritious diet is a must. It must be high in usable protein and in use at least three to four weeks *before* the onset of training, thus enabling the dog's brain to work in all its complexity. When you examine the chapter on set-ups it should be readily apparent that it is important for the dog to be able to think out the content of the set-up. The nutritional status of the dog influences its ability to decode what you are trying to teach it.

To briefly summarize what I have previously written about nutrition: I believe that canned foods should be used in moderation and semimoist foods not used at all. Nonfixed-formula dry foods should be carefully evaluated because it might not be possible for the dog to eat enough of the food to get the promised amount of protein, and protein works the brain. Obviously I prefer the so-called speciality foods. These are dry foods that are made in small amounts and usually have a 3:2 ratio of protein to fat. As an example, a food that is 30 percent protein should contain 20 percent fat. In my opinion this 3:2 rule is a benchmark for a quality specialty food. The correlation between the two percentages is important because there must be easily digestible fat, and enough fat to supply energy to *use* the protein with just enough fat left over for a nice shiny coat. Yet there must not be so much fat left over that it becomes the source of other problems such as large stools, obesity, an overly greasy coat or, worse yet, medical problems such as a fatty liver. Use a specialty food with good quality control and a terrific track record. This means selecting a specialty food that has been in production for at least seven years. Because the dog food industry is changing faster than ever before, it is impossible to indicate specific brands, but if you use the 3:2 protein to fat guideline and do a little research at your local pet supply or food outlet (which may involve calling some of the 800 numbers listed on the backs of different bags), you should be able to zero in on the best food for your dog.

Let's talk about nutrition as it pertains to particular behavior problems. My comments here might help to illuminate the decisive role proper nutrition can play in behavior modification. Remember, you can concoct a sterling set-up, but if your nutrition is a no-no the results will be no-go!

Housetraining

If owners of new puppies or older dogs who have "fallen off the wagon" simply remembered that what goes in has to come out, the housetraining process would be greatly simplified. Canned foods in particular present major problems. These foods are 50 to 78 percent water, and added to the water that a growing puppy already drinks, it's harder for the puppy to "hold." Canned foods also contain ingredients like iron oxide and dyes that are not digestible and irritate the lining of the intestine, making mistakes more likely. Again, use canned foods only as a flavoring for a quality dry ration. Hold the line at one, two or three *teaspoons* added to the dry ration. No more!

Specialty foods usually contain a fibrous substance such as beet pulp, bran, corn cobs or even peanut husks that help the growing puppy or older off-the-wagon dog to maintain control. This gives the possible house soiler more time to alert the owner or simply make it to the desired spot for elimination. No one knows how much time is gained when a dog eats a food with a felicitious fiber substance, but my experience has been that even if only one minute is gained, it's worth feeding that food. Yet it never ceases to amaze me how many otherwise educated owners will be in the thick of the housetraining task and yet feed their charges foods with no fiber, and worse, foods with ingredients that will actually trigger on-the-spot elimination. You wouldn't try to toilet train your kid on prunes, so why try to housetrain your dog on junk food?

I also have a big beef with breeders who intelligently recommend specialty foods but then send their clients home with elaborate instructions to add supplements like B and C vitamins, coat conditioners or dairy products. All of these additions can cause diarrhea. The addition of these substances to the diet should be held off until the housetraining process is over. I stress again that what goes in has to come out, and it is often the *owner's* choice, not the dog's, as to whether what comes out is deposited decently or destructively.

Aggression

The favorite food of all aggressive dogs is whatever you're eating. Grouches are adept at conning their owners and others into surrendering their food or giving excessive treats. Point nine of the RRRR says cut off all treats for the problem dog. Don't take this advice lightly. *No treats.* Also remember not to feed your doggie dictator any people food—even if you are adding it to its normal ration as flavoring. The dog knows that it was once yours—after all the dog smelled it when you prepared it for yourself—and it's important that the Alpha does not share food with a subordinate, at least not a problem subordinate.

Because set-ups for aggressive dogs often demand split-second timing and fully engage the dog's mind, it is important that the dog's nutritional life be sound. The hypothalamus, the gland that to a degree controls behavior, must be calm and regulated. In my experience the higher quality foods are beneficial in this respect, as long as the dog is properly exercised. I also feel that *two* daily feedings keep aggressive dogs calmer. Try feeding one meal in the early morning and one in the afternoon so that food is kept in the dog's stomach during its waking hours and the hypothalamus kept happier.

It's possible that a trainer will recommend the use of food treats to facilitate a set-up that will help your aggressive dog. As long as the previously stated food rules of the RRRR are adhered to, and as long as the treat is used only *within* the set-up, give the ploy a chance. Sometimes food works as a training tactic for aggressive dogs. However, some aggressive dogs can no longer be manipulated with food, even if they know how to manipulate to *get* food. If food fails, clearly it needs to be removed from the set-up. Trust your trainer, but you owe it to him or her to state in advance whether you have abused food in your relationship with your dog by feeding the dog from the table or bribing the dog with treats, or if the dog has a history of stealing food or displaying aggression when eating food.

A quick tip to breeders: Computer analysis of my client records reveals a direct correlation between large litter size and later problems with aggressive displays toward owners while the dog is eating food. Perhaps this problem has early roots stemming from too few available feeding plans during early weaning. The pups soon learn to jostle each other around the food pan, the dominant pups getting the lion's share of food. These pups later turn out to be food grouches and food guarders. Breeders can help by providing one pan for every four puppies, thus eliminating fanatical food fights—and later problems for owners. However, if you do own a food grouch, don't hesitate to devise a set-up to correct the problem unless you can simply use creative avoidance to circumvent it. Sometimes it's simply not worth the effort to correct feistiness over food, especially if the problem is isolated, infrequent, easily avoided and doesn't connect up with other displays of aggression. A good trainer can usually decode whether or not it's essential to correct an aggressive dog over food or simply leave the dog alone when it eats.

Jumping Up

A dog with a jumping up problem often receives double messages from its owner when the owner allows the dog to jump for a treat but forbids the dog to jump otherwise. If you have a jumper you must realize that you can't have it both ways. The dog must be taught to sit and stay for *all* treats. In fact, if the dog is a serious jumper you should put it on the RRRR program, which will forbid the dog any treats for one month anyway. After the jumping subsides and you are "allowed" to reoffer treats, try to curve your hand above and over the dog when offering the treat. If the treat is held too closely to your body the dog will be more tempted to jump up on you than if your hand is extended and curved downward.

Be sure that children do not tease the jumping dog with food. Kids sometimes enjoy running around, enticing the dog to grab food from their hands. This can result in serious accidents and calls for parental supervision. If this type of teasing and play isn't curtailed the dog could become a spring jumper—and I don't mean the season, but rather a dog that springs into the air so quickly that most lay owners will simply not be able to correct the dog fast enough. Remember, jumping up is not simply a search for love and attention, but also a form of dominance.

Destructive Chewing

There is considerable anecdotal information from trainers and behaviorists that poor-quality foods containing high levels of red or yellow dyes are connected with the development of destructive chewing. Semimoist foods seem to be the main culprits, but it might not just be the dyes and preservatives that produce canine "beavers." It could very well be that these foods do not have any natural crunchiness that allows the dog to alleviate some of the natural desire to chew hard objects. Again, a diet of specialty foods would be in order.

Don't make the tragic mistake of rewarding your dog for not chewing by offering food treats, especially if the reward is given after the fact. The dog simply won't get the connection. Destructive chewers can also be helped by feeding them two or even three meals a day. Keep that hypothalamus happy!

Not Coming

Obviously, never offer your dog a treat as a bribe to get it to come to you. This sound advice has been in training for decades, but a recent spate of food-oriented training books advises that it's OK to break this once cardinal prohibition in training. The theory is, of course, that the food treat can be used early on as an inducement to get the dog to come and later can be phased out. This is nice on paper but overlooks the fact that in daily life food is often abused by the owner (with the best of intentions) and the acquisition of it becomes a major obsession for even younger dogs.

Just as housetraining difficulties are, in my opinion, the biggest closet secret amongst dog people, bribing dogs with food to get them to come when called probably ranks as the second most prevalent "dirty little secret." Very few owners—especially professional dog handlers—are proud of the fact, or will even admit (except under experienced cross-examination), that the only way they can get their dog to come is via food bribery. Of course this *isn't* anything to be proud of, but rather something to be concerned about, because often a dog who won't come ends up as a dead dog. What I am saying is that food bribery is much more widespread than is generally acknowledged and many owners feel trapped and terrified. After all, they have to get the dog *somehow.* Yet they are ashamed that they have to use food to do it.

If you are stuck with this problem, follow the directions in the chapter "To Come or Not to Come" carefully. Photocopy the training chart and put it on your refrigerator door so that you'll be sure to follow the program exactly. Turn to the RRRR and apply that program immediately. If you follow both training regimens at the same time, you can stop food bribery as of today, because your dog simply will not be away from you to cause you to cheapen yourself by proffering a treat, and the RRRR forbids all treats anyway. Presto: You've won round one!

You can see from these nutrition notes that intentional or unintentional misuse of food aids and abets many major behavioral problems. There are probably deep psychological reasons why humans enjoy offering dogs food so much. It is a deep-seated human need to be liked and loved. Many of us are taught in childhood that the way to a dog's heart is through its stomach. I disagree. The true way to a dog's heart is via friendship and leadership.

20

In the Trenches: Inside Information for Individuals "in Dogs"

VETERINARIANS, groomers, boarding kennel operators, obedience class instructors and, of course, trainers are on the front lines in the battle against problem dogs. A look at the articles in trade and professional journals or even a cursory glance at speaker lineups at professional conferences readily confirms this "in the trenches" mentality. Veterinarians sometimes risk limb and even life dealing with upset, aggressive patients—not to mention upset, aggressive human clients. Every groomer has a particular dog whose arrival at the shop is a dreaded event and sometimes a day-long ordeal. Boarding kennel operators sometimes feel more like wardens of maximum security prisons or supervisors in mental institutions for the criminally insane—depending on the particular batch of dogs occupying the kennel at a particular moment. Obedience class instructors may never know who in the lineup of students will strike.

Professional trainers have it worse. I've given my fellow trainers a separate chapter. They are employed to change the dog's behavior and thus place themselves in the direct line of fire for assaults. Years ago, I applied for disability insurance. After a review of my application the company told me that my rate would be the highest. I was in "group four." Other occupations represented in group four are fire fighters, high-rise construction workers, theatrical stunt performers and lion tamers. I rest my case.

Seminars for groomers now routinely feature speakers on canine behavior—usually behavior that involves attempts at biting (usually a groomer). I often teach canine behavior at various veterinary conferences. The draw for my talks at the Michigan Veterinary Conference, for instance, was over 700 veterinarians and technicians. At the Ohio State conference, over 1,000 practitioners flooded the conference hall. Simultaneous surgical and clinical presentations drew far fewer attendees. Obviously, behavior has come of age and is receiving the attention it has always deserved. But the explanation might be much simpler—professionals are tired of being bitten! I don't blame them.

Aggression is by far the biggest problem for those "in dogs." But first things first. The perspective of the given professional is also important. Of the groups mentioned, only trainers have the specific task of training dogs and counseling owners. Naturally, veterinarians, groomers and boarding kennel operators are often asked for advice, but their attitude toward giving it should include the realization that they are not necessarily qualified to dispense it. All too often these professionals overstep the boundaries of their chosen fields in a sincere attempt to help clients who have a canine behavior problem. But true training and correct counseling involve interviewing skills, the ability to catalog information and intricate instructional skills that assure that clients fully *understand* what is being taught. It's next to impossible to employ these procedures correctly over an exam table in a clinic setting, over a grooming table with an unruly dog or at a boarding kennel when perhaps all the dog wants is to get *out* of the kennel, into the car and home. Also—and this is very important—clients in such settings are usually not *paying* for the proffered advice, and thus do not necessarily fully appreciate it.

Just as I do not groom dogs, board them or perform clinical or surgical procedures on them, other professionals should not assume to train them. Besides the fact that the quality of the advice can be shoddy, the well-meaning professional puts an unnecessary pressure on himself or herself. Inevitably this lessens the quality of their primary service. It's hard enough to be in dogs in any capacity and not get bitten, pummeled, goosed, dragged, barked at, wet or otherwise assaulted *yourself*—so why complicate matters by playing trainer unless you are one?

The advice included here, then, is intended to help professionals in given fields protect *themselves* and their employees. It is intended to help them run their clinics or businesses in a smooth fashion. The chapter for trainers is also geared in this fashion, but since trainers also need information on how to advise clients, I have added some "people tips" and I would suggest they also read *The Evans Guide for Counseling Dog Owners.*

Veterinarians: Viciousness and Vexations

Veterinarians do not want to become disabled veterans. They should take time to consider the concept of *territoriality* in dogs. A lack of appreciation for how territoriality operates in the canine mind is the root cause for many unpleasant incidents in clinic settings. Dominant or aggressive dogs often claim territory as they go. It's a moving concept of territory that includes protection of the dog itself, the owner and as much as a six- to ten-foot area around the dog and owner. So when a dog barges into your waiting room, dragging its owner behind, that dog has already claimed your clinic. Smell trouble? Your sense of smell is excellent.

There's not much you can do to prevent this with a first-time client, but if the practice continues, the receptionist or the veterinarian can inform the client that barging makes the dog feel that it is boss. Frequently, it's better if the aggressive or extremely unruly dog is removed from the waiting room, and its owner, and placed in a holding pen in the rear of the clinic. A diplomatic way of approaching this separation is to say, "One of the jobs your dog thinks it has is to protect you. If you are not around, there will be nobody to protect, and it might be easier for us to give the dog proper care." Naturally, what *isn't* being mentioned is that a dog that feels it has to protect its owner in a veterinary waiting room, where there is no threat to life or limb, probably has a pretty mixed-up, leaderless relationship with said owner—but then again, we're not being employed to train the dog that's in this situation, just treat it.

It's far better for the practitioner to be in the exam room *before* the aggressive dog enters. While this is the opposite of usual procedure, it makes eminent sense, given the territoriality of most dogs. Naturally, if it's the first time you've ever seen a given patient, you will have no way of setting this up in advance. But if the patient is a known troublemaker, try to arrange to be in the exam room so that the aggressive dog perceives *you* as having claimed it already. The alternative is to stuff the unruly dog and ineffective owner into the exam room (often to maintain peace in the waiting area) and then let them "comfort" each other. The owner then lets the dog "get used" to the room by sniffing (claiming) everything in it, and soothes the dog with faulty paralanguage and body language—cooing to and fondling the dog. By the time the poor veterinarian enters the room the dog feels perfectly at home and ready to go into action. It is on guard: "This exam room is *mine!*" Reversing the usual procedure throws the dog off guard—it's entered *your* turf.

Some troublesome dogs are better treated on the floor, but it's touch and go and has to be evaluated on the spot, for other dogs are disoriented by being elevated onto an exam table and thus more manageable. With the advent of mechanically operated tables that rise to the desired height with a minimum of motion or noise, some happy compromises can be made.

My advice to veterinarians if they even slightly suspect that a patient will become aggressive is to muzzle the dog. While, in general, muzzling *increases* tension in dogs and encourages resistance, the fact is you have procedures to perform, treatment to give and time limits. The medical exam must be completed. If a trainer muzzles a dog, it is simply a stopgap measure, but for a veterinarian to do so is simply sane and right. Remember, in every single case in which a veterinarian has brought suit against an owner for being bitten, the veterinarian has lost. Bites are considered occupational hazards and litigation is a lost cause. Self-protection, advance planning and psyching out each client and patient behaviorally are the only safeguards available.

Remember also, it is quite feasible that trusted clients can sue *you* if *they* are bitten by their own dog—if they can prove that the veterinarian placed them in a situation that insured that a bite would take place. Malpractice suits of this nature are on the rise. I know we live in a litigious society, but some instances are truly sick, tasteless cheap shots at well-meaning vets. It seems incredible, but owners of known aggressive dogs have actually collected hard cash because they were bit while the veterinarian tried to help their untrained, unruly pets. The cases I've studied show that there is almost always a history of aggression by the dog and a corresponding lack of leadership and neglect of obedience training by the owner. This again points up the necessity—and possibly money-saving value—of veterinarians clearly advising such owners to secure training early on. The suggestion should be backed up by giving the client the actual phone numbers of prospective trainers, and this should then be noted on the patient's chart. If training is not pursued, and the dog later acts up during an exam and bites the owner, the veterinarian will have an excellent line of defense since he or she *did* suggest training.

I usually advise veterinarians to schedule known agitators for the early morning hours, when the waiting room is less crowded, the clinic quieter and the practitioner's patience highest. Also, there is absolutely nothing wrong with refusing to treat an aggressive dog unless it is properly restrained. "Properly restrained" might mean that you will have to *insist* that the owner leave the dog's presence so that his or her negative thought waves, body language and paralanguage aren't affecting the patient. A technician (or two or three!) can then be called in to restrain the dog. A metal ring screwed securely into the wall can be handy because the dog's leash can be passed through it and the dog pulled toward the wall. The dog's head will now be tethered and the remaining task is to simply block in the rear end. A tech can work the rear end and another can keep the leash taut so that the dog cannot wheel around and retaliate. It's sad when veterinarians and technicians have to engage in such tactics. After all, they studied animal medicine, not rodeo routines. The absent owner should be informed, not of every difficult detail that was involved in securing the dog for treatment, but certainly that treatment was a torture and training is strongly indicated.

If you are presented with an older, grouchy patient, trying to sell training can be difficult—especially if the owner is content with the dog as it is or too lazy to seek out help. With young puppies, the best course is prevention. Ask, "What are you planning to do about training?" during the very first examination. Be sure to button your lip and let the client answer. Don't just say, "Are

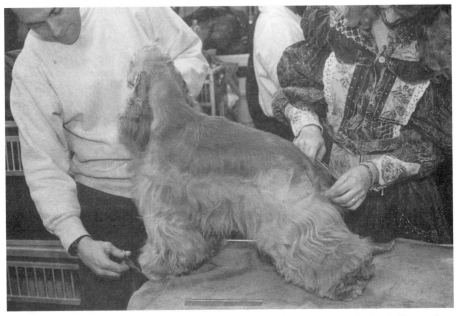

Frontal control by one person often enables a veterinarian or groomer to "work the rear" more effectively. The dog cannot whirl around as easily. *Kevin Smith*

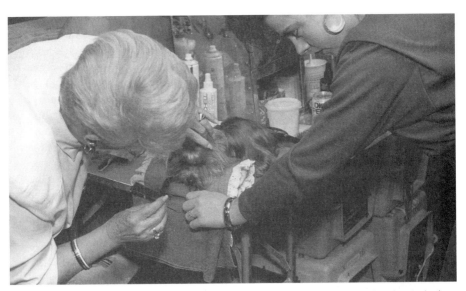

Groomers are "in the trenches" with a great motivation: They just want the dog to look beautiful! *Kevin Smith*

you going to train this dog?" because the answer will, of course, be "yes." What the client means is that the dog will be trained to sit for a treat at home: end of "training." The former wording places the client on the spot and indicates that there is something to be *done, they* have to do it and you know they *should.* Remember, clients view the veterinarian with deep respect. Since you are probably the first contact who speaks with authority concerning the dog, you owe it to your clients to indicate early training. The long-term benefit will be a patient that, hopefully, lives for many years. Note: Trained, unstressed dogs live longer than stressed-out dogs. Trained dogs are a joy to have at the clinic—in the waiting room or on the table. Moreover, such an early suggestion clearly shows the client that you are concerned with the *whole* dog, body and mind. The AVMA has targeted behavior as an area that needs more attention from rank-and-file practitioners. Bravo for your heeding the call.

Doom and Groom: Trouble on the Table

I've met many groomers who are closet trainers—but not many trainers who are closet groomers. In short, groomers are often behaviorally oriented but behaviorally uneducated—a situation that can be remedied—while most trainers would rather pick up a dinner tab than a grooming brush. More communication is desperately needed between the two groups.

Groomers are in the trenches like no one else, because sometimes they have to battle to confer beauty on a beast! Groomers sometimes overstep the boundaries of good sense by refusing to restrain or muzzle an unruly canine customer, and instead tranquilizing or harshly disciplining a dog. If you want to take the risk, that's regrettable, but most groomers agree that more flies are caught by honey than vinegar. Groomers, you can throw all my previous admonitions about not using food aside. While I do not suggest the use of food for standard training, we need to remember that in this case, the dog is the customer, not a student. Your job is to make the dog look beautiful, and if food helps, use food.

The traditional grooming table is really quite nicely designed from a behavioral standpoint, so use it. The metal bar allows the groomer to "string up" a dog so that the head is held high—and biting attempts thwarted. Just be sure to watch the dog's rear end, as, even if properly tensioned in the overhang bar, many smaller dogs can easily rotate, sending themselves into a panic. Often an assistant can be at table side, with hands palm down on the table edge, not restraining the dog but ready to if necessary. Some dogs allow grooming if they feel they are being *watched* but are *not* restrained. Read over the chapter on aggression in this book and watch for the classic hardness of the eyes. This is when a well-timed "No!" can be of great value—minus any physical discipline. Some aggressive dogs do better if left to sit and stew in a crate or holding pen while observing other dogs being groomed.

Naturally, grooming the head and shoulders presents the biggest problem when dealing with "the ungroomables." In extreme cases, it's not unacceptable to let the owner do the grooming under your direction. The tool can be passed to you without much fanfare and you can add a few strokes before completing the job. The next session, perhaps one side of the face can be done by the owner and the other by yourself. Advise owners of known or potential menaces to feed only one-half the normal ration if you plan to use food as bribery for cooperation. Remember, aggressive dogs do not like sudden movements. Try to have all clippers, scissors and other implements laid out in advance so that opening drawers, slamming cupboard doors and any delays can be avoided.

There are some groomers who have enough experience to incorporate elements of training, via a set-up, into the grooming procedure—if only in order to complete the task at hand. Follow the steps for a set-up listed earlier. A typical set-up would include warning the potential grouch *as you pick up the first tool,* retreating immediately if there is a snap or other retaliation (a growl should suffice) and *quickly* yanking the tether that is attached to the overhang bar. Repeat the process if necessary, but try food first, set-ups second. You do not have to have a love affair or leadership role with this little (or huge) monster. You just have to get the dog groomed nicely and out of your life—at least until the next appointment.

Quiet soothes and often mystifies aggressive or bouncy dogs. Grooming shops are, unfortunately, sometimes the rivals of rock concerts for decibel output. Especially if you run a drop-off-and-pick-up service, a shop full of screamers can be an everyday fact of life. If there is a quiet nook you can escape to, even if it means going into a backyard, do so. Dominant dogs tend to like noise and confusion, as the humans then become distracted and exhibit erratic body language that is easily decoded as a threat. Sometimes a simple walk around the block or building on leash will display the dominance needed to change some hellions into demure devils. While most trainers would not trade places with most groomers, many groomers would make excellent trainers. If you find yourself training more than grooming, consider a career change—we trainers need all the soldiers on the front lines we can get!

Boarding Kennel Operators: The Keepers and the Kept

The biggest problem boarding kennel operators face besides aggressive clients is, of course, aggressive dogs. I used to run the boarding/training kennel at New Skete Monastery. The monks had developed a reputation for being able to rehabilitate aggressive dogs. Unfortunately, because of our cloistered status we were unable to go directly into the lion's lair so to speak—the domicile of the aggressive dog. Instead, owners simply deposited such dogs with us and after a careful interview would fly off to Rome or Tahiti while we were left with a kennel full of dogs resembling the ones in Stephen King's *Cujo.*

Just realizing the fact that the kennel will often be populated by problem dogs somehow helps the boarding kennel operator deal with the issue. There is always a chance that a given boarder will be aggressive. Perhaps even as

Boarding kennel proprietors should not underestimate the value of a well-timed "No!"—especially to squelch fence-fighting. *Judy Emmert/Dealing with Dogs/TV Ontario*

many as one out of ten dogs will exhibit aggression while in your care, so some coaching is in order. Aggressive dogs do not endure stress well. They are often neurotically dependent on their owners and do not want to transfer their love or loyalty to anyone else—and certainly not to you, bozo! Trouble is, if you run a boarding kennel, you are *ipso facto*—at least to a degree—asking dogs to be dependent on you. The aggressive dog doesn't want this transfer to take place and will marshall all its forces to prevent you from taking over. The scene is set for problems early on in the dog/owner interactions, before the dog even reaches your doorstep.

Owners have often been cooing to, coddling and generally placating the hell out of their aggressive dogs for days, even weeks, before the dog gets to you. If you have contact with the owner before the dog arrives, especially when the owner is actually preparing to leave on a trip, tell the owner to hide all signs of imminent leave-taking from the dog. Suitcases should be packed on the sly, housecleaning done normally and even the discussion of the upcoming boarding avoided. After all, an owner chitchatting on the phone in a nervous, worried way, constantly interjecting the dog's name, is being listened to by the dog—which does know its name and recognizes the worried tonalities. The boarding, instead, should be sprung on the dominant dog with little preparatory fanfare. On many levels, aggressive dogs don't like sudden surprises, but this ploy is a "structured" surprise that will have payback potential. The dog will simply not have time to rev itself up into a frenzy about the upcoming separation.

When owner and dog arrive at the kennel, it's best—although not always possible—to separate the two on neutral territory. A good place is halfway between the owner's car and your entrance way. Second best is to separate the two within the kennel. Unfortunately, since aggressive dogs claim territory as they move, the dog may already have claimed your kennel. If the dog had claimed the parking lot it's not as bad—after all it won't be camping out there. If you take some time to explain what it is you'd like to do, most owners will be willing to accommodate you. Whichever site is chosen, have the owner hand the leash to you. Do not reach toward the owner or dog and simply take over—this could result in a bite. Remember, the aggressive dog is set on defending three things: itself, its owner and the territory it has just claimed.

Preregistration phone interviewing is very desirable in preventing incidents with aggressive dogs in a boarding kennel situation. Watch out for code sayings like "Just leave him alone and he'll be fine," or "She just gets a little uptight sometimes and gets grouchy," or "Whatever you do, don't corner him." These statements are all dead giveaways that you have a problem pooch coming in. A code system can be developed listing dogs that are to be suspected of acting up on arrival.

Remember, you cannot afford to get bitten. You make your living with your hands, and if the aggressive dog gets in one good zap, your authority is lessened. Plan out in advance just how you are going to whisk "little Hitler" back into the kennel. Be sure to have passageway doors propped open in advance because dominant dogs often take advantage of passageways and act up—and act out—in them. There is a way of taking the dog from the owner and having it ensconced in its kennel so smoothly that the dog literally doesn't know what has taken place. This beats trying to "make friends" with the dog while the owner coos to it, unintentionally informing the dog that you are the warden of this "lockup" and not a friend at all.

Once the dog is placed (or plopped) in its kennel, simply leave the grouch alone. Don't try to make friends or warm up to the dog. On the other hand, if the dog is growling at you, issue a stern "No!" and then quickly look away aloofly. Some dogs will stop growling, others will continue, but you will have employed a bitch basic that registers with the dog. Even seasoned boarding kennel operators sometimes underestimate the power of a well-timed "No!" accompanied with a withering stare and the aloof look away. In my kennel, I often stopped fence-fighters using this method and sometimes a squirt bottle. Aggressive dogs love to fence-fight, and often need to be placed on the end of the line so that they have only one partner, preferably a submissive dog who does not care to fence-fight or will simply ignore the dog. Turn to your older, more experienced boarders for this invaluable service.

There are some boarding kennels that simply do not accept aggressive dogs. After all, in most cases, you are not being employed to untrain the aggression anyway. There are also some boarding kennels that find that aggressive dogs do better if handled by female employees. Women seem to telegraph less ego than many macho men. While I've mentioned the value of a well-timed verbal reprimand, sheer force usually will not make the dog accept its fate with equanimity. Try to assign female employees to care for such dogs, as long as direct physical contact with the dog can be avoided. If not, be certain they possess the necessary skills.

When interviewing owners of dogs being admitted to the monastery boarding/training kennel, I was often informed that a given aggressive dog "hated men." The owners often volunteered this information innocently, then suddenly realized that a monastery is an all-male community. While often I felt like replying, "Thanks for nothing," I kept my monastic cool and usually replied that monks are gentler than most men—and in general, monks are. Knowing that aggressive boarders often calm down when cared for by a woman, I would be sure to give that particular dog a good look at myself in full monastic habit. That usually smoothed the psycho's psyche. I'm sure the dog thought I was an exceptionally ugly woman in a black dress!

21

The Trials of Trainers

IF VETERINARIANS, groomers and boarding kennel operators are in the trenches in the war with problem pooches, trainers are truly on the front lines—minus any protective trench. While medically treating, grooming or boarding a difficult dog can be potentially dangerous, only trainers are charged with the task of changing the behavior of the dog. As if this isn't enough, trainers also deal with the dog's owners in a counseling setting. The trials of trainers include burnout, sexism and tolerating repetition—and it's these dilemmas, and others, I'd like to address. Trainers, prick up your ears, this is for you from me.

Tolerating Repetition

How can a trainer manage the monotony of repetition? How does one learn to tolerate it? I learned a lot about repetition during my years at New Skete Monastery where we sang Matins, Vespers and other services day in, day out, 365 days a year, with small changes in the service except for perhaps a feast day song. After eleven years of that, I might be crazy or I might be able to offer you some tips on tolerating repetition. Because I don't want to face the first prosect, however true it may be, I'll opt for the second and offer some help.

1. Facing down the fact that repetition is, well, repetitious is the first step in tolerating it. Of course you are going to be called in for countless housetraining consultations, and of course it will be boring

to dish out the same advice each time. On the other hand, even though housetraining consultations will be among the most boring and repetitious you will face, your client desperately needs the information, otherwise he or she will sour on the dog and get rid of it because it is "dirty." The way I get through such consultations is to remind myself that if I fail to be informative, lively, caring and complete, the dog's death will possibly be on my hands. Drastic? Not really. Try it, it works.

2. Some advice books on repetition will counsel you to focus your attention elsewhere in the room or off the subject of repetition. This is absolutely bogus, false and potentially hurtful advice for private trainers. *Never* do this. No matter what the effort, keep you attention fixed on the client and dog—especially if it is an aggressive dog. Trying to divert yourself to spare yourself boredom is a losing game and you will be mauled in the process.

3. Instead, try to rearrange your material, perhaps explaining eye contact last instead of first, even if it seems more natural to open a consultation stressing its importance. There are some clients who simply want the cold info on crating, confinement, schedules, foods, etc., rather than a lot of philosophical verbiage. Feel free, when repetition is unrewarding, to depart from your standard, rehearsed speech. You'll give yourself the break you need, but be sure to provide all pertinent information within the consultation, if only rearranged.

4. I have another trick for you from my monastery days. Since we followed the Eastern rite, the services were rich, ornate, mystical, inspiring and *long.* Indeed, the Russian Orthodox have a standing joke that all churchgoers develop legs of steel since standing is the preferred position during worship. No matter how much you love a particular religious rite—or your dog training and counseling sessions—the fact that the sessions are lengthy can be bothersome, especially if material is old hat. I used to tell myself during a particularly arduous service, "This service can only go forward, it cannot go backward." It was my way of reassuring myself that time does, indeed, pass, despite the timeless quality of some services. It can be your way of enduring a session during which a client prattles on endlessly about the dog's faults or virtues, or surviving an interview where careful interviewing and note taking is essential. Repeat it like a mantra to yourself: "This session can only go forward, it can't go backward." Know what? You'll probably free yourself from feeling trapped by time and have a better session for it.

5. On the other hand, some private trainers cook their own gooses by simply trying to give too much during a session. An initial session, in my opinion, should not last more than two hours, even if the dog has severe problems. After a while, clients simply feel overwhelmed

with information, even if you leave everything in writing, and even if you are a laid-back, low-key counselor. I'm quite the opposite, I'm told, and I have learned to trim my goods to the necessary essentials so that I don't leave clients with their head spinning. Other trainers feel that the more they give, give, give, the more they talk, the more information they impart, the more they are doing quality work. Not necessarily so. Much depends on your delivery style, the educational level of the client and how much you can endure repeating yourself for such a long time. "Trimming your goods" by having a fellow trainer sit in on your sessions and offer frank evaluations of what to cut and what to add can be invaluable in helping you tolerate repetition.

6. Finally, it may seem odd to include a section on repetition as a "trial" trainers endure, but I've identified it as one of the major causes of burnout among private trainers. More on burnout follows. The sooner a private trainer develops techniques against repetition before being bored by it, the better. And who knows, tomorrow you may get a new, *exciting* student for training—like a Rottweiler that waits until you are settled for twenty minutes and *then* attacks your buttocks as you rise, rather that than three Maltese who defecate behind couches—all of course owned by separate persons, and all three consultations, of course, on the same day. You'll be thankful for the Rottie problem—*if* you avoid that butt bite.

Trainer Burnout

Burnout has been getting a lot of press over the last few years, and its sister, rustout, isn't far behind. Burnout, even in the dictionary, means, simply, *exhaustion;* rustout means you're nearing burnout. If you've experienced burnout, or are nearing rustout or burnout as a trainer, this section is for you.

First, let's face reality. Learning for dogs and for people is stressful. If you've ever studied for an exam, the probability was that you were under pressure and had a strained, uptight and tension-filled expression on your face. Learning isn't easy, and teaching is *worse!* So just take it as a given that training pooches and people is going to involve looking at stressed, depressed and even ugly canine and human faces. I mention this because it is the virtual sea of sad-sack faces that gets to a good many trainers and seminar givers. "They all look just, I don't know how to say it, so *out* of it," one trainer told me about her classes. Well, it's the teacher's responsibility to infuse the class with so much energy that the participants no longer look so out of it—but in doing so the teacher can readily burnout.

It takes a lot out of a person to consistently go into a class setting, see private clients, welcome newcomers to a veterinary practice or work at an animal shelter and *not* burnout within one to five years. If this person also tries to juggle a show or obedience career, the chances of burnout are much higher, since by virtue of the way trials and shows are set up they produce only a fraction of winners and a plethora of losers.

In reality, losing or winning doesn't really stop burnout. It is a syndrome that affects winners and losers, and in fact, consistent losing may be a blessing in disguise, motivating you to make decisions to curtail activities that *would* have led to burnout. Burnout victims often don't realize one important rule: You can't do it all.

Upon entering the dog game, many newcomers will attempt to conquer every aspect of the fancy—showing in obedience and confirmation on the weekends (often with the ubiquitous RV complete with appropriate decals), training all week (maybe running classes), plus volunteering at the local Humane Society (very laudable) and perhaps penning a column for the local newspaper or club newsletter. In between all this they fit in a KPT class, the fly-ball team and hosting the club's monthly meeting every so often.

Then there is the phone. Very few dog people learn to curtail their phone chatter, ringside verbiage being the only other vocalistics they have an even harder time refraining from. Phone consultations can quickly lead to burnout. The facts are: Phone consultations take an extraordinary amount of time as the caller feels he or she has your OK to prattle on forever; phone calls effectively prohibit you from doing anything else; finally, they *don't work* if you attempt to give advice via them, which of course adds to your feelings of ineffectiveness (a classic sign of burnout). You simply can't help someone over the phone with a dog problem because you must usually see the owner and dog interact. Simply saying, "I'm so sorry, but I can't see you and your dog together, so I'm sure you'll understand why I can't be of any help to you over the phone," seems to be a near impossible statement for many trainers to croak out.

Of course, preventative medicine is the best response to the problem of burnout. Making a decision early on to limit your time on the phone when it comes to doggie matters, carefully charting your activities and involving yourself in only the activities you can realistically handle are, of course, the best ways to avoid burnout.

But for most of us, burnout will be there before rational thought is. Here are some signs of burnout for the dog trainer and some remedies:

- *You have to teach a class or see a client, but you just don't care about it.* A classic sign of burnout is not caring about anything—yet, you do . . . of course you do. If you absolutely *can't* get out of teaching or seeing that client (and preferably take a vacation—more on that in a second), just focus on the dogs. Pick out a comical canine face and play to it—perhaps use that dog as a demo dog. *Fake it,* for that night, and then reevaluate your priorities.
- *You are confronted with a complex behavior problem (like aggression or destructive chewing) and your mind goes blank, even though you*

know what you need to say. Burnout frustrates giving complex information in a logical sequence—even if you know your materials and remedies! Don't be frustrated with yourself. Your inability to think straight about a situation you are perhaps well versed on is symptomatic of exhaustion and a signal for rest. Give the client the best outline you can—often writing it out will help your mind to focus—and personalize it for the client. Now, heed the warning. The very next day, cancel all unnecessary appointments and rest. Do not take phone calls. If you don't have an answering machine, get one (preferably *not* voice activated, but with a prescribed message time limit). Don't worry, you're *not* losing your mind, and you don't have to bone up on what to do for house soiling problems—you're just bone tired. You're burned-out.

- *You come home from class (or a private client or from the shelter or veterinary office) and you break down and cry. Or perhaps you cry while on the job—and you can't figure out any reason.* You're really burned-out—unless the crying is the result of some other kind of stress. Assuming everything is A-OK at home and otherwise, the crying could be a reaction to stress. Wash your face (always a good temporary remedy) and go back to work—for that day. After work, talk to your boss (if it's yourself, sit yourself down and have a talk with yourself) and explain that you are overworked or at least overextended. You most probably will not get fired. You will most probably get a few days off (or give yourself a few days off if you're the boss). But that's not enough.

- *After a few days off you feel just as strung out, tensed up, preyed upon and awful as you did before you had the respite.* Get a newspaper or job placement tabloid and look for the nearest seminar or expert on stress and/or time management. You need to learn how to handle stress and organize your time and to set priorities. The fact that the brief vacation didn't help clearly signals that more work must be done if you are to escape burnout.

- *You got bitten in class or while seeing a private client.* Chances are, your timing was off, unless you simply are not skilled in handling such dogs. Were you overtired? Preoccupied? Overextended? In an extraordinarily perceptive and honest piece in the February 1986 *Off-Lead* magazine, veteran trainer Roy Hunter recounted a time when he had suffered from jet lag and "started a brand-new training class at 9:30 A.M." the next morning. He wound up getting zapped by a small dog that spun itself around enough to also injure itself. His observations are to be well noted. *Never* work with an aggressive dog when you are tired or out-of-sorts, and have the wisdom and humility of Mr. Hunter to admit that such was the case—and give yourself a rest.

- *Try to get into the habit of taking short three-to-four-day vacations several times a year instead of one long two-or-three-week vacation.* (Of course if you can get that length of time, too, go for it!) I've found that people who work with dogs often do better under this system. Short vacations spaced periodically will give you something to look forward to, and be sure that they are at least three days long (one or two days are too short). If you are self-employed (many trainers are) these should be easy enough to arrange; in fact, they might be more desirable than closing down completely for two or three weeks.

Above all, don't laugh at burnout or make light of it in any way—many do, thinking, "it won't hit me." It *can* hit you, very easily, and a healthy respect for burnout and related syndromes can help you prevent it in the first place. Protect yourself from burnout and you'll also be protecting the dogs you train as well as their owners.

Sexism in Dog Training

Didn't that subhead grab you? I thought it would. But the fact is, dog trainers confront sexism on the job constantly and discuss it among themselves frequently. Yet I've never seen a mention of it in print. It's time to remedy the situation.

Women suffer the most from sexism. Almost every female trainer has a story about how some butch male resented her handling his dog, or assured her in advance that she would never be able to handle anything larger than a Pekingese. One trainer in New York City told this story:

> I walked into the house, and the husband was lying on the couch watching a football game. The dog, a German Shepherd Dog, was running around the dining room with a kitchen towel in his mouth, shaking it frantically. The wife was in hot pursuit, trying to retrieve her dish towel, do the dishes, answer the phone, which was ringing, and let me in all at the same time. As soon as the husband noticed me, he lifted his head ever so slightly and said in a low drawl, "Oh, you're the trainer? I was expecting a man. You'll never be able to do anything with *him.*" Indicating, of course, that this lowly female would never be able to rehabilitate such a male maniac.

Some men will seem subtly proud of their male dog's naughtiness, and "agree" to training for the sake of the wife's sanity. The truth is, they have no idea of how to control the dog and most of their attempts to do so have met with outright rebellion. Now, here is this *woman* who is going to shape things up. It's everything some men can do to hide their interior humiliation.

How do you handle such binds? First, don't be insulted. Sexism is endemic in our society. There are still double standards, especially in dog training, even though so many famous trainers have been women. Respond by educating. To "You'll never be able to do anything with *him,*" respond by laughing and saying, "Well, have *you?* Maybe we can try together." Push through the implications and elevate the situation to a new level—and begin training.

Sometimes it's impossible to involve a husband in training. This has frequently happened to me, even though I agitate to have the whole family present at all sessions and particularly at the opening session. In one recent situation I was called in to solve a housetraining problem coupled with destructive chewing. I sat down at the kitchen table with the wife, and the husband was (you guessed it) watching a football game on TV, beer in hand. I asked Mrs. Travolinni (not her real name) if Mr. Travolinni would join us, and she replied, "Good God, no—don't bother him, he's mad enough at the dog as it is." Mr. Travolinni did get up, though, to come over to the table to coach us. "Now, you listen to him carefully, honey," he said, "and get to the bottom of this messing in the house." He then returned to his post at the television. Housetraining and picking up after the destructive dog were strictly women's work.

I had sized up the situation and decided to use it to my own advantage. We set up a program for housetraining that night and agreed to start active training the next session, beginning with the heel. Mr. Travolinni again stopped by the table when I arrived, after grabbing a beer from the fridge, and was headed back to you-know-where. I stopped him though when I said, "Mr. Travolinni, today we are going to start some of the more *active* phases of training, starting with the heeling, phases of training when more *control* must be exerted. . . ." For the key words "active" and "control" I cast a quick glance at Mrs. Travolinni, who looked down at the table smiling. She knew exactly what I was doing, and she didn't care: She wanted to get the dog trainer and her husband involved. Mr. Travolinni appeared suddenly concerned, and in a low voice asked me, "Well, do you need help? I mean, do you think she can handle it?" I replied that I'm sure that *both* of them would make fine handlers, and we went out for the session together. Then, as Mr. Travolinni worked on the heel (he was terrible, by the way), I gave him all the information on housetraining and destructive chewing I had given his wife earlier. He never missed another session, although I had to plan our appointments around the NFL games.

The classic situation where sexism rears its head is when the dog trainer suggests neutering a male dog. Spaying a female is rarely a mental problem for men or women, but the specter of castrating a male is reason for a crisis. The reaction on the part of some men is so visceral that I've had men immediately cross their legs when I introduce the idea. I've been told by female trainers that the reaction is even worse when they suggest the surgery. I plow right through this reaction without even noting it. I do not have time to deal with the emotional issues right away, although I do back up and talk about them later.

My first priority is education about neutering. I explain what the studies (especially the one conducted by Dr. Benjamin Hart, University of California at Davis) have shown about neutering as a tool in behavior therapy, and explain that male dogs secrete testosterone in *two* locations (testicles and adrenal glands) and that only one production zone is being removed. While this is not clinically kosher, because the greater amount of the hormone *is* produced in the testicles, it is one way of taking the sting out of my suggestion. I also explain other health benefits resulting from the operation, such as the elimination of prostate cancer. I explain all this slowly, absolutely calmly, even though I know my client's head is spinning with emotional distress. Then I back up and ask my client's feeling on the matter. Their emotionality then hits the solid wall of education I've laid down. Every trainer has had difficulty with this one. As public education increases, the problem will lessen, and it will be easier to suggest neutering and talk about it calmly.

Some sexism exists within the professional training community itself, although I am not aware of any inordinate degree. In general, men and women participate in obedience competition on an equal basis, and collaboration between male and female trainers is good. In fact, compared with other dog-related fields—veterinary medicine for example—training is remarkably free of discrimination and sexism. A man will just as readily pick up a book by Wynn Strickland Carlson to gain knowledge and information as a woman will use a book written by William Campbell. We don't look at whether the author or seminar or clinic lecturer is a man or a woman—we look to see how they train dogs. The many husband-and-wife trainer teams present in the dog-training field are also an inspiration to us all and wonderful examples of cooperation and mutual respect.

When it comes to sexism, a trainer's major problems and hurdles remain the attitudes of clients, which are, in turn, a product of the society at large. While these attitudes can sometimes hinder us in our work, and occasionally make it impossible to work with some clients, they are responses that people in other helping fields have to deal with also, and handled with humor and tact, can be overcome.

Rhythm, Timing and Training

Most trainers develop a sense of timing quickly, but few develop perfect or near-perfect timing. What's timing? To most trainers it is the ability to move with the dog and to deliver praise or correction (usually via the leash, but not always) at just the right moment—and the right moment from the *dog's* point of view, not the trainer's. This usually involves speeding up bodily movements and tightening up hand, forearm and leg coordination so that praise or correction registers with the dog in split seconds. Most trainers are too slow at the start of their careers. They do not realize how quickly they can work a dog, and how much vocal animation is needed. But occasionally—rarely, but occasionally—a trainer will be *too* quick for the dog, and will need to learn timing by slowing down. When a trainer has good timing, he or she is in tune with the dog and there is a seemingly effortless flow of energy and communication between them.

I have heard "perfect" timing described as everything from "dancing with the dog" to "as wonderful as good sex," and I'd have to agree with both statements. Timing cannot be *learned* from a book or an article—the importance of timing can only be *pointed out* in print. The budding trainer needs to be directed to other sources to learn more about it. The number one source for learning timing is a trainer who has it. The only way you will learn whether she or he has it is to observe her or him in action with dogs. Some trainers have wonderful timing on static exercises (like sit-stay) and horrendous timing on active exercises (like the heel). This search for learning will involve seminar and clinic attendance and general snooping around. Even then, don't make the foolish mistake of asking the trainer with perfect timing to "impart" his or her secret to you. Timing comes from within, and the trainer, no matter how dearly he or she may like to share it with you (and remember many do *not* want to share it with you), simply cannot "give" it to you. All you can do is watch, listen, *try* to move your body like the trainer does. One hint: When you see a trainer with perfect timing, or at least timing you admire, *stop looking at the dog.* Look only at the *trainer* for at least twenty minutes, imagining yourself as the dog. Watch the trainer's hands, watch his or her eyes, study the way the trainer holds the torso (very important). Watch the whole body of the trainer, the neck, the way the head is held. Don't just watch the extremities—many beginning trainers get hung up on what to do with their hands, and they forget that the hand is connected to a forearm, which in turn is connected to an arm, a shoulder, etc. All of these are communicating something to the dog. Remember: Watch the trainer's *eyes!*

Remember, too, that the concept of timing has also to do with other essential questions: What *time* of the day is it? What is the *timing* of the dog's meals? What *time* in the dog's life span is it? And on and on. Consider the overall *concept* of time when perfecting your timing.

Where does timing come from? Even though I've clearly indicated that timing can be learned, acquired, perfect or near-perfect timing, in my opinion, flows out of an innate sense of rhythm, specifically, *musical* rhythm. Take a man like the late Jack Godsil. I had the benefit of an extended, one-on-one personal clinic with him. Here was a man who was essentially a ballet artist who trained dogs. This man was grace in action, as on his toes in his given craft as Baryshnikov is in his. He was an accomplished guitarist—and it's no surprise. He was able to time his training moves because of an innate sense of rhythm, coupled with a good frame (it always helps to look imposing) and a certain quiet charm and poise that dogs, well, just *felt.*

This gift of rhythm is the underpinning of many trainers' sense of timing. Don't be fooled—the timing was developed, worked hard for, by observation, study, trial and error. But to some degree the sense of timing flowed out of rhythm, which is a gift, an inborn drive, a desire to be at one with a "beat."

Can you develop what may be a dormant sense of rhythm that may lead to better timing and better training? Sure! Why not take a swing at it? I've known of trainers who play march music while they train, timing automatic sits during heeling patterns to an oompah-pah beat. I know one trainer who trains to a waltz, "The Blue Danube" or other 3/4 rhythm pieces. Then I know of some trainers who play disco, although the steady, pounding 4/4, 120-beats-per-minute drive of most disco songs may make it hard to train most breeds, I know of Dobermans trained to disco. Disco Dobes, in other words.

All kidding aside—do what you can to free yourself to hear life's beat, usually heard most clearly in music, and to develop whatever rhythmic abilities you have. Out of that will flow timing, and out of that, happy, well-trained dogs. And what does rhythm *itself* flow out of? Well, the philosophers have a lot to say on that. Some say that musical rhythm developed not just out of humankind's urge to entertain itself, but out of a longing for a hookup with a more universal rhythm that first shaped our world. Scientists would call this a "life force" and religious people would call it "God's rhythm." Is it any surprise that the evolutionary theory widely accepted now is called the "big bang"?—a pretty rhythmic phrase if you ask me! As a trainer, you are in touch with life's rhythm, expressed in and through yourself and in and through another living being—the dog. It is a great opportunity, something that might be thought of as granted only to artists, but available to all of us who work with dogs, for trainers are artists also.

Competition or Craziness?

One problem I deal with constantly in seminars, on the phone and in working sessions is the complaint about the "ring-wise" dog. The seemingly malicious dog that runs out of the obedience ring during the recall or the off-lead heeling process, but always performs well at home. In fact, if you are to believe the stories, the dog in question always performs *perfectly* at home. Just as lay dog owners have tons and tons of folklore and mythology they hold dear concerning their pets, so do professional obedience persons. And one of those myths we want to hold on to is this nonsense about the ring-wise dog. You see, such thinking makes mistakes very understandable: We can project the blame onto the dog. But who is really to blame?

Paralanguage is the original tongue of your dog—the sublanguage it learned while still in the litter. The puppy's mother growled at it to assert her Alpha role, but littermates whined at it—and this whining was a signal of distress, loneliness or separation from the mother. The mother *never* whined at her puppies—only littermates whine at each other. In this book we've talked about the placating owner who tries to cajole his or her dog into good behavior by using a whining tone of voice. This placating behavior often becomes a general life stance toward the dog, keeping the dog in an infantile state and in a type of low-grade distress, since the owner is read, by the dog, as a littermate talking about littermate concerns. Remember, littermates don't perform for each other—they just play with each other. Obedience competition is not play. It is work. It can be fun, but it is not play.

But the dog owned by a placating owner can quite possibly perceive the whole obedience ritual as pure play, especially if the owner alternates the play with some Alpha leader-type behavior in the form of corrections. "You'd better play—or else." This effectively screws up signals enough so that the dog plays until no corrections can be given. Further, often the placating owner will do an about-face on the dog on the way to the trial. These owners turn on their dogs on the way to the trial site and begin to blame or scold the dog in an effort to get the dog ready to perform perfectly in the ring. All this does is make the dog wary of the ring. The dog is bewildered at this sudden sense of "command" and presence from an owner viewed, essentially, as a bimbo and a wimp who loves to play. "Why the sudden switch?" the dog wonders.

Conversely, owners who *blame* their dogs as a way of relating to them (see description of the blamer in chapter 7) will often pull an about-face on their dogs and try to *placate* their dogs into good behavior (performance) just before they enter the ring. ("Pleeeeeze Tippy, pleeeeze do the off-lead heeling, okaaaaay. Pleeeeze.") These owners do *not,* by any stretch of the imagination, talk with their dogs this way the other 364 days of the year. Why blame the dogs for being totally bewildered, strung-out, absolutely spaced-out because of *our* faulty paralanguage, *our* abrupt about-faces? Again, the problem lies within the relationship itself, the faulty relationship between dog and owner, and the tension the owner brings into the ring.

It is standard practice for obedience competitors to refrain from feeding their dogs prior to a trial. I disagree. Be sure to feed your dog something before a trial. Remember, there is a center in your dog's brain called the hypothalamus. It controls behavior, to a degree. If you feed your dog normally other days of the year and then cut off food on the one day you want *top* performance, thus "hyperventilating" the hypothalamus, it's small wonder that your dog is edgy when entering the ring. The rationale for *not* feeding is that if the dog eliminates in the ring, the team will be excused and disqualified. If you're concerned about this, try feeding just one-half the dog's normal ration before a show. But *do* feed.

Obedience competitors can visualize success in much the same way Olympic athletes do. Right before you go into the ring, calm yourself and close your eyes. Envision the ring ritual and recall successful practice sessions. Reach down and massage the centering spot on your dog's forehead with your thumb. Breathe. Breathe deeply. Now, go out there and knock 'em dead!

Two other problems affect clear thinking on the ring-wise syndrome. First, some owners think the real problem lies in the area of technique, and secondly, some owners think their dogs are simply too intelligent and are bored with AKC obedience work. Again, we have more human-centered, anthropomorphic thinking. Technique certainly *is* important, but some seminar givers would have their participants think that if they would just hold the little finger of the left (or right) hand one millimeter lower (or higher) during off-lead heeling, then the dog would not run out of the ring (or wander, or go lick the steward, or go to a spectator with a hot dog, or whatever it is the ring-wise dog does). The distraught owner is thus offered a cure by technique that effectively lets him or her off the hook in terms of examining underlying problems. When I bring up the subject of relational problems, owners of ring-wise dogs often tell me that this is *not* what they want to hear. What they want to hear is that they were holding the third finger of their left hand slightly off where it should have been (depending on whose information they are following) and *that's* the real reason Tippy didn't complete the recall. That's easier to stomach. A mechanical problem is often easier to solve than a relational one.

The my-dog-is-too-intelligent-for-this-stuff school of thought is a kissing cousin to the above syndrome. A recent piece in *Off-Lead* magazine details the escapades of yet another ring-wise dog that thwarts her owner at every turn because she is a German Shepherd Dog and thus too intelligent for AKC ritual. At one point the owner reports having turned on the dog after a particularly poor performance and said, "I hope you're satisfied!" One wonders what kind of paralanguage roller coaster this Shepherd rides before and after each show, and just how very deeply it must affect her.

Professional obedience people get a good deal of laughter out of this ring-wise business. If the problem stayed on the level of laughter, I'd have no complaints. Of course there is always a bad day for almost any dog, even if the paralanguage is completely kosher, even if the owner has good technique and wonderful timing. But the laughter most often blames the dog, ascribing to the dog that failed spiteful motives that are purely human projections and consequently a great source of confusion for the dog. That's the really sad part—the blaming and the subsequent stress for the blamed dog. And all because we'd rather spend time figuring out why our dogs are ring-wise than why they are wise to us.

What to Do When You Walk In

What do you do when you enter the household of an ineffective owner with an unruly, bratty dog? It never ceases to amaze me how crazy and off-the-wall the dogs (and some of the owners) are during that first session. There is a variety of often-used approaches. If any of these sound familiar, you are not alone.

- Trying to calm the dog down by petting it
- Ignoring the problem dog and going on with your work
- Screaming over the pronounced barking and/or defending yourself from physical maulings, pummelings, goosings, shovings and other forms of canine abuse

I've tried them all, too. They don't work. The fact is, most private trainers need to take a behavior case history during that first session, and to try to do so with a canine terrorist trying to hijack the session can be torture. By the way, if you are not in the habit of taking a complete behavior history and you call yourself a private trainer, you are probably undertraining and undercounseling. For forms, guidance and process see the classic *Behavior*

Problems in Dogs by William E. Campbell (American Veterinary Publications, 1975), or my own *The Evans Guide for Counseling Dog Owners*.

In my book I state that it is preferable if the dog is *not* present at the first session, as owners tend to lie less about their pooch when it is not physically present. Further, the absence of the unruly dog helps facilitate the interview process. However, I wrote that portion of the book when I was fresh out of New Skete Monastery, where I had an office for interviewing clients and a convenient kennel in which to stuff their crazed canines. If you have no such facility, and if you work in your clients' homes, you will not have this option.

In fact, this was exactly the situation I confronted when I started my business in New York. I would arrive at a household and immediately the dog would begin to molest me. There was a temptation to immediately correct the dog for jumping up, nipping or whatever canine crime it was committing, but I've always refrained from administering a correction until I have had an opportunity to explain my theory and interview the owner. Some private trainers *do* correct dogs right away, and I can only say that while the dogs' owners might be impressed with the efficacy of a jumping-up correction, they will *not* mentally catalog it (since they are stunned and in awe of your ability) and they most definitely will not like you for "manhandling" their dog so immediately. "Ego" trainers who want to "get the dog in line" quickly might disagree, but we should never forget that our work is 80 percent people work and only 20 percent dog work. Correcting a dog too quickly and too harshly will not endear you to your client, and if your client does not *like* you, you might as well pack up your training collars and leashes and go home.

Since I suffer from an inferiority complex, I have always been concerned with getting people to like me first and teaching them later. I have seen brusque, even brutish trainers enter a household or open a class by walloping an unruly dog with such force that the owners, to a man and to a woman, simply cringe. Believe me, that trainer has cashed in his or her chips when it comes to the trust of the clients. Of course, lay clients are in awe of us, so they don't say anything, but you will have hurt them deeply if you correct their dogs too soon.

What to do then? I can only offer my own procedure, developed over six years and three thousand clients in Manhattan. In each and every case, I was in the home of the dog's owner.

Here is my procedure:

1. Greet the owner *first,* even if the dog is crazed. Make direct eye contact with both unless the dog is aggressive. Smile, smile, smile— yes, that means smile even if the dog has slammed itself into a part of your anatomy that is especially sensitive. Male private trainers are now nodding their heads in sympathy at this statement. *Do not* correct the dog.

2. Ask if there is a *table* where you can sit and talk. Some owners will instinctively guide you to the living room. This will not work. You need a table in order to do your case history. You also need a table because you need a higher chair in order to sit on a leash to get a certain spoiled monster to lie down, pronto.

3. You have to get the dog quieted down fast in order to do your interview. If you hold the leash, you will give the dog enough slack so that the dog will fool around. Many dogs only see a leash when it is time to go outside and will immediately go into high gear when it is produced. This is especially true of city dogs. Just get the leash on and then sit on it. Yes, sit on it.

4. Measure out only as much lead as the dog needs in order to lie down, no more. You can estimate by simply pushing the dog down once to see how much leash is necessary. Do not say "down"—there is no sense in giving a command to an untrained dog until it has begun to learn the word, and believe me, if the dog you have tethered really knew "down," you wouldn't be there.

5. The dog will start to test its options. If it jumps up on you, snap the leash down smartly, saying "no." By now you should be into your interview, which should distract the owner, who is sitting opposite you. Yes, you *can* interview and snap a leash at the same time, and if you can't, get out of private training fast, as most of the work of a private trainer involves doing more than one thing at a time. If the dog chews on the leash, snap the leash diagonally up toward your body. When the dog pulls against the dead weight of your body it will become quickly apparent that the object (your body) is immovable, and, like most of us do when straining to move an impossibly heavy object, the dog will give up trying.

6. With this method, and as long as the private trainer cancels all unacceptable options such as jumping up, chewing on the leash, crying, whining or yodeling, most dogs calm down and hit the dust within ten to twenty minutes, many sooner. Some real recalcitrants and hyper types will remain standing or sitting, but at least they will not bother you. They will often simply stare at you in disbelief. This is an excellent moment to make some piercing, mean, frozen-eyed eye contact and then look away with aloofness and continue your interview. In fact, this is the exact look a bitch would have given a puppy that was bothering her while she tried to do something other than pay attention to the pup. If the dog does hit the dust quickly, *do not praise.* No command was given, no command was fulfilled, thus no praise is warranted. The dog simply figured out the options (basically, none) and deduced that it was smarter, more convenient, safer and certainly more restful to lie down while you do one heck of a job taking one heck of a complete behavior case history—the taking of which will enable you to become the Sherlock Holmes the owner hired you to

be and quickly solve the canine crime presented. At least with this method you can do so with style and grace. Try it—it works!

What to Do When You Walk Out

It's one thing for a trainer to know what to do or not do when walking *into* a client's house, but what do you do if you have to walk *out?* Sooner or later every trainer meets a difficult client who blames everybody but himself or herself for the dog's problems—including the dog's trainer. These clients are usually blamers. It sounds perverse but there are people who will call in a trainer, pay hard cash and yet deliberately thwart the trainer in his or her efforts to help. Such souls are really very insecure and lonely people beneath the haughty and superior facade they present to the world.

When I need to terminate a client—a given individual I sincerely feel that I do not want to work with—I indicate this *immediately.* I listen to the first strong gut feeling that registers inside myself, because without client cooperation and trust there is little or nothing I can do to help the dog. In my early years of training I ignored such gut feelings hoping that the difficult client would become less manipulative and more cooperative in time. Unfortunately, this rarely happens. My advice to trainers is to listen to that inner voice. If it tells you that a relationship with a client won't work, terminate that client. Do this immediately, as soon as you get the feeling.

How? Simply look your client directly in the eye and say, "I'm sorry but this session isn't going well. I'm afraid I'm not the trainer for you." That's it! You needn't say anything else. Simply wait for a reaction and if the client seems to be in agreement, immediately collect your training materials and exit. However, many clients will express surprise and even shock, especially if they are quite aware that they have been behaving obnoxiously. If, and I mean *if,* you sense the client is sincere, you might mention that client cooperation is essential if the dog is to be helped. Pause again and wait for another response. If the client becomes apologetic or repentant, you can then make the decision whether to continue.

Most of all, don't take such situations personally. Difficult clients are usually difficult with everyone, and you're no exception. Of course you will feel sorry for the dog, but perhaps the client will behave more civilly with another trainer. However, *do not* refer such clients to fellow trainers. Let these clients find other trainers on their own. If you do decide to continue the relationship and are a trainer with some experience, please remember that you probably have worked with problem clients in the past—and successfully. There is a tendency to forget this fact. Every time a troublemaker comes into a trainer's life it feels like the *first* time. Of course it isn't. As long as the air is cleared immediately and proper boundaries set up, most difficult clients will respond to consistent, firm friendliness.

In my twenty years of training I've had to terminate only fifteen clients out of over seven thousand. One particularly nasty woman, the owner of a

Maltese bitch with the habit of redecorating her Fifth Avenue apartment with the results of Nature's calls, drove me so batty that I called my own father to ask him to search his library of psychological books and journals and send me anything he had on difficult people. He informed me that he would have to photocopy half his library. Instead, I flew home to Michigan and did research with my psychologist pop for one week. I felt better after that, but I still had to leave the *lady*—and her poor Maltese.

22

A Panoply of Problems

S TAGING STERLING SET-UPS should be sufficient in
your attempts to rid your pooch of problems. Sometimes, however, a set-up
can be enhanced by using other methods specifically related to the problem at
hand. I'll detail these "extras" in this chapter and I hope these added steps will
insure eradication of problems. We'll round out the chapter with questions
concerning a variety of canine conundrums.

Jumping Up

You now know how to concoct a set-up to put the jinx on jumping up.
All you have to do is trick your dog into doing it and administer the three-part
correction: Whip the tab or leash down *forcefully* and say *"no,"* pull up on
the tab or leash and say *"sit,"* flash the stay signal in your dog's face and say
"stay." Naturally it helps if you have been teaching your dog the sit-stay. So
if you have a jumper, go immediately to the section on the sit-stay and begin
teaching these words.

Now that you know what to do to stop the jumping up it's important
that we take a moment to examine what you absolutely should *not* do when
a dog is jumping. First of all, under no circumstances should you hold the dog
up by its front paws with your hands since this will be taken as approval of
the action. One ineffective correction for jumping that has been dished out for
years is to firmly grasp the dog's paws in your hands and squeeze them tight
or pinch between the dog's toes. By the time owners of jumpers get their hands
positioned correctly and learn to squeeze the paws hard enough, the dog has
interpreted the fact that the owner is supporting it as approval for its action.

Another mistake owners make is to simply turn away as the dog is jumping. At the same time the person being jumped on usually whines "no" or "stop it." Two things are wrong here. First of all, the body language is incorrect. Turning away looks like exposure of the flank to a dog. Did you ever watch two dogs playing in a field? The submissive dog will roll over and expose its belly or flank, saying, "you win." The submissive dog will also whine or whimper at the same time—precisely what people unintentionally do when jumped on. The faulty body language and paralanguage then says to the dog—at least in the way the dog interprets what it sees and hears—"Please jump on me again," which, of course, the dog does. So don't turn away and don't appear to whine. Get that tab or leash—or, if all the dog has on is a collar, get that—and whip it down hard, saying, "No!" Some owners of chronic jumpers might have to literally scrape the dog off of themselves so forcefully, in a firm downward yank, that they may feel that they have lost control and hurt the dog. If you're such an owner, don't worry—you're probably showing just as much force as the situation really merits. Remember, if the dog is jumping on someone else who does not know, or will not execute the correction, the same correction is still administered—by you.

Another classic goof that owners of jumpers make is to say the wrong words for a correction. I once purchased a classic sweat shirt at an obedience trial. The front of the shirt is covered with muddy dog paws, and the words "Down, boy, down" are emblazoned on it. "Down" is not the correct correction word here since the word "down" means, or should mean, that the dog is to recline on the floor. "Off," "no" or even "scoobie-doobie-do" would be more appropriate—anything but "down." Professional obedience people, the saleswoman told me, readily got the joke behind the sweat shirt—few lay persons did.

One last point: There is a tendency when administering jump corrections to concentrate on the person the dog is jumping on. This is a normal reaction because, of course, one is terribly embarrassed that one's dog is accosting another person. The trouble is, concentrating on the person being jumped on will distract you from yanking the leash down firmly and delivering a correction concisely. This is when a set-up can be of great help—because during a set-up, since it is preplanned, and hopefully because the jumped-on person is preenlisted, you need not pay special attention to your assistant and act apologetically. Instead, you can deliver a sharp correction with sufficient speed to startle your dog. Remember, your dog, if it is a confirmed jumper, has already become used to your delayed reaction as you apologize, explain, snivel out excuses and even offer to mend destroyed or soiled clothing—even as your dog clenches onto the offended person. So concentrate on correcting your dog *immediately* rather than paying attention to the person, place or thing it scales. A good technique—especially if your dog seemingly spring jumps onto people—is to simply watch your dog's two front paws. If both paws are off the ground, that's the beginning of a jump. If you concentrate on the two front paws, and on nothing else, you will be able to jinx most jumping.

Destructive Chewing

You can stage set-ups until the cows come home to cure your dog of destructive chewing, but if you don't examine the problem holistically, the set-ups might not take. Be especially careful about how you say hello and good-bye to your chewer. Overemotional hellos and good-byes keep the dog on edge. If you make a big production out of leaving, the dog will be ready to tumble into an emotional black hole by the time the door clicks shut in its face. It will chew to alleviate owner-induced frustration. On the other hand, if your dog is overanxiously awaiting the sacred moment when you arrive home—because this moment is when it is petted and fussed over the most—the dog may decide to munch down on valuables just before you get home. God forbid that you are held up enroute and Fido's sacred rite is postponed. Don't make a thing over greetings and departures. When you leave, present Rascal with a toy—a special toy. Keep the toy up out of the dog's reach and preferably out of sight. This toy is offered only when you leave the house. When you are actually ready to leave, and not before, sit your dog, make eye contact and in a friendly, but not anxious, voice tell your dog to watch the house, and just as you leave, scent the toy by rubbing it firmly on your palm or, still better, put some of your saliva on it. As you exit, offer this toy. If your dog doesn't grasp it in its mouth, simply drop it nearby. If your dog gets frustrated when you are gone, it may decide to masticate on this toy rather than on forbidden objects. The ploy works with some dogs and has no effect on others—but it's worth a try, and to a degree justifies correcting the dog even after the fact (but remember, you must have some proof to convict the dog) since you did, after all, provide a chewing option in the form of the scented toy.

When you return, greet your dog calmly. A simple hello should suffice. Of course, whether you have been gone twenty minutes or two hours the dog will inveigle you to put more "umph" into your greeting. Don't give in. Keep it simple. If you are returning home after staging a set-up, skip any greeting at all and simply search for proof. If there isn't any, say a simple hello and go on with your life. If there is, follow the instructions in the chapter "Do Dogs Feel Guilt or Shame?"

Besides staging set-ups, it's a good idea to try to make the environment itself look like it is disciplining the dog. You can use substances like Tabasco sauce, bitter apple or cayenne pepper (Vaseline applied to the surface first makes the pepper stick better). Jalapeño peppers are my favorite—but wear gloves when rubbing them on surfaces you do not want chewed. Mousetraps are an old trainer's ploy and can be set and placed on couches, chairs and other surfaces. Obviously, don't put bait in the trap! This is training, not torture. I once had a client who did put bait in the mousetraps she set on the couch—she figured using bait would speed up the training process.

I'd suggest blitzing your dog with set-ups when you can grab a free day. Leave with a proper good-bye and offer the scented toy. Stay away for just fifteen minutes. Return, check for proof and if you find some, discipline. Leave again, this time for a half hour. Return, check for proof and discipline if necessary. Leave again for one hour. Start adding half-hour increments and try to build up to two hours during your first blitz. Each time you leave, offer the scented toy, but each time you return, pick the toy up. The length of the interval between leave-takings should be only about ten to fifteen minutes. The point of the blitz—much like the bombing in England—is to stun the dog into accepting several hellos and good-byes from an Alpha figure. By coming and going so fast and frequently you are telling the dog that you are the leader who comes and goes from the den at will—and it is the subordinate who must hold the fort and behave. Remember, underplay all hellos and good-byes. If the dog "flunks" a section of the blitz, stay home for fifteen minutes and then repeat that part of the blitz again and call it a day. You can always try to build up to a longer time span another day. The blitz is best done on a free day, obviously, and this also accomplishes something else—it tells the dog that even on free days you might have to come and go—and it still cannot, must not, chew your belongings. You see, especially for some "weekend dogs"—dogs that see their owners basically in the evenings or on weekends—the contrast between when the owner is home and when the owner is absent is just too stark and must be minimized. When you are home, the dog feels like it is the center of the universe, and probably is. But when you are gone, the dog feels demoted to nothingness. The solution is to lessen the contrast, and this is done by leave-takings on weekends and during the evening.

You ultimate goal should be an adult dog that can be left to freely roam most of the house and not chew inappropriately. While I have nothing against crating destructive chewers, this goal will never be achieved using a crate—unless the crate is phased out over time. Obviously, young puppies have to be confined and are too young for blitzing. But older chewers, if simply crated, never learn to respect the house. Crate if you must, but when it's blitz time allow the dog house freedom, room by room. For instance, start the first blitz in a relatively chew-proof room like a bathroom or the kitchen, and then add a room each time you stage a blitz—but don't add more than one room at a time and don't add any rooms at all if the blitz bombs. Is there a risk factor in staging blitzes? Of course! It's not "cute" to try this technique and come home to a wrecked room. On the other hand, most dogs quickly become responsible and seem to appreciate freedom to move about more liberally, even if they can't munch at will. If your dog absolutely refuses to cease chewing, and you really feel that you have staged fair, humane, yet forceful set-ups, then you must simply practice creative avoidance for one month. Crate or otherwise confine the chewer for one month, and then grab a free day and blitz away. It goes without saying that such a recalcitrant should be placed on the RRRR program for one month.

Finally, don't feel guilty that you have to leave Rascal alone at times. Someone has to go out and work in order to buy the dog food—and it certainly can't be Rascal, can it? You have a life to live, friends to see and places to go. Besides, you are the Alpha, and even a mother wolf leaves the den to search out food or simply to take care of her own needs. Your dog is your dog, not your Siamese twin—for that matter, not even your identical twin, although it's spooky how many dogs look like their owners!

Housetraining

Getting your puppy or dog to realize that cleanliness is next to godliness can be accomplished by following the ACCESS plan I outlined in my book *The Evans Guide for Housetraining Your Dog*.

A   is for *Alpha*—that's you.

C   is for *Corrections*—that's what you give.

C   is also for *Confinement*—that's what you provide.

E   is for *Establish*.

S   is for a *Schedule* (which is what you establish).

S   is also for *Selecting* a dog food that will aid you in getting your dog housetrained.

You know all about how to be Alpha already, so remember to establish eye contact formally twice a day as previously described. Correct your dog for housetraining mistakes by quietly taking the dog to the proof itself, sitting the dog, focusing his eyes (*not* his nose) on the proof and delivering the shake or swat correction. Remember, no screaming and no overphysicality! If correction after the fact doesn't work don't just keep disciplining! Confine the dog in a crate or a small room and try another housetraining set-up later.

Stick to your schedule of walks and select a food that will help, not hinder, housetraining. Stay away from unlabeled generic foods, dairy products and superoily foods. Remember, what goes in comes out!

I've found that most owners who tolerate unhousetrained dogs either trust the dog too soon and too much, granting the dog more area than it can really handle, or they just cheat on the ACCESS plan and then blame the dog for goofing up. An exception is the dog that is physically ill. If you are having any problem with housetraining, get the dog to a veterinarian! After that, assuming your dog has a clean bill of health, I'd offer you my tips here, my book on the subject and my sympathy! Don't worry though, given time and consistency, most dogs *do* clean up their acts.

Dear Job: Questions—and Some Answers

Here is a potpourri of questions about various pooches and their problems. These are actual questions that I have fielded over the years in seminars and via letters and phone calls—although I hasten to add that I do not make it a habit to reply to unsolicited inquiries via phone or the mail. At seminars the questions were either asked aloud and taped or submitted in writing at the podium. Questions concerning elimination problems (which owners consider a "dirty" topic and thus kept closeted) and questions about shyness (surprise, surprise!) were almost never asked aloud. Knowing owner psychology after twenty years in this field, I understand this reluctance, especially on these two topics. This is precisely why I've always provided seminar participants with the option of submitting written questions. This has paid off for myself as well: I believe I get a truer reading of the problems really bothering owners, much in the same way a priest will eventually hear everything in confession. Anonymity sometimes aids truth.

I deliberately have not arranged these questions in any precise topical order, but rather mixed them up because often problems overlap and owners of problem dogs—always on the lookout for a quick-fix solution—have a tendency to falsely categorize their dog's difficulties. Nor have I changed the wording of the questions as transcribed from the tapes or question cards. Often the wording and phrasing of a question give an insight into the owner's psychology. So plow on through—you'll find problems of interest everywhere.

I have two nine-month-old Sheltie females (littermates). One is submissive and one is dominant. When we pay attention to the submissive one, the dominant one will start attacking her. How do we train the dominant dog not to attack the submissive dog?

First, I am always suspicious when owners decree who is dominant and who is submissive among their pets. My expeirence, more often than not, is that a substantial amount of owner miscalculation fouls up any set-up that might be concocted to stop such fighting. I would urge you to drop such classifications and instead place both dogs on the RRRR as soon as possible. Separate the dogs for one week using crates, confinement or whatever type of creative avoidance measures necessary. After one week on the RRRR the dogs will sense a change in the household atmosphere and you will be ready to stage a set-up. Put tabs on both dogs, deliver your warning with eye contact, discipline if necessary and *do not* separate the dogs if there is an outbreak of fighting. Instead, place them on down-stays if they know this exercise. If they don't know how to hold a long down, get busy teaching it pronto using the techniques in this book. If the dogs don't know the down-stay, simply tether them three or four feet apart in the same room after the fight. Even if you have to stand between them during this time and rediscipline them, *don't separate the dogs.* This is what they want! Since Shelties are a small breed and slight of build, you might be able to handle this set-up on your own. If you have the slightest suspicion that you will need some assistance make certain to procure it before staging the set-up. Good luck in your efforts and let's hope for serene Shelties.

You talk a lot about owner personality types such as the placater and blamer. Can one personality type be "pushed" into another by sheer frustration over a dog problem?

Babies and dogs can be great pals—especially if the dog knows a solid long down and there is proper parental supervision.   *Judy Emmert/Dealing with Dogs/TV Ontario*

Of course, it happens all the time. The most common scenario is for a placater to become a blamer. As the dog's problems get worse and worse, usually because of continued placating and lack of leadership, the owner reaches a point of feeling trapped and begins to blame the dog for anything and everything. The switch doesn't happen overnight but is rather a gradual change, yet it is still extremely confusing for the dog. If you feel you've reached this juncture, don't simply back up into your original placting mode, but instead read over the section on *leveling* with your dog and try to avoid extremes of placating or blaming completely. Actually, your evolution is a plus because usually placaters who become blamers *are* developing some leadership skills and Alpha attitudes, if only by accident.

Could you please discuss how to introduce a newborn baby into the household? We have a one-year-old Golden.

First be certain to have taught your dog the long down. Being able to tell your dog to go to its place and stay will be essential. You wouldn't think that an ex-monk would know a lot about babies, but I am also the oldest boy from a family of eleven children. My mother was never *not* pregnant. I was four feet tall before I ever saw her face. I know that baby care involves rituals that are easily interrupted by a cavorting canine. If your dog doesn't know the long down you will find yourself constantly banishing the dog to the backyard or to a crate—which tells the dog that it doesn't rate anymore and can produce jealousy. By using the long down the dog can be included in household life, not excluded. Before your baby arrives practice long downs in the room that is planned as the nursery. It's a good idea to dry-run diaper a large baby doll, watching Rascal out of the corner of your eye for any breaks in the down-stay. Follow the corrective sequence for long down breaks that you'll find in this book.

The long down can also be used to let the baby socialize with the dog. You can stage set-ups by gently warning your dog to be nice, placing the dog on a long down and then placing the baby next to the dog. You can kneel nearby or even lie down with your child and dog to let them relate. If your dog uses its mouth or paws in too rough a fashion on the baby a slight swat under the chin or on the dog's paw itself should show the dog that gentleness is mandatory. Check with your veterinarian to be certain your dog doesn't harbor any parasites or other contagious diseases that the child can contract, and if your child has been ill, inquire with the pediatrician along the same lines.

How do you select a private trainer if you have a problem dog? How do you determine who is qualified? How do you determine if a person's methods are humane and sensible before hiring him or her?

Since training is an unlicensed field it is quite possible to hire a poor trainer. There have been some attempts to regulate the profession, but as of this writing, no definitve structures have been set up. So buyer beware are the watchwords for anyone looking for a trainer. Here are some hints. First, any decent private trainer will begin by taking a behavior case history—carefully interviewing you about your dog's problems as well as your needs and desires in training. Some class trainers now do this also. Bravo for them! Beware of trainers who skip this step or simply do an oral interview and do not take any notes. Even longtime trainers simply cannot remember what each client and student needs unless they write it down.

For a referral, begin by asking your veterinarian. Veterinarians have a vested interest in affiliating with good trainers because they are queried so often about behavioral matters, yet often do not have the time or skill to provide full answers. No veterinarian will remain associated, however loosely, with a trainer who consistently turns in bad results or if clients complain about the trainer's services. And believe me, the veterinarian will be the first to hear about any poor quality services. Don't worry—if you are the skeptical type— that there is any "arrangement" between the trainer and the veterinarian. Veterinarians are forbidden by the ethical guidelines of the American Veterinary Medical Association from taking any kickbacks for referrals. This is still another safeguard for you.

Do you feel comfortable with the trainer? Some persons prefer to work with a male trainer, some with a female. When you ask questions about the trainer's background—and you should—are answers clear and concise? Has the trainer published? While this is not absolutely necessary, if the trainer has authored a book or has written for training trade journals, there is more of a chance that he or she has been up for peer review and taken the criticisms and compliments publication usually brings.

You might also ask about methods over the phone—without expecting a detailed account of every method the trainer uses. Ask also if the trainer has worked with dogs of your breed, and be especially wary of negative comments concerning any breed. Be careful, too, of the unfortunately ubiquitous sales verb "guarantee." "We guarantee results!" some ads will scream. This is patent nonsense. Your dog is not a robot you are sending into a repair shop to be fine-tuned. It is a thinking, feeling, living being that has a relationship with a leader figure—hopefully you. Since there are three parties involved in the training process, yourself, your trainer and your dog, I fail to see how one party can guarantee the performance of the others. If all three parties cooperate and are willing to learn, change, identify problems and restructure life to alleviate those problems, training most often succeeds.

I have a one-year-old Border Collie. If I hadn't already named him I would have called him Saint because he practically is one. I know you're probably saying, "Oh sure, sure," Mr. Evans, but I really haven't had any sizeable problems with him. I've taken him to obedience school and feel my leadership is "in place" in his mind. I'm wondering about one thing though. I'm heading into a career period when I'll have to be away for longer periods of time. I understand about staging set-ups and your suggestions for blitzing the dog to correct destructive chewing—but is there anything else I can do to circumvent chewing? A kind of "preemptive strike"?

Yes. You can teach your dog avoidance of *verboten* items by leading him to the objects and issuing a *light* reprimand. Begin by placing your Border Collie on lead and making eye contact. Lightly touch his centering spot so that he will know that he should concentrate. Now calmly lead him to forbidden objects and make those objects attractive. For instance, let's say you fear that he might undo the fringe on an Oriental carpet. Take him to the carpet fringe, lift the end of the carpet about a foot in front of his face, wiggle the fringe enticingly and say, "No! Don't touch," or some similar phrase. Be sure to use the same phrase you would use to reprimand the dog for chewing something inappropriate if he did it when you weren't home.

Have handy the special scented toy discussed in the section on destructive chewing—the toy you usually would give your dog only when you are leaving. Right after your gentle reprimand, offer the dog that toy. He might take it or he might ignore it. If he takes it, praise him and let him chew or lick it for a few seconds, then move on to another no-no knickknack. If your dog looks bewildered and doesn't take the acceptable toy, simply lead him on to a few more items and call it a day. If you don't want your dog on the couch when you're gone, lead him over to the couch, sit him, lift one paw up onto the couch and give it a light but firm tap. Be sure to run several such sessions by your dog before you start to leave the household for longer periods of time—but, and this is important—don't center the dog's attention on more than five forbidden items a session, otherwise you'll overload his circuits and confuse him.

You've done so many things properly already—taking your dog to school, establishing yourself as Alpha and getting a preliminary understanding of set-ups—that you hopefully won't have any problem. One last tip: Dogs who engage in destructive chewing almost always lack aerobic, sustained exercise, the kind that truly dissipates excess energy. Especially with this breed, exercise is important, so don't shortchange your dog in this area. Frankly, you sound like the type of owner who never will.

What are your suggestions for staging a set-up for a digging dog? My backyard resembles a nuclear bomb test site.

First, my sympathy. Secondly, this advice: I hope you are being fair with your dog and leaving it in the house as much as possible. People who banish dogs to backyards usually wind up with yards that look like yours. I also hope that you've had your dog in school so that it has some words to live by, such as "down," so that it can be, in fact, a member of the household. When owners complain of this problem, my first thought is always "Why is this dog outside anyway?" Assuming all of the above is kosher, my advice would be to put the dog on the RRRR program for one month and practice creative avoidance for the first two weeks of that one month. In other words, simply do not leave the dog alone to dig. This might involve using a crate or confining the dog inside for two weeks. Once the RRRR kicks in, reestablishing your leadership, and once practicing creative avoidance has bought you and your dog some time and simply broken the daily habit of digging, you can grab a free day and blitz your dog for digging.

Take your dog to the back door and sit the dog. Issue an advance warning touching the centering spot and using eye contact. Release your dog to the backyard and hide out in the house, peering out a window secretively. At the first suggestions of digging—in other words, when the dog's paw starts to scrape dirt—heave a large handful of boulder-type marbles at the dog. Naturally, you'll have these ready to go in a bowl near the back door, which of course you've left slightly ajar for quick opening. BBs work well, too, but often don't deliver a strong enough correction. You should have a tab leash on your dog as well. Charge out toward the dog just as you throw the marbles, get the dog, give a good shake. Sit the dog at the excavation spot—do all of this quickly yet calmly—and take one paw and scrape it on the earth as if the dog is digging. Give the paw a good swat—and quickly lead the dog back to the back door. Reissue your warning, again using the centering spot: "Sport, I *told* you not to *dig!*" Now release the dog again. A nice flourish is to show the dog a handful of marbles just as it is (now dejectedly) marching out to the backyard. Hide again and observe. Repeat the process and extend the blitz by leaving the house for fifteen minutes, returning and checking for excavation, disciplining if necessary and leaving for a half hour, building up to two hours.

Again, your sequence in shorthand would be: Issue advance warning, release dog, hide out, if digging commences heave marbles, *charge!*, grab tab, shake dog, sit dog, scrape paw on ground, swat paw, race back to house, sit dog, reissue warning using *same* warning phrase and emphasizing same phonics, brandish marbles and show them to dog, rerelease dog and repeat all of the above, lengthening the period of time you leave the dog alone.

Finally, if you don't have an enclosed backyard, you'll have to use a leash longer than a tab to get your dog when you charge out—and frankly, if you don't have an enclosed backyard your dog has no business being left alone unattended there anyway. There are some other old ruses that might, I repeat, *might,* work and they are worth listing: You can try filling in the holes, but first bury some of your dog's feces about three inches underneath the top of the soil. Mousetraps set near the holes sometimes work, as do unpleasant lotions and potions such as Tabasco sauce—although the ground tends to simply soak up whatever potion is applied. Further, these ploys often simply convince the dog to shift earth-moving ventures to another portion of the lawn. It's my feeling that the discipline should come directly from the owner, but you can't go wrong if you try the above measures as well.

Are Dalmatians stupid? Everyone says so. Can they even understand a set-up? Aren't there breed differences to be taken into consideration in staging set-ups for bad behavior—or even using them at all? If you don't want to answer this question to the whole seminar group, you can contact me in Room #347. I'm staying in the same hotel as you.

Let me quote directly from my taped answer to this submitted-secretly-at-the-podium question: "First, folks, this is an actual question submitted today by an actual person. I am going to have it framed. No, I cannot rendezvous with this person in room number 347. Yes, I will answer the question, not in private but to the whole seminar group. This is a funny, but ignorant, question. The only smart part of the question, I'd like to think, is the suggestion at the end! Dalmatians are not stupid. Further, this person obviously doesn't realize that I *have* one! Most people just assume that I have a German Shepherd Dog, I suppose, because I was once with the Monks of New Skete, who are famous for raising them. But no, my friend, wherever you are in the audience—and I think I can pick you out because there is only one crimson face in this sea of people—I have one of those 'stupid Dals.'

"In my opinion most breed qualifications are bunk when it comes to correcting problem behavior. I repeat, *bunk.* I find that, more often than not, owners simply use what they have heard about a given breed as an excuse to settle for a less-than-well-behaved dog, as a cop-out against taking the time to stage set-ups or even simply train their dogs in the basic words every dog needs to know. There is no such thing as a dog that cannot learn to heel, sit, stay, down itself and hold a long down. No such domestic canine exists unless it is medically or psychologically impaired—and this is very rare. If a given dog can learn those words, that same dog can, in my opinion, understand a correction and its connection. The foil, however, as we know, is an owner who has already decreed in advance that dogs of a given breed are dumb. This is a form of *blaming,* a way of hanging the dog without a fair trial. Of course there are breed idiosyncrasies, small behavioral quirks, that can be noted. For instance, it might be harder for a Siberian Husky or a Terrier to understand a set-up meant to eliminate digging, since a Siberian may really like to dig a cooling hole, and Terriers, by virtue of the fact that their very name comes from the Latin word for "earth," certainly like to burrow. Sight hounds and coursing hounds might be a tad more difficult to teach the recall to, and large, protection-oriented breeds might have a propensity to defend territory. But all of these are simply traits, not dictums, and can be modified, indeed must be modified in order for a given dog to fit into a given situation. I doubt whether the person who asked this question truly believes that Dalmatians are stupid or that any breed is impossible. Instead, most probably this person is issuing a cry for help—in his or her own peculiar way—because the person is frustrated by a problem dog. But the problem really isn't the dog, nor the dog's breed, is it? The 'problem' is registered in room number 347. So I've changed my mind: I'd be pleased to have dinner with you tonight. Let's see what we can work out together." (By the way, readers, when I read back the question to the group I changed the room number to protect the party involved. I used my own room number instead. I got a call later that night from a seminar participant who didn't recognize my voice and said I had a lot of nerve trying to see Mr. Evans alone.)

Here's the problem: My dog is working on his CDX, but I'm afraid he'll never earn it. As you know part of the "obedience ritual" to earn that title (Companion Dog Excellent) is that the dog has to hold a sit-stay and a down-stay while the

A set-up for an obedience foul-up: disobeying during the long sit. Warn the crash-landing Collie by tapping the "centering spot." *Levon Mark*

Immediately give the verbal command and visual signal for "stay." *Levon Mark*

Devise a method to watch from afar, and when the dog begins to sink into a down, quickly return. *Levon Mark*

handler is out of sight. This exercise is taken as a group and therein lies the problem. During the long sit my Collie lies down, goes into a play bow and starts to solicit attention from the other dogs! If they ignore him, he simply goes into a full down, ruining the exercise. I've tried everything. I've gone back and simply repositioned him without scolding. I've gone back and scolded him and I've even stationed helpers nearby behind him so that he always feels that someone will correct him if he breaks the sit-stay. He will never earn this title at this rate. I've heard of this problem with other Collies. Is it specific to the breed?

It *is* possible and preferable to stage a set-up for this problem and I'll tell you how. But before I do I need to tell you that my gut feeling is that something more serious is happening here than just a simple mistake on the dog's part. Let me simply ask some questions—questions every owner with such a so-called ring-wise dog should mull over.

You mention several times what the *dog* does that is wrong. You say twice—in a short question—that "he" won't earn the title at this rate. "He" won't earn the title? What about "we?" I thought obedience training involved teamwork. Is it possible that you are *drill, drill, drilling* your dog in this and other exercises to the point that he just doesn't give a good gosh darn about the whole ritual? My advice is to back off and employ some creative avoidance here. Simply *don't* train your dog at all for two weeks. Play fetch, go for long walks in the woods, go for a run on the beach, but other than usual household training, don't do any formal obedience training. Just enjoy each other.

I know this sounds anthropomorphic, but I firmly believe that many competition dogs can tell when they are being "used" to further an owner's goals. They pick it up via owner paralanguage and body language—especially before and after obedience trials. The owner, of course, in an attempt to deflect this "criticism" from the dog makes his or her goals the dog's goals, thus, "He will never earn the title at this rate." What if the dog just doesn't *want* to "earn" the title? Why does he have to "earn" it? What if you are pushing for it too hard? Very, very few professional obedience persons ask these kind of questions, often because they are fixated on achieving goals—goals that they have neatly transferred to the dog. The moratorium period on formal training will show your dog another side of yourself that your Collie might miss. A change in his psychological attitude might be what you need to correct this problem. So it's time to call "time-out!" and relax and reflect.

However, you'll still have to stage a set-up for the specific problem. After the two-week no-training period has passed, stage a set-up as follows: Leave your dog with a light warning, using a distinctive phrase, "OK, Tommy, you *sink* and you're *dead,*" emphasizing *sink* and *dead.* Remember, the phrase could be, "OK, Tommy, *mushrooms,* mushrooms, *mushrooms,* zucchini, mushrooms," just as long as it is consistent and does not include an obedience word. Tap the centering spot as you deliver your warning phrase. Now give the stay command and leave. Remember, there is no law that says that just before you disappear from sight you cannot reissue the warning command again. Of course, you will be secretly watching the dog from afar. Perhaps you

Do not simply reposition the dog into the sit. Instead, give the Collie a good shake and stern scolding—but no hysterics! Quickly reissue the command "stay" simultaneously with the visual signal and leave again.

Levon Mark

Remember, as you leave to disappear from sight again, there is no law that says you can't give a *second* warning—just be sure to use the same phrase consistently, emphasizing the same words.

Levon Mark

could try hiding behind the high jump, peering out at your dog through the slats. This is a nifty ploy because jumps are set up in various rings at trials, and your dog may never know which one you are hiding behind. As soon as your dog sinks into the play bow, charge back, repeat the warning phrase emphasizing the same phonics, give your dog a good shake correction, then reposition the Collie into the sit. Give the stay command again. Move! There should be a smooth, strict flow to this scenario. Don't go back and negotiate with the dog about its "fall from grace"—just repeat the warning phrase, discipline and get out of sight again.

The missing ingredient in your previous recipe was that you did not issue a warning, but instead hoped against hope that maybe, just maybe, this time the dog wouldn't sink into the play bow or simply crash. Repositioning the dog without any reprimand made the ritual into a game—and repositioning a dog is not correcting a dog. Finally, this dog obviously feels a need to solicit attention from other dogs, even in formal circumstances. Does he get to play with other dogs? Or is the only time he relates to members of his own species in such matches or trials? Try to let him play more around other dogs, cutting the play sessions midcourse and immediately going into an obedience exercise. If, on the other hand, your dog really does get to relate with other dogs frequently, he is simply playing "Mister Congeniality" with too much fervor and the set-up should show him that such an award, while awarded at beauty pageants, is definitely not awarded at obedience trials, and never to males in either circumstance.

I have a shy dog. She is fearful of loud noises, sudden moves, practically anything spontaneous. I am afraid she will become a fear biter, as she is already growling at people. What can I do? By the way, I'm shy, too.

(This question, like a good many queries I receive on shyness, was not asked aloud during the seminar but instead submitted in writing and placed on the podium during a break. Characteristically, the handwriting is extremely small, barely legible and scrunched. My purpose in pointing this out is not to criticize, but rather to point out that if an owner is underconfident—shy—often the dog will be, too. As a joke, I'll often say, "OK, who submitted this question? Stand up!" If one cannot joke about one's shyness, I believe that person will remain forever shy. I am shy outside of seminars, people are surprised to find out. But I can laugh about it, and my dogs aren't shy. Funny, but not shy.)

Forgive me in advance for being blunt but I'm concerned about this owner and dog. You don't have just a shy dog, you have an aggressive dog as well. You are in potential trouble unless you start training pronto. Put this dog on the RRRR today. Immediately read over the RRRR chapter and my open letter to owners of aggressive dogs in this book, then come back to this answer. Back already? I hope you read those chapters. I know you were probably protesting, "But why am I reading this, the dog's *shy,* not aggressive," but, my friend, if a dog is growling, that's aggression in my book, and aggression that could lead to a bite. No one will care, once bitten, that your dog is shy.

The bite will feel the same to them. So tackle the aggression first. From this moment forth, it is simply unacceptable for your dog to growl at anyone or anything. Repeat: Unacceptable. You must firmly discipline any such actions. Remember, often with shy dogs the corrections need not be very harsh. Indeed, you may get away with only stern leash corrections, but if the aggression is pronounced, regardless of the cause, stop it in its tracks.

Bear in mind that I understand that your dog may be, in fact, shy. But first things first. We have to stop the aggression and simultaneously socialize the dog out of shyness. The first step in rehabilitating any shy dog is to teach the dog a rock-solid, proofed, secure sit-stay and down-stay. If these commands are taught and adequately proofed the dog will be forced to face the prospect of disobeying a command word in order to cater to shyness. You will need these words, "down," "sit" and especially "stay" to stage set-ups for shyness. These words must be tight in the dog's brain. These words must be proofed. You can use these words to conquer shyness. At first the dog may only "do" the word in order not to incur your wrath—even as people pet it—but the word "stay" will save this dog. Does your dog *really* know "stay"?

Begin by having some guests over, seated in your living room. Let the dog see the guests enter the home, insisting on a sit-stay at the door. The guests need not touch the dog, but rather can simply nod, say a sweet (but not too sweet) "Hello, Shy Sam" and proceed to the living room. Bring your dog in and place the dog on a long down. If the dog doesn't yet know the long down get busy teaching it today using the methods in this book, and for now simply sit on the leash to keep Sam anchored. Have some conversation. Don't talk about the dog—shy dogs, like most, know their names and can tell when the name is interwoven into stressed, whiney paralanguage. Just ignore the dog, even if the dog is straining to get away, run and hide. Don't allow this, and don't touch the dog at all, unless it is to discipline obnoxious whining. After fifteen minutes, have the guests leave.

The next day repeat the process adding a warning to Shy Sam not to be shy. Remember, consistent phrase, tap the centering spot, make eye contact. Let the guests stay a half hour with no interaction with the dog. The following day, repeat all of the above, but leave a six-foot lead on your dog. Enclose the dog in the room and simply pass the lead around to each guest. In this Round Robin Recall the dog is called from person to person and praised. If the dog stalls, the person should haul the dog in firmly, but not pet the dog. If there is stalling or any sign of aggression, all praise must cease immediately. Only one person at a time should praise the dog, and if the dog clings to the owner, the owner should stare the dog down, issue a stern "No!" and look aloofly away. Try to blitz the shy dog with such set-ups for fourteen days. But, as the New Agers say, "Don't push the river." Once you have obtained the set-up goal for that day, call it a day. You can always stage another set-up tomorrow. Naturally, there is a risk factor in such set-ups, and if you feel that they would result in friends being bitten, you simply *must* secure the help of a qualified trainer or behaviorist right away. Shyness always gets worse, not better, unless checked by training, so don't delay. Good luck! At the risk of being presumptuous, you might seriously consider some assertiveness training for yourself. Most cities offer such services. Perhaps you are afraid to get tough with your shy dog because you yourself are shy. I fully identify because I am, off-stage. Even one session might work wonders. I'd suggest books on the topic, but my experience is that shy owners read them submissively and need personal confidence building.

My husband and I are concerned for our four-year-old son. We have a six-year-old, mixed breed, spayed female who constantly runs after him, nipping and trying to bowl him over. Worse though, and this is what we are really concerned about, three days ago the dog growled at our son when he approached us while we were still in bed. It was a Saturday morning and we wanted to sleep late, but our son knows that he can come into the bedroom then so that one of us can get up and turn on the TV for him. However, he also has a problem—pretty typical with children his age, I think—of trying to get into bed with us at night. Following a therapist's instructions, we simply walk or carry him back to his own bed each time he tries to get in ours. We tried simply telling our son to go back to his bed, but that didn't work. Our dog sleeps on our bed, always has since the time she was a puppy. The growling incident was on the morning after we had to escort our son back to his bed about six times. What can we do about our dog's behavior, and, while you're at it, any tips for our son's behavior!?

Some maids don't do windows—I don't do kids. But I do do dogs and I can assure you that there is a kid/dog interplay here that is essential for you to understand. Since your dog probably thinks of herself as number three in the family hierarchy (for that matter, maybe she even thinks she's number one), she definitely thinks that the "new puppy"—your son—is number four—and should stay in his place. You confirm this faulty notion each time you lead your son back to his sleeping quarters, even if you do so calmly. The dog watches this carefully and probably with a great deal of satisfaction; after all, she's been on the bed for six years. Who is this interloper? And, no, the dog does not necessarily know that this is your son, whom you love and cherish. Nor would she necessarily care if she did know. The dog probably feels that her place in the family hierarchy is threatened, or at least changing, and wants to preserve the status quo. So, obviously, get the dog *off* the bed, *pronto*. You will probably have to tether her to prevent her from trying to fling herself on the bed. Do not demote the dog from the bedroom, just off the bed.

Let your son have a walk session with the dog on leash. This can establish even a small child as an Alpha figure who has some leadership skills. If these two ploys don't work, and if within two days there is still hostility, place the dog on the RRRR program and leave her on it for one month. Put a short tab leash on the dog right away and be quick to grab it and deliver a *stern* leash correction if the dog chases or corrals your son—at this juncture all of this is aggression, not just simple play, and must be stopped. Don't just yell at the dog from afar, go and give a physical correction.

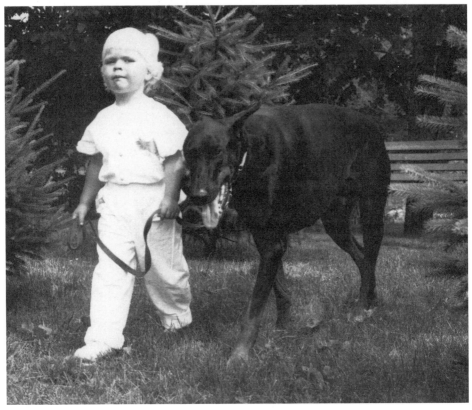

A child can establish some dominance over a dog by having a parentally supervised walk on-leash. This also increases the child's self-confidence and introduces the ideas of training and discipline. *Dealing with Dogs/TV Ontario*

One night of obedience class can be structured so that the children are included. The kids hold the leash, seemingly "in control," but only mimic the adult's commands and signals—a kind of obedience "Simon Says" game. *Lionel Shenken/Visual Productions*

You can concoct a set-up by issuing a warning and then releasing the dog near your son at a time when you know the child is bound to be playful or cavorting about. Zap the dog by grabbing the tab and disciplining if things get too rough, reissue the warning and release the dog again. Naturally, parental supervision of the child is a must. No tail yanking, ear pulling or other roughhousing should be allowed, and a four-year-old is old enough to understand being told to cease such behavior.

Chances are, in your efforts to allow the two to become friends, you've unintentionally allowed too much rough play. It's time to tighten up the controls now, before an unfortunate accident happens. Meanwhile, even if you wind up putting the dog on the supertough RRRR, you have my permission to modify it slightly by adding this step: Twice a week, each of the adults should take your pet for a long walk, alone, just you and the dog. The other parent can stay at home with your son. This will show your dog that you still love her and care enough for her to give her her own personal time alone with you. If there are woods nearby, try going there for the walk, even if it has to be on leash. This adds to the sense of intimacy the dog will feel with you. Good luck!

I've had it! I don't have a dog, I have a Hoover vacuum cleaner! I'm so frustrated I could scream! Well, let me back up. What I have is a garbager. I live in New York, and every walk I take with my dog, a five-year-old Cairn Terrier, is a trial because she snarffs up anything and everything she sees on the street. I yank the leash up hard, sometimes raising her front two feet off the ground, and scream, "Drop it!" and sometimes she does, but two seconds later she just snarffs up something else. It's a wonder she hasn't gotten sick from the filth she sucks up, or had a chicken bone caught in her throat. And don't ask me to just walk her where there isn't any trash on the street. This is New York! Oh, I forgot, you live here, too . . . well, then, you already know. . . .

I know you are trying your best with your Hoover, and I appreciate your attempts. There are several reasons success has eluded you. When you yank the dog up and away from "treats" you are simply *repositioning* the dog, not correcting the dog. Because the dog drops the trash doesn't mean that the Cairn will not try to pick up the next piece. Your walks have become games, and unpleasant to boot. I would advise you to stage a set-up that will involve issuing a warning, and then deliberately gliding your dog over some choice tidbit of trash. You should have no problem finding trash—I fully agree that even in the better areas of our city, it abounds.

Take your dog out on a proper training collar and a six-foot lead. Don't allow the dog to barge out of your building before you, as this only sets up an atmosphere that will make the tendency to garbage greater. Once you see the refuse you intend to use, stop about ten feet in front of it. Sit your dog. Tap the centering spot and deliver your warning, emphasizing key phonetics, "OK, Rascal, you *touch* that *trash* and you're *dead!*" Now glide over the garbage. I know you're shocked—after all, you've probably made it a habit to steer clear of as much garbage as possible, which means that in New York you probably look like a drunk walking a dog as you weave all over the sidewalk trying to avoid trash. Now here I am telling you to walk Rascal right over trash! The reason, of course, is so you can let Rascal garbage.

Watch for the moment her head dips to snarff and yank the leash up, *hard*. Now lean down and give Rascal a firm tap under the chin. Don't use the shake for this problem—the delay time is too long and the correction will be lost on the dog. If, by chance, the Cairn has already chomped down on the garbage and has it in her mouth, don't wrestle with her by sticking your fingers down her throat and trying to scrape the garbage out. Some "vacuum" dogs actually *like* this kind of interaction and consider it part of the game, especially if they sometimes manage to swallow the tidbit anyway. Instead, if the trash is of sufficient size, grab the end of it and yank the *dog* away from the trash, holding the trash steady, not vice versa. If the piece of garbage is too small to hold steady and yank the dog away from, try this: Place your left hand over the dog's snout, slipping a finger of that hand under the collar so as not to lose the dog. Place your right hand, palm up, under the dog's mouth and cup your thumb and index finger into the dog's mouth near the incisors. Firmly shake the dog's head downward to expel the trash. This method limits hand interaction with the dog's mouth and lessens the chance that the dog will interpret attempts to remove garbage from its mouth as a game and a challenge.

Regardless of whether the dog dropped the trash or had to have it removed, don't forget to give the disciplinary swat, immediately reissue the warning and heel forward. Now double back quickly, repeating the warning, and glide over the *same* trash. If the dog still garbages, chances are your initial correction was too slow or too soft.

Finally, you're right—garbaging isn't cute, there are real health risks involved. If the problem continues, you might have to call in a trainer—although most owners can rehabilitate "Hoovers" (sounds like a new breed, doesn't it?) themselves without too much difficulty. If you do need a trainer, and this is the only problem you have with your dog, one or, at most, two sessions should be all you need.

Bayou, my eleven-month-old Golden Retriever, has been baring his teeth and snarling at me and at other people since he was seven weeks old. Usually he does this when he is verbally corrected for his extremely destructive behavior or when he is touched (brushing, toweling him dry, pulling him off furniture). He has never actually bitten anyone. I obtained Bayou at age seven weeks from a reputable breeder and have contacted the breeder several times about his behavior. The breeder claims that there is no problem with the dog and just tells me to be firmer with him. My veterinarian has examined Bayou and ruled out medical causes for this behavior. Bayou was neutered at seven months but his behavior did not improve. He also attended obedience school for ten weeks and was the worst in his class. Bayou can be very sweet when he wants to be but I don't really feel I can trust him. I would appreciate any suggestions you can give me.

First, something that should be obvious to all, Bayou and, probably more importantly, Bayou's owner need to work with a qualified trainer or animal behavior consultant *in the owner's home.* While I'm happy the owner sought out obedience training, the class atmosphere is too hectic, even in well-run classes, to center in on the problems of a growling, snarling dog. In fact, obedience class training might have made the situation *worse,* especially since Bayou did not do well and probably got into tons of little dominance fights with the owner when they attempted to do the assigned homework between classes. An intelligent class instructor would have indicated this to Bayou's owner (it was probably apparent after the first class) and directed them to private training. Perhaps because the dog was so young, the instructor just thought the bad behavior would get better in time.

But all that's water over the dam now. I mention it for the sake of obedience class instructors who admit and keep aggressive dogs in their classes. You are doing the dog and the owner no favor. They should be directed to a private trainer or specialist. Often problems of aggression are easily treatable, and even one private session can work wonders. The dog can then come back to class or continue with the private training.

Since this was a written submitted question, there are many questions I need to ask the owner. I would need to interview Bayou's owner quite extensively. For now I'll just speculate since I can't interview owners during a seminar or as they read a book anyway.

While aggressive behavior is not generally genetically predisposed in Golden Retrievers, it does crop up occasionally. I would need to ascertain for sure if the puppy truly began displaying aggression at age *seven weeks.* Unless the breeder placed the pup at six weeks (a sign of an uninformed breeder), that means that the pup was exhibiting aggression from the time of placement! Yet the owner says that the dog was procured from a reputable breeder. My response to all this is simply, "Hmmmmm . . ." Very interesting, wouldn't you say? Why didn't the breeder catch it? Aggression in a seven-week-old Golden? Remarkable. Why didn't the breeder see the signs of aggression before place-ment? Or is this *owner* hyperbole—obvious and intentional exaggeration to impress me with the urgency of the problem? In order to ascertain this, and thus distinguish whether this problem has a genetic base or is owner-related, I would have to have the owner in a situation where I could ask him or her many questions. There are ways of asking trick questions so that the truth comes out.

If I were able to conduct a complete interview and work with the dog, and *if* the owner's statement that the dog was aggressive with him or her *and* others from seven weeks of age on was true, I would say there is a strong case that the dog is genetically defective. That will make rehabilitation and subse-quent management very difficult. I would then counsel the owner to return the dog to the breeder if possible, or if the owner refused to be separated from the dog I would set up a program similar to the one that follows, with the provision and warning that the dog will always be a management problem.

I highly suspect, however, that this case is not one of genetically predisposed aggression but one of owner mismanagement. Let's face it, friends: You have to really *work at it* to produce a Golden Retriever that is genetically aggressive and "baring his teeth and snarling" at age seven weeks!

If the owner has intentionally or unintentionally bungled the leadership role I would prescribe the following:

1. Immediately employ a qualified trainer or specialist to help you in your home. The trainer will help you to devise set-ups so that the bad behavior is elicited from Bayou and can be corrected.

2. Since the dog has a problem with physical contact, all corrections must be distanced—collar corrections while the dog is on a leash or tab, which should be on whenever the owner is home. The owner should *not* use the shake or swat corrections I usually suggest. This is one of the exceptions to using those techniques.

3. I would advise the owner to immediately institute (the verb is correct) the RRRR program.

4. The private trainer or specialist *must* be sure to educate the owner as to *paralanguage*—indicating clearly that any stressed or whimpering tones of voice will simply demote the owner to littermate status in the dog's eyes. Some playacting might be necessary here and a lot of humor. I can assure the trainer that the academic approach will backfire here. Don't be afraid to mimic the littermate sounds and instruct the owner as to why these sounds, this paralanguage, will be misinterpreted by the dog and will lower the owner to littermate status in the dog's eyes. (By the way, as a quick aside to the trainer or behaviorist who might get this case—this is a blamer owner. I'm almost certain of it. Worse, he or she is also a placater. The dog gets placated and the breeder—and probably any trainer who gets called in—gets blamed. Tricky.)

5. Finally, the owner has to be taught how to refrain from *escalating* incidents when going after the dog for destructive behavior or grooming—often owners tense up, put tension on the lead (*if* they have one on to begin with) and create an atmosphere of high anxiety that the dog learns to anticipate and fight. Good luck to both client and trainer!

My dog chases cars. Not every car that passes by, only some. She also gets carsick on every ride. What can I do? How can I break her of these habits?

If this dog was not hanging around outside, undoubtedly off leash and unsupervised, such a problem would never develop. Get the dog in the house pronto, except for elimination and on-leash walks. If you are ever going to be able to trust her outside, even under your supervision, you must institute a moratorium period on any and all off-leash outdoors freedom. Break the car-chasing cycle! Do this for two weeks and then you can try a set-up. I'll describe one in a second, but, I hasten to add, if you simply let the dog return to an outdoors-all-the-time, unconfined life-style, you will probably *never* break the dog of car chasing. Instead, your dog will break something else: her neck, her leg, her back—get the picture?

After the moratorium period has passed (and during that time you should also be practicing formal recalls as described in the chapter "To Come or Not to Come"), you can stage a set-up. Put a six-foot lead on your dog and simply let the dog walk around the house with it on for two full days. You need to secure the help of a neighbor and another family member in order to stage this set-up. The neighbor will drive the car the dog will chase, and you will be hiding in that car. The family member, preferably the person in the family the dog thinks of as the second Alpha figure, will deliver the advance warning. Coordinate with each other as to the time the car will *slowly* pass the house. This can be announced by strategic horn honks just before the car will appear. At this point the helper sits the chaser, taps the centering spot, makes eye contact and delivers the warning, "OK, Road Runner, you chase that *car* and you're *dead.*" The helper then releases the dog and returns to the house, surreptitiously peering out. The decoy car should then roll by at a slow, enticing pace. The main Alpha figure should be hidden in the backseat, ready to charge out, grab Road Runner, who of course is wearing the six-foot lead it's gotten used to, and give two or three disciplinary swats under the chin. Yes, swats. In my opinion, this car-chasing problem is big-time and deserves the swat, not just the shake. Big canine crimes are better disciplined with the swat—especially when they involve a threat to the dog's own life or to the lives of others—as this crime definitely does.

The car driver may have to break suddenly, so be sure that you stage the set-up for a time when the road is not busy, and be sure that the driver announces to the person secluded in the car exactly when the breaks will be applied. If you do not manage to catch the dog for discipline, the indoors helper, who will be watching secretly, should simply prop open the house door. The dog will probably run inside, where that person can deliver the discipline or, better yet, trot the dog quickly back out to the scene of the crime and let the main Alpha discipline at car side. Repeat the process again, securing the help of still another neighbor in a different make car. At the start of the set-up, the two decoy cars can be parked together a short distance away. After the first part of the set-up, once discipline has been delivered, Alpha number one turns the dog over to Alpha number two and hitches a ride to decoy car number two with the driver of decoy car number one. Got it? Need three decoy cars? Well, get them.

I've found neighbors are only too willing to help with this ruse—as their cars are often the very ones being chased. They would rather participate in a set-up than run the gauntlet every day and risk injuring the dog or themselves. Owners of car chasers are often also owners of in-car howlers. They have gotten used to such behavior from their dogs inside and outside of cars. What they rudely don't consider or have any sensitivity about is the sheer panic almost all other drivers experience when the car is charged by a chaser. It's literally impossible to tell if the dog in at the side of the car or under it, and most drivers tense up terribly and swerve around dangerously, endangering themselves and others.

If you are fast enough exiting the decoy cars, your dog should be totally *shocked* to find you coming after it. The element of surprise, and the fact that the correction comes from a leader figure, puts the shine on this set-up. You might have to have a practice dry run minus a dog, so that driver, discipliner and house helper can coordinate their movements. One last point: During the two-week moratorium period, don't allow the dog to urinate or defecate anywhere near where the car chasing occurs. In other words, if the chasing happens in the front yard, confine all elimination to the backyard. Dogs claim territory by eliminating on it, and the chances are the dog thinks the front yard and thus the road and the "big shiny dogs" that "run by" there belong to it. If you believe in the myth that a dog "needs to be outdoors" or "needs to enjoy the country air," at the risk of sounding blunt—you are misinformed. Properly socialized, your dog is a pack animal that would far prefer being inside with the rest of the pack. But it might not know that this is best for it. It's up to the pack leader (that's you) to inform the dog what's best. As for fresh country air, unless you live in the Arctic, these days the air is most probably fresher indoors rather than outdoors.

For the second problem, set-ups minus discipline still work. Begin with short rides, gradually building up to longer ones. If the dog gets sick in the car, do not discipline the dog. Try not feeding the dog anything for two or three hours before a short drive out and then back into the driveway. That's all—not even around the block; do that tomorrow. The next day, drive a half mile, and the day after that, one mile. Ask your veterinarian about drugs that can help with this problem. If you have dual car conundrums—your dog chases cars and gets sick in them—you'll probably resolve the second problem by staging a set-up as described above for the first problem. The car-chasing set-up will deglamorize cars in your dog's mind and connect your authority and Alphahood up with the very presence of an automobile. This may very well aid in composing your dog inside cars.

I am going to Europe and am considering sending my two-year-old Rhodesian Ridgeback to a boarding kennel that also offers a training course. He has problems with destructive chewing and is still not 100 percent on his housetraining. Do you think the training will be successful in stopping these problems? He'd be at the kennel for almost one month.

I doubt that the type of training your dog will receive at a training kennel will include correction of chewing and housetraining problems. Since your dog will be kenneled, with only acceptable toys, how will he even have access to unacceptable chew objects in order to make mistakes and get corrected? As for housetraining, think about the word itself: *house*training. Seems to me the procedure is best accomplished in someone's *house,* specifically, yours. It is not just a mechanical process but rather has to do with how the owner is viewed by the dog, which food is offered, adopting a schedule, discerning whether the dog can be disciplined after the fact and then disciplining correctly. This can hardly be accomplished in a boarding kennel setting.

On the other hand, your dog most likely *will* learn the basic command words, and if his trainers take the time necessary to train *you* to train your dog, this will be beneficial in terms of the way the dog views you. Be sure to be carefully interviewed as to your needs and desires in training when you drop your dog off, and be sure that the trainer who takes your dog into the kennel is the same trainer who will give you an exit lesson when you come to call for your dog. The idea sounds workable, especially since you are going to Europe and need to board your dog anyway, but don't expect your dog to come home a saint. As William E. Campbell says, "I've worked with a few thousand problem-dog owners who have hustled their little 'Caesars' off to obedience classes or called for private instruction with the idea that what the dogs need is just 'a little training.' In truth, that's too easy; too much like a free lunch. The shoe is on the wrong foot. It's the owners who need the training, along with a change in their perspective and attitude and, hence, a change in *their* behavior, which will be followed by a change in their dogs' behavior."

My dog goes berserk when there is a thunderstorm. I mean absolutely nuts. As in off the wall. I've tried confinement and she screams in her crate. I've tried drugs, all under veterinary supervision. She fights through every drug she's ingested. The veterinarian says it is a behavioral problem. Around July 4th, she begins to freak out over firecrackers. What can I do other than move to the Sahara Desert or try to find a country that never celebrates anything with firecrackers?

Every July 4th, my answering machine is flooded with hysterical calls from owners on the battlefield. For some reason, especially in Brooklyn, Queens and the rest of the USA (other than the island of Manhattan), firecrackers are as American as Mom and apple pie. Funny, nothing similar occurs in Canada on July 1st (Dominion Day) or in other countries—although dogs in Greece suffer shell shock each Easter.

Often in the background I'll hear a dog screeching and bombs detonating. Occasionally, I can't even hear the distraught owner's voice. Usually this is because the owner is cradling the upset dog in his or her arms, and the dog's vocalizations outdo the owners.

The biggest mistake owners make is trying to soothe their puppy or older dog out of being fearful of such sounds. This usually begins in puppyhood. It doesn't take long for the dog to realize, "Mommy and Daddy pay lots of attention to me if I just act frightened during a storm or on the Fourth—and besides, I really *am* frightened . . . well, sometimes." It's interesting that many such coddled dogs simply do not freak out (at least not as much) when a storm comes up or a firecracker goes off and Mommy and Daddy are not home. Many scared dogs simply find a niche—behind a couch, in their crate or down in the basement—and wait things out. So if your pet has such a niche, I'd say let the dog retreat to it. Stop any petting or comforting of the dog. You will simply unintentionally train the dog's fear *in,* tighter and tighter.

There are some tape recordings and phonograph records of storms and firecrackers that are touted as a cure for storm shyness or Fourth freakouts. I've tried them but never had much success with them, but they are worth a try as a desensitizing ploy. In my experience, the tapes or records just can't reproduce the sound of thunder or firecrackers with enough decibels or suddenness to simulate the real happenings. Then, too, lightning (especially heat lightning flashes) usually *precedes* the sound of thunder, so the preconditioned dog takes its cue to get ready to freak from the lightning flash, which many dogs can perceive even if you draw all the blinds. Again, I'm for anything that works. Not everything works with every dog, so the tapes might be worth a try.

If you decide on such sound effects and you find that your dog is doing no better, just leave the dog alone. If, on the other hand, the dog engages in destructive behavior, runs about too much or screeches bloody murder, you owe it to your dog to lessen its stress by disciplining it and placing the dog on a long down. Your dog must know that even during a storm, even when firecrackers go off, hysterical behavior is simply unacceptable and you believe it can do better.

Sometimes a dog will become so hysterical during a storm or another disturbance—especially if coddling is cut off—that the dog resembles a person at a funeral who is so deeply grieved that he or she is out of control. It's standard policy in some cultures to give this person a good shake, or even a slight slap on the cheek, just to bring the person back to reality. The bereaved one is then advised to sit and relax. If your dog flies out of control, this type of action may be necessary, and the long down-stay is the equivalent of having your dog "sit and relax."

OK—I've listened all day and I think I've come up with fifty-five different set-ups for fifty-five different problems my dogs have. So, thank you. But I have a problem I'll bet even you can't stage a set-up for. It's overbarking, and I don't mean one overbarking dog, I mean seven. They live partially in the house and partially in an outdoor kennel in runs. When someone comes to the door, all hell breaks loose. It resembles the psychiatric ward in One Flew Over the Cuckoo's Nest. *If they are out in their kennels and I pick up the telephone (they can see if I'm on the phone by looking in the kitchen window) all seven go nutzoid. One trainer told me that this was jealousy. He said they probably think I'm holding and talking sweetly to another dog because the phone is held close and has what looks to them like a tail. That's a cute explanation, but it doesn't help me to stop the problem. Actually, it's not so far off the mark. Come to think of it, I'm usually talking to my mother, and she can be a bitch. If you can solve this one, Job, I'll cook you dinner. And, yes, they are Terriers. I know you're probably thinking, "Well, she deserves everything she gets."*

No, I don't think that. Instead, I was thinking, this woman deserves the very best, because you seem to have a lovely sense of humor, and despite some problems (most of which you feel you can alleviate or eradicate), I just sense that you deeply love your dogs. Some people think staging set-ups is mean or unfair, but this just isn't so, because the motivation for staging them comes out of love. Indeed, parent to child, owner to dog, discipline *is* love.

So you've already taken an important step just by listening to the seminar today and doing some work on yourself. If you do those fifty-five other set-ups (really fifty-five?!), you might find that much of the overbarking simply subsides. But—never one to avoid direct advice—let me describe some sample set-ups for your specific problems.

For the in-house doorbell vocalistics, you are going to have to teach each dog a rock-steady stay at the front door. Take each dog, one by one, for just three minutes a day and run the Volhard sit-stay progressions past the dog near the front door. You'll find them described in "Words Dogs Live By." On day two, have a helper ring the doorbell as you run each individual dog through these paces. Get ready, the dogs will freak out and you'll have to be superstrict about enforcing the stay *and* disciplining any barking.

On day three, admit the person to the house, again working with only one dog at a time. Enforce the no-bark rule. If you secure the help of an assistant who knows in advance that you will enforce the stay and discipline barking if necessary, you will not have to worry about greeting the person or being ashamed as you correct the dogs.

If you feel that individual dogs are controlling their barking, stage a set-up employing a helper and working, on leads, with two dogs. Start with the leader Alpha dog and the most subordinate dog in the "pack." You most probably know who's who. If you don't, which is unlikely but possible, ask a knowledgeable dog person who knows your dogs. They'll tell you who's who. Since other members of the pack will tend to mimic the top dog, you can cash in on disciplining it and having it filter down to the others. This type of mimic behavior is called *allelomimetic* behavior and can be a great aid in staging set-ups. Now work inward into the pack order, staging the next set-up with the second most authoritative dog and the next up in submissiveness. Your next step would be to do a sting operation using a helper and the four or even five most cooperative (which means newly silent) dogs. Set-up schedules are touch-and-go, and you have to set the pace according to how quickly the dogs learn that silence is golden.

If your dogs participate in a lot of random, sporadic, spook-type barking (for instance, at perfectly acceptable outdoor noises, at household machines, etc.) you must stop it all. Some dogs have been unintentionally taught to live just on the edge of a bark and are constantly "on." I think this is one heck of a stressful life-style for any dog, and the amount of stress such noisemakers will experience by being disciplined for inappropriate barking is really nothing compared to the ongoing stress of feeling that they have to be ready to "spook-bark" at anything that is in the least unusual.

Don't worry that you'll destroy the protection potential of the dogs and that they will suddenly become mute and never bark when undesirable intruders threaten. They will, trust me. You will be simply teaching them discrimination and poise rather than condoning random overbarking. Besides, even if they do inhibit their barking somewhat, by virtue of the fact that you are asking this question, you seem to be saying that this would be perfectly fine with you! But don't worry, especially with Terriers, a propensity to bark comes in the genetic bargain. The propensity for it simply has to be shaped and controlled.

For run barking when the dogs are confined, you might try verbal corrections and a squirt gun filled with water and lemon juice. A plant-misting bottle with the squirter dialed to deliver a sharp spray rather than a mist is often better than a squirt gun—it shoots a longer distance. The trouble with a set-up here is that the corrections would be delayed as you fiddle with the gates to get to the dogs. But it's still worth a try to stage one. The sequence would be: Start with one dog, warn, tap centering spot and leave a tab lead on, confine in kennel, leave, charge back and discipline if barking, rewarn and repeat. Use the worksheets found earlier in chapter 10 of this book.

Owners of overbarkers need to map out in writing their set-ups because it's so easy to lose one's cool in the face of such yodeling, screeching, yapping and general confusion. Don't bark back at the dogs! Screaming *"No! No! No-no-no-no!"* is faulty paralanguage and will make you sound exactly like the barking dogs, even if you use the word "no." Even if the dogs really know the word "no," they will opt for the paralanguage and bark back. All eight of you will simply have a bark-fest. Keep your voice low and firm and go into action. The dogs will learn quickly that you mean business.

I have really been "at it." I have really laid down the law with my aggressive dog. And I have been making headway—a lot of headway. I had "misdiagnosed" his aggression as shyness and he really was just damn overprotective, precisely, of me. So we have been on the RRRR for about three weeks. I realize that the program is as much for myself as for my dog. Now, however, we have entered a period (about the last two days) during which my dog's behavior has gotten even worse. He's been making so much improvement—now this. What gives?

Here's what gives. Your dog has reached a point of rebellion. It's quite understandable—and explains why sometimes bad behavior becomes even *worse* once any kind of behavioral therapy is begun. This regression often mystifies owners, since they assume that once they clamp down, the dog will quiet down. Not so simple. At the risk of sounding anthropomorphic, let me paraphrase it from the dog's point of view: "OK, bozo, what is this RRRR business? Whether you know it or not, we had life set up a certain way around here. Basically, I was in charge. Now you tell me that *you* are Alpha, that I can't get on the bed, can't finagle any treats, can't get petted unless I earn the praise, can't have any people food, can't do this, can't do that. What am I?—*grounded* like some rebellious teenage kid? Well, don't expect me to buy it! I'm going to do everything I can to get things back to the status quo—the way things used to be. And don't you try to stop me, bozo!"

Your "reply" to this little tantrum/speech (although there needn't really be any at all) is to say, "That's right, you've got it just right—ride it out." You need to hang in there. You're doing many things right, and this rebellion period will pass. Again, if you think about it from the dog's point of view, it's all quite understandable, if unenjoyable. So just stick to your guns and hang on for better times, sweet times you and your dog will enjoy together.

I have lost my dog and I am heartbroken. I heard you say once in a seminar, "If dogs don't go to heaven, then I don't want to go there." That comment helped me, in fact, made me cry, and I noticed that many around me were crying also. Many of us have been through the death of a dog, it seems—really, I guess we should expect it, after all, dogs just don't live as long as we do. Still, I feel so empty, alone . . . can you say anything to me . . . will I ever see my beloved friend again?

I do believe you will. As far as I have been able to determine, with the exception of some radical, fundamentalist sects, no major Christian or Jewish denomination has ever issued a definitive pronouncement about what happens to animals after death. You are free, regardless of your religious preference, to believe what you will.

I would say the following to comfort you. First, feel sad and don't be ashamed of it. Of course you are sad and there's nothing wrong with that—it's quite natural. I really, *really* worry about owners who lose pets and do not feel sad or grieve. Among professional dog people, I've seen this stoic reaction often. It's as if the dog was a member of a livestock herd, a commodity to be traded, bartered, sold. I think this is one reason lay owners often feel so gypped when they turn to some breeders or trainers for comfort after the death of a dog and run up against a brick wall of "unemotion."

I've written elsewhere about how to deal with the death of a dog. Over a decade ago, the first dog writing I ever penned, the book I coauthored with the Monks of New Skete, *How to Be Your Dog's Best Friend,* dealt with this issue for perhaps the first time. Now it is standard for authors to address this all-important question. Thank God, for, after all, death is part of life.

Still, I find myself floundering, hemming and hawing as to what exactly to say. I once read in the excellent Barbara Walter's book *How to Talk to Practically Anyone about Practically Anything* that sometimes (oftentimes, she implied) the best thing one can do for the bereaved is to listen and say, "I know, I know . . ." The stupidest things to say, she says, are "I know exactly how you feel" (because you don't), or worse, "Everything will be all right" (it isn't and it won't be).

Just keeping it simple and saying "I know" seems like sound advice even now—even in the new age during which we've been tutored on how to accept death. I suppose Elisabeth Kübler-Ross started this trend when she mapped out the stages she observed in terminal patients nearing the end: shock, denial, anger, bargaining and, finally, acceptance. Neat, huh? Trouble is, what Kübler-Ross reported were simply *descriptions* of what she had observed in near-death patients—but the descriptive quickly became *prescriptive,* especially at the hands of her disciples.

The fact is, very few persons want to face death squarely, not the death of their dog and certainly not their own! We live in a death-denying, seemingly death-defying culture. But all reasonable dog owners know that, unless they are very old themselves and own a younger dog, most probably their dog will die during their lifetime. So for many a dog's death places the mourner squarely in the face of the incredible mystery of death itself—for perhaps the first time. Scary stuff—especially when others, insensitive to the death of a dog (and the other losses and potential losses it signifies), caution the bereaved to "get over it," because, after all, "it was only a *dog.*" Neat, huh? And the death-denying culture we live in "wins" once again, if only by default. The grieving owner is left to sort out emotions all alone.

I think that the Kübler-Ross paradigm is accurate, to a degree. But not everyone goes though similar stages in confronting death—their dog's or their own—and mourners shouldn't be expected to follow a script, however in vogue. For some owners, the death of a dog is instead a roller coaster of events and emotions. This is especially true if the dog has been euthanized because of behavioral difficulties. The fear, guilt and incredible distress an owner can feel in such a situation is lessened only by the fact that if the dog were allowed to live, serious harm might have befallen many innocent souls. But the owner is often too distraught to see this fact, and that's understandable.

So don't feel you *have* to go through any prescribed stages, and don't be critical of yourself for feeling so blue. Deliberately try to stay away from insensitive souls who make silly comments that minimize or trivialize your grief. On the other hand, if after two or three months you are still deep in grief, perhaps you should seek out some counseling. It's quite possible that the loss of your dog is bringing to the foreground other losses that you might have experienced in the past and for one reason or another refused to acknowledge or simply squelched down in yourself. This type of delayed-reaction grief is very common, but if worked on, it can help you grow. As a positive action, you might consider making a memorial donation to an organization that helps animals. The Delta Society (321 Burnett Ave. South, Third Floor, Renton, Wash. 98055) or the Morris Animal Foundation (45 Inverness Dr. East, Englewood, Colo. 80112) or your local humane society are all good possibilities.

Something strange has happened in my household. I recently lost Copper, my oldest Golden Retriever. He was nine years old and pretty much ruled the roost vis-à-vis the other dogs in the household. I have four others, all Goldens. All are bitches of various ages. Copper had been under observation at my vet's office but he rallied and came home. Two days later he took a turn for the worse. I was upstairs cleaning and suddenly felt an urge to go down to the kitchen. I found him dead in the kitchen, on his favorite rug. All of the other dogs were surrounding him in a semicircle—they looked like someone had put them all on sit-stays, and when I entered the room they all continued to look down at Copper. It was like a wake; they all looked extremely sad. Are dogs aware of the death of another dog? If they are, does this mean that they have religious sensibilities?

I just can't get over coming upon that scene. Although I was devastated when I realized Copper was dead, I was somehow comforted by the way the "family" had gathered. What do you think?

I think that you were blessed to see all of your dogs at a very private, special moment. The hand of God had just touched Copper and you were lucky enough to be passing by. Yes, I believe that dogs can grieve. They must experience emotional pain when such a prominent member of the pack passes away. I also believe that the dogs probably sensed that Copper was weakening, and perhaps expected his death. It's interesting how they were all so strangely quiet, although gathered together, and that even upstairs you felt drawn to the scene. I have had similar experiences myself. While I know you are sad about Copper's death, you can know, practically for certain, that your dogs join you in grief.

The thing to do now is to make all of the remaining dogs as secure and happy as possible. When one owns a "colony" of dogs (in behavioral terms, this is what you have) there is a tendency to do everything en masse. Especially now, take each dog for a long walk, in the woods if possible, alone—just the two of you. This will reassure each dog and help them to reorder the pack—with you as the featured Alpha. Strange as this may sound, put each dog through its obedience paces—as mind work helps to lessen grief. Your question is not at all out of line and is, in fact, quite sensitive. You are a very lucky person and you sound like a top-notch owner and steward. Your dogs are lucky to have you to lead and love them.

In Closing

So now we come to the end of the subject. Well, almost. I'm glad I've answered these questions about death submitted at seminars, because this is an inevitability almost all owners will have to face. Of course, besides not wanting to face the pain of loss, the real problem behind our unwillingness to deal with the issue of pet loss is our tremendous fear of our *own* eventual death. Yet, as far as I know, three out of every three people on this earth will die, so there is no escape. Here, our dogs can teach us an invaluable lesson about facing reality and about living one day at a time and cherishing each day. While I believe that dogs grieve and feel loss, and perhaps sense that they themselves will die, I don't think they obsess on it or become preoccupied with it. They live life, as fully as they can, one day at a time. They are an inspiration for us all, in life and in death. They can teach us much about what we need to know about love—if we let them and if we are open to their message and to the message of all nature. As the wise monk Father Zosima said in Dostoevsky's *The Brothers Karamazov*

> Love the animals: God has given them the beginnings of thought and untroubled joy. So do not disturb their joy, do not torment them, do not deprive them of their well-being, do not work against God's intent. Man, do not pride yourself

on your superiority to the animals, for they are without sin, while you, with all your greatness, you defile the earth wherever you appear and leave an ignoble trail behind you—and that is true, alas, for almost every one of us!

Love God's creation, love every atom of it separately, and love it also as a whole; love every green leaf, every ray of God's light; love the animals and the plants and love every inanimate object. If you come to love all things, you will perceive God's mystery in all things; once you have perceived it, you will understand it better and better every day. And finally you will love the whole world with a total, universal love.

Bibliography

HERE IS an annotated bibliography of books that concentrate on problem dogs—and their owners. I have not included standard training books that simply teach the obedience exercises and do not address problems. The information in the following books usually complements advice in this book. The novice seeking to stage sterling set-ups can find helpful tips galore—and the *professional* trainer owes it to himself or herself and to clients to be fully informed on just who has advised what, and when, for dealing with behavior problems. Accordingly, I've added two books at the end of this list that are somewhat archaic in style and technique, but will be of interest to professionals who wish to get a broader, historical overview of how people have "put up" with problem pooches.

Benjamin, Carol Lea. *Dog Problems.* 1981. Howell Book House, 866 Third Ave., New York, N.Y. 10022.

   Benjamin, probably our finest dog writer, has a sound theory: Anticipate problems with your dog, and if you already have them, don't remain passive about them. Practically every problem is handled: chewing, digging, aggression, shyness, car sickness and more. Highly recommended.

———. *Mother Knows Best: The Natural Way to Train Your Dog.* 1985. Howell Book House.

   Another top-notch book, the key chapter for owners of problem pooches is chapter 7, "Trouble-shooting." Geared more to the puppy owner than *Dog Problems,* it's a book that trainers try to get new owners to read before problems occur.

————. *Second-Hand Dog: How to Turn Yours into a First-Rate Pet.* 1988. Howell Book House.

If you've adopted a dog from a shelter, this is the book for you. Included is the excellent "Alpha Primer" that has similarities to the Radical Regimen detailed in this text. Again, as in all Ms. Benjamin's writings, the emphasis is on the dog/owner relationship and the quality of leadership in that bond.

Campbell, William E. *Behavior Problems in Dogs.* 1975. American Veterinary Publications, Drawer KK, Santa Barbara, Calif. 93102.

The chapter "Problem Owners and Characteristics" is classic—and completely turns the tables around from the "blame-the-dog" approach found in many books. Get ready: Hardly anyone escapes criticism. But you'll love Campbell's breezy style and valuable tips. The book is a must-read for professionals who, in any capacity, must deal with problem dogs or problem owners. A companion volume, *Owner's Guide to Better Behavior in Dogs and Cats,* appeared in 1986 and is geared to the lay person. This is a pioneering, essential author.

Evans, Job Michael. *How to Be Your Dog's Best Friend* (with the Monks of New Skete). 1978. Little, Brown & Co., 34 Beacon St., Boston, Mass. 03410.

————. *The Evans Guide for Counseling Dog Owners.* 1985. Howell Book House, 866 Third Ave., New York, N.Y. 10022.

————. *The Evans Guide for Housetraining Your Dog.* 1987. Howell Book House.

————. *The Evans Guide for Civilized City Canines.* 1988. Howell Book House.

Since these books have been alluded to in the text, I'll simply say if you are a first-time owner you'll love what I always refer to as "the Monks' book" (although I wrote forty of the forty-four chapters). If you have a dog that has fallen off the housetraining wagon, read the housetraining guide—pronto! If you live in a town with more than one stoplight, *Civilized City Canines* will be of great help, and if you must talk to dog owners in any capacity—veterinarian, breeder, trainer or concerned friend—*Counseling Dog Owners* is the guide for you.

Hart, Benjamin L, and Lynette A. Hart. *Canine and Feline Behavioral Therapy.* 1985. Lea & Febiger, 600 Washington Sq., Philadelphia, Pa. 19106.

This academic guide is long on observation and short on specific, workable tips to aid the owner of a problem dog—and some of the protocols would try the patience of a saint—but it is, nevertheless, worth a look-see, especially for professionals.

Holmes, John. *The Family Dog.* 1957. Popular Dogs, 17-21 Conway St., London, W1P6JD.

I have always admired the way the English write about dogs. Invariably UK authors are blunt, strict about "proper" behavior in dogs, yet loving and caring. There is a good section here on various problems, including one Holmes simply calls "pestering." This means, of course, the dog that bothers its owner by constantly wanting to play ball, catch a stick, get a treat or just get praised for looking cute. Holmes doesn't sympathize with this kind of canine pest. "Any tendency to develop a 'thing' about anything should be discouraged in the dog or corrected before it becomes established." Bravo!

Milani, Myrna M., DVM. *The Invisible Leash.* 1985. New American Library, 1633 Broadway, New York, N.Y. 10019.

Dr. Milani has a six-step procedure for sizing up and solving many problems. First, recognize that probably the "bad" behavior is normal, then define the problem, list all possible solutions, collect information, select the best solutions

236

and then evaluate the results. Sound too neat? Give this book a good examination and together with the understanding you'll gain, you'll feel a calm—your dog isn't out to "get you" after all.

———. *The Weekend Dog.* 1984. Rawson Associates, 866 Third Ave., New York, N.Y. 10022.

Have a dog you see only nights and weekends? Don't hang your head in shame—such an arrangement *can* work—but some problems are bound to crop up. They are all covered here, including separation anxiety, housetraining, nutrition, even a chapter on "Sex and the Weekend Dog." That should peak your interest. An excellent book.

Quakenbush, Jamie, MSW. *When Your Pet Dies: How to Cope with Your Feelings.* 1985. Simon & Schuster, 1230 Avenue of the Americas, New York, N.Y. 10020.

Is the death of a dog not the ultimate "pooch problem"? Truly it is, but there is no conceivable set-up that can be concocted to avoid it. Here, in a moving text, is a guide to acceptance of the event, or even the eventuality. A section entitled "In Spite of It All, We Miss Him Terribly" details the emotions surrounding the death of a biting dog—by owner decision, and may be of help to those facing this difficult juncture.

Siegal, Mordecai, with Matthew Margolis. *When Good Dogs Do Bad Things.* 1986. Little, Brown & Co., 34 Beacon St., Boston, Mass. 03410.

There is a directory of problems in this book that is as exhaustive as any in print, and a variety of solutions and steps that will aid you in setting up set-ups. It's well written, concise and has an appealing format.

Smith, Dr. M. L. *Eliminate on Command.* 1984. Masterworks, Inc., P.O. Box 901, Friday Harbor, Wash. 98250.

The no-frills title means exactly what it says—you can convince your dog to defecate or urinate practically on a dime. Who would want such a service? Try millions of city dog owners who must stand shivering waiting and waiting for their pooch to answer the call, or for that matter anyone who wants to speed up this process to enjoy more quality time with their dog—and that includes all of us.

Tucker, Michael. *Solving Your Dog Problems.* 1987. Howell Book House, 866 Third Ave., New York, N.Y. 10022.

While this book resorts to the old ploy of labeling dogs instead of owners ("The Clever Dog," "The Difficult Dog"), it contains solid tips for better behavior and should be examined. Aggression, car chasing, chewing and show-ring problems (which are often disregarded in other books) are covered.

Veterinary Clinics of North America. Small Animal Practice series: *Animal Behavior* (November 1982) and *The Human-Companion Animal Bond* (March 1985). W. B. Saunders, W. Washington Sq., Philadelphia, Pa. 19105.

These two somewhat technical volumes will be of interest to specialists and trainers and cover various behavior problems, mostly from an academic perspective. Authors like Drs. Borchelt, Voith, Hart, Houpt, Tuber and Wolski are represented in the volume on behavior. Articles by Drs. Bustad, McCulloch, Marder and Beck are offered in the human/animal bond issue. These are important names in the academic area of behavior studies and professionals especially will find much of interest here.

Volhard, Joachim, and Gail Tamases Fisher. *Training Your Dog: The Step-by-Step Manual.* 1983. Howell Book House, 866 Third Ave., New York, N.Y. 10022.

While this excellent training book concentrates on the nuts and bolts of training the traditional exercises, it does address behavior problems in one top-notch chapter. Professionals will also be interested in a companion volume, *Teaching Dog Obedience Classes,* for which I wrote the foreword (also Howell Book House).

Finally, two older books I came across at the AKC library, which is an invaluable resource to all interested in canine behavior and is located at 51 Madison Ave., New York, N.Y. 10010, 20th Fl., phone (212)696-8245. These two gems, while full of misinformation, can be read to get an overview of how techniques have changed over the years and how ethics, cultural influences and even sexism have affected dog training and problem solving.

Woodhouse, Barbara. *Difficult Dogs.* 1950. Faber & Faber Ltd., 24 Russell Sq., London, WC1.

   While the late Ms. Woodhouse was controversial within the dog training community, she *could* write, and in a charming, if somewhat bratty, style. While many of the actual training techniques are old school, her view of owners is accurate. "I would very much like to hear what some dogs think of their owners," she declares. "I have a horrid suspicion it would not be too complimentary." Meanwhile, with a few exceptions, modern-day dog writing avoids criticizing dog owners—after all, they might get psychologically depressed. Woodhouse never gave a whit about that. By the way, English dog writers adore the adjective "horrid."

Badcock, Lt. Col. G. H. *Disobedient Dogs, and Other Matters.* 1933. Herbert Jenkins Ltd., 3 York St., London, SW1.

   Another English author, Lieutenant Badcock is full of opinions, some of which have merit, but many of which truly betray the "state of the art" at that time. On Terriers: "Of all the mischievous varmints, except perhaps a Labrador puppy, Terriers of all breeds are the worst. I think one of the troubles of dogs in after years of being such nuisances to other people is the fact that their owners allowed them to run riot too long." So much for Terriers! But wait, Badcock has opinions on *people,* too. Lady Kitty Ritson, who wrote the foreword, warns us that "Col. Badcock has little opinion of the female 'handler.' I am convinced he wrote this book with the 'females of the species' in mind. I can hardly blame him. The average woman is a terror with dogs, for either she shouts at them (generally eliciting no response) or she nags them . . . a disobedient dog is a horrid dog, and dogs are never horrid of their own free will, it is some human who has made them so." I would have loved to be a fly on the wall during a blind date between Ms. Woodhouse and Lieutenant Badcock! But I doubt any such event ever occurred.

Most of all, enjoy your reading!

Index